Basic Education beyond the Millennium Development Goals in Ghana

A WORLD BANK STUDY

Basic Education beyond the Millennium Development Goals in Ghana

How Equity in Service Delivery Affects Educational and Learning Outcomes

Peter Darvas and David Balwanz

THE WORLD BANK
Washington, D.C.

© 2014 International Bank for Reconstruction and Development / The World Bank
1818 H Street NW, Washington DC 20433
Telephone: 202-473-1000; Internet: www.worldbank.org

Some rights reserved

1 2 3 4 16 15 14 13

World Bank Studies are published to communicate the results of the Bank's work to the development community with the least possible delay. The manuscript of this paper therefore has not been prepared in accordance with the procedures appropriate to formally edited texts.

This work is a product of the staff of The World Bank with external contributions. Note that The World Bank does not necessarily own each component of the content included in the work. The World Bank therefore does not warrant that the use of the content contained in the work will not infringe on the rights of third parties. The risk of claims resulting from such infringement rests solely with you.

The findings, interpretations, and conclusions expressed in this work do not necessarily reflect the views of The World Bank, its Board of Executive Directors, or the governments they represent. The World Bank does not guarantee the accuracy of the data included in this work. The boundaries, colors, denominations, and other information shown on any map in this work do not imply any judgment on the part of The World Bank concerning the legal status of any territory or the endorsement or acceptance of such boundaries.

Nothing herein shall constitute or be considered to be a limitation upon or waiver of the privileges and immunities of The World Bank, all of which are specifically reserved.

Rights and Permissions

This work is available under the Creative Commons Attribution 3.0 Unported license (CC BY 3.0) http://creativecommons.org/licenses/by/3.0. Under the Creative Commons Attribution license, you are free to copy, distribute, transmit, and adapt this work, including for commercial purposes, under the following conditions:

Attribution—Please cite the work as follows: Darvas, Peter, and David Balwanz. 2013. Basic Education beyond the Millennium Development Goals in Ghana: How Equity in Service Delivery Affects Educational and Learning Outcomes. World Bank Study. Washington, DC: World Bank. doi:10.1596/978-1-4648-0098-6. License: Creative Commons Attribution CC BY 3.0

Translations—If you create a translation of this work, please add the following disclaimer along with the attribution: *This translation was not created by The World Bank and should not be considered an official World Bank translation. The World Bank shall not be liable for any content or error in this translation.*

All queries on rights and licenses should be addressed to the Publishing and Knowledge Division, The World Bank, 1818 H Street NW, Washington, DC 20433, USA; fax: 202-522-2625; e-mail: pubrights@worldbank.org.

ISBN (paper): 978-1-4648-0098-6
ISBN (electronic): 978-1-4648-0100-6
DOI: 10.1596/978-1-4648-0098-6

Cover photo: Ghanian schoolgirl. © Peter Darvas. Used with the permission of Peter Darvas. Further permission required for reuse.

Library of Congress Cataloging-in-Publication Data

CIP data have been requested.

Contents

Foreword		xi
Acknowledgements		xiii
About the Authors		xv
Abbreviations		xvii
Overview		1
	Inequity: The Central Challenge	1
	Basic Education in Ghana: Main Findings	4
	Teacher Policy Dilemmas	18
	Basic Education in Ghana: Recommendations	19
	Notes	24
Chapter 1	**Introduction—Why Focus on Inequity?**	27
	Report Framework	30
	Notes	34
Chapter 2	**Country Context**	37
	Rapid Growth and Change	37
	Recent Progress in Education	39
	Persistent Challenges	39
Chapter 3	**Education Reform History**	41
	Education Reform: 1951–2008	41
	Recent Policy Initiatives	44
	Notes	45
Chapter 4	**Equity**	47
	Overview	47
	Equitable Access	49
	Equal Distribution of Inputs	54
	Equitable Outcomes	59

	Social Mobility and Reproduction of Inequality	64
	Results of Equity-Improving Policies and Programs	65
	Notes	73
Chapter 5	**Quality**	**75**
	Overview	75
	Learning Outcomes	77
	Factors Affecting Learning	84
	Qualified Teachers	87
	Literacy Instruction	90
	Closing Notes	91
	Notes	92
Chapter 6	**Efficiency**	**95**
	Overview	95
	Internal Efficiency: Teachers and Instructional Time	97
	Internal Efficiency: Output Production, Other Inputs	102
	External Efficiency	105
	Notes	105
Chapter 7	**Education Expenditure**	**107**
	Education Expenditure	107
	The Wage Bill	116
	Notes	122
Chapter 8	**Management, Finance, and Accountability**	**123**
	Overview	123
	Strategy and Influence	126
	Fragmentation of Financing	131
	Planning, Implementation, Evaluation	133
	Accountability	135
	Decentralization and Teacher Policy and Management	140
	Notes	143
Chapter 9	**Options for Policymakers**	**145**
	Recommendations	145
	Notes	150
Bibliography		**153**

Boxes

1.1	Definitions of Key Themes	30
4.1	Providing Basic Education for Children with Disabilities	53

4.2	GES Experimentation with a Resource Allocation Model	60
4.3	Improving Girls' Access to Secondary Schools in the Three Northern Regions	66
4.4	Zones of Exclusion Framework	71
4.5	Equity, Quality, Efficiency in Rural Schools	72
5.1	The Teacher Community Assistant Initiative (TCAI)	83
5.2	Multigrade, Multilevel Schools	86
5.3	National Standards of Performance	90
5.4	Private Schools	91
8.1	Expanding Senior High School	142

Figures

0.1	Primary and Secondary School Net Attendance Ratio, by Wealth Quintile and Urban-Rural Status, 2011	5
0.2	Primary Net Attendance Ratio, by Region, 2011	6
0.3	Primary PTTR, by SES, 2008/09	7
0.4	Percentage of P6 Pupils Attaining "Proficiency" in English and Maths, by Urban-Rural Status	8
0.5	Percentage of P3 and P6 Students Achieving Proficiency in English, by Region	9
0.6	Percentage of P3 and P6 Students Attaining Proficiency in English and Maths, 2011	11
0.7	Percentage of P3 and P5 Students, by Reading Comprehension Score	11
0.8	Percentage of Trained Teachers in Primary School and JHS, 1987/88–2009/10	12
0.9	Percentage of Students Reaching Minimum Competency and Proficiency, by Classroom Type, P3 English, 2011	13
0.10	Instructional Time in Basic Schools in Four Countries	14
0.11	Sources and Flows of Funding and Resources for a Primary School in Ghana	17
1.1	Attendance Rates, Ages 6–14 Years, by Poverty, Gender, and Region, 2003–08	28
1.2	Conceptual Framework for Basic Education in Ghana	32
1.3	Themes and Interventions System Improvements in Literacy and Numeracy	34
4.1	Primary and Secondary School Net Attendance Rate, by Wealth Quintile and Urban-Rural Status, 2011	50
4.2	Primary and Secondary Net Attendance Rate, by Region, 2011	51
4.3	Primary and JHS NER, by Wealth Quintile	51
4.4	Private Enrollment as a Percentage of Total Enrollment in Primary Schools, 2010/11	53
4.5	Proportion of Primary Teachers with Training, by Region/District, 2008/09	55

4.6	Primary PTTR, by SES, 2008/09	55
4.7	Degree of Randomness of Teacher Allocation	57
4.8	PCE, by District, 2008	59
4.9	Percentage of P6 Pupils Attaining Proficiency in English and Maths, by Urban-Rural Status	61
4.10	NEA 2007 Scores (P6), by District Average and Wealth Quintile	62
4.11	BECE English and Mathematics Pass Rates, by Region, 2010/11	63
4.12	BECE English Pass Rate (2008/09) in Districts, by Income	63
4.13	Primary and JHS Completion Rate, by Wealth Quintile	64
4.14	Progression of Students to SHS, by Wealth Quintile	65
4.15	Access and Zones of Exclusion in Primary and JHS	72
5.1	Percentage of P3 and P6 Students Achieving Proficiency in English, by Region	78
5.2	Percentage of P3 and P6 Students Achieving Proficiency in Maths, by Region	78
5.3	Percentage of P3 and P6 Students Attaining Proficiency in English and Maths	79
5.4	Percentage of P3 and P5 Students, by Reading Comprehension Score	80
5.5	Zero Scores in Reading Words and Comprehension, by Grade and Age Group, 2009	80
5.6	Comparative PISA Math Proficiency, by Country Income Status	82
B5.1	Percentage of Students Reaching Minimum Competency and Proficiency, by Classroom Type, P3 English, 2011	86
5.7	Percentage of Trained Teachers in Primary School and JHS, 1987/88–2009/10	87
6.1	Student-Teacher Scatter Plot (Primary, 2008/09)	97
6.2	Student-Teacher Scatter Plot for Northern and Upper East Regions, 2010/11	98
6.3	Instructional Time in Basic Schools in Four Countries	99
6.4	Effective Instructional Time Basic Schools in Four Countries (EQUIP2)	99
6.5	Distribution of KG, Primary, and JHS Schools, by Enrollment	103
7.1	Public Education Expenditure as a Percentage of GDP	108
7.2	Total Education Expenditure, by Source, 2011	110
7.3	Total Education Expenditure, by Budget Category, 2011	112
7.4	GoG Education Expenditure, by Budget Category, 2011	113
7.5	Relative and Absolute Measures of Per Primary Pupil Public Expenditure in Several Countries in Sub-Saharan Africa, 2010	115
7.6	Public Current Expenditure Per Tertiary Student as a Ratio of Current Expenditure Per Primary Student (Selected Countries)	116

7.7	Composition of Per Student Recurrent Expenditure by Subsector, 2011	117
7.8	Distribution over the GES Salary Scale, 2009	120
7.9	Distribution of Salaries and Entry Levels, 2009	121
7.10	Average Teacher Years of Service, by Region, 2009	121
8.1	Influences on Education Priorities and Expenditure	126
8.2	Sources and Flows of Funding and Resources for a Primary School in Ghana	131
8.3	Funding Flows for MoE Budget Category	132
8.4	Annual Planning, Budgeting, and Monitoring Cycle	134
8.5	Partners with Whom MoE Negotiates to Secure Resources	134
8.6	Interrelated Dimensions of Teacher Policy	142

Maps

0.1	Percentage of Trained Primary Teachers, by Region, 2011/12	7
4.1	Percentage of Trained Primary Teachers, by Region, 2011/12	54
4.2	Poverty Headcount, 2003–06, and Average PTR, by District, 2006/07	56

Tables

0.1	Enrollment and NER in KG, Primary and JHS 1990–2011/12	5
0.2	Per-Child Expenditure in 2008 GHc Measured at District Level	8
0.3	Overview of Selected Equity Improving Programs	10
0.4	Factors Explaining Teacher Absenteeism	14
0.5	GoG Budget Share, by Budget Category and Execution in Relation to Budget Amount	16
4.1	Enrollment and NER in KG, Primary, and JHS 1990–2011/12	49
4.2	Per-Child Expenditure in 2008 GHc Measured at District Level	58
4.3	Basic Education Demand- and Supply-Side Measures in Ghana	67
4.4	Overview of Selected Equity-Improving Programs	70
4.5	Share of Students Receiving Capitation Grants and School Meals, by Deprivation Index	71
5.1	Selected Mathematics and Science TIMSS Scores	81
5.2	TIMSS Content and Cognitive Domains, 2004	81
5.3	DBE Programs and Output of New Teachers	89
6.1	External and Internal Efficiency	95
6.2	Factors Explaining Teacher Absenteeism	100
6.3	Cost Per Primary Completer and Cost to Produce a P6 Student Proficient in English	102
6.4	Efficiency in Core Textbooks Distribution in Primary and JH, 2004/05–2008/09	104

7.1	International Comparative Analysis of Public Spending on Education	108
7.2	Education Expenditure, 2003–11	109
7.3	Expenditure by Level of Education as a Percentage of Total Expenditure, by Source, 2011	111
7.4	Subsector Expenditure as a Percentage of Total Education Expenditure, 2008–11	111
7.5	PE as a Percentage of Total and GoG-Only Education Expenditures, 2011	113
7.6	GoG Budget Share, by Budget Category and Execution in Relation to Budget Amount	114
7.7	GETFund Expenditure as a Percentage of Total Education Expenditure	114
7.8	Education Unit Costs across Different Subsectors	116
7.9	Payroll Numbers GES Payroll Figures, 2008	119
7.10	Staff in the Basic Cycle, 2008	120
8.1	Incoming Government Policy Commitments, 2008	128
8.2	Excerpt from ESP 2010–20, Vol. II, Basic Education Section	129
8.3	Frequency of Head-Teacher and Circuit Supervisor Activities, 2003	138

Foreword

Over the past decade, Ghana has seen a number of very significant achievements: GDP has increased fivefold, the number of families living in poverty has been cut in half, democratic traditions have taken root in the political system, and women and girls are increasingly gaining skills, voice and access to power. In 2010 Ghana celebrated its transition to lower-middle income country status. Will these successes be built on and multiplied in the next decade? The future holds great promise in Ghana, but also considerable challenges.

Education in Ghana also reflects these general trends. More children are now in school than at any time in the history of Ghana, and learning outcomes and literacy have started to gradually improve. *Basic Education in Ghana* notes these achievements, but also points out that, despite major gains in improving access to education, over 300,000 school-age children in Ghana are not in school. Further, while a small number of children perform well, there is a now a "missing middle" in terms of learning outcomes: every year an estimated 350,000–400,000 students (65 percent of sixth-grade students) leave primary school without having become proficient in English or mathematics. The majority of these pupils are from Ghana's northern regions and deprived districts, poor and rural households and ethnic and linguistic minorities. These students, who require the most support, tend to be the most neglected by the system. Given that people are a nation's most precious resource, such inequities in education service delivery undermine progress toward broader national development goals of poverty reduction, economic growth, democratic development and social cohesion. Given that Ghana's population is still growing and youth will continue to represent the majority of the population, the country can reap a demographic dividend only if its young people acquire the literacy and the basic mathematical skills that are absolutely essential to progress further in their education or find well-paying jobs.

The report offers an extensive analysis of the dimensions of inequity in basic education, and documents the extent to which management, finance and accountability systems serve to perpetuate or mitigate inequities. It also takes stock of the many dilemmas that challenge educators, planners, politicians, and policymakers. Importantly, this report presents evidence on several initiatives designed to improve demand for education, support deprived areas and target poor and vulnerable populations.

Over the next decade, Ghana's promising trajectory could see gains in inclusive economic growth, grounded, in part, by efforts to ensure basic skills and competencies for all, and to avoid the types of social unrest frequently seen in societies where investments in people are inequitable. While this report is about Ghana, it offers important lessons for other countries making progress toward and beyond the Millennium Development Goals and middle-income status.

We sincerely hope the data and insights from this report inform a lively and productive debate on the future of basic education in Ghana and beyond.

Yusupha B. Crookes
Country Director, Ghana
The World Bank

Ritva Reinikka
Director, Human Development Group,
Africa Region
The World Bank

Acknowledgements

This report was authored by Peter Darvas and David Balwanz. It grew out of the very positive reception and an emerging consensus that was generated by *Education in Ghana: Improving Equity, Efficiency and Accountability of Education Service Delivery* (World Bank 2010). This earlier report also led to a new policy agenda which became the basis of a new Global Partnership in Education Project for Ghana, which is now the most critical undertaking by the Government in basic education and is supported by all major Development Partners. As such, we are greatly indebted to Alexander Krauss, a co-author of the earlier report as well as various analyses completed for the earlier report by Prof. Albert Akyempong, Jesper Steffensen, Michele Savini, Paud Murphy, Peter DeVries, Quentin Wodon, and George Joseph. Burton Bollag and Rumit Pancholi provided editorial support as well as advice for the final publication. Without the expertise of staff from the Ministry of Education and the Ghana Education Service and access to their extensive warehouse of data and evaluations, this report would not exist. Special thanks go to MoE staff in Planning, Budgeting, Monitoring and Evaluation and Education Management Information Systems and GES staff in the offices of Basic Education and the Financial Controller. The Ministry of Education and the Ghana Education Service have both played critical diagnostic and program development roles in supporting the recent Global Partnership for Education Grant in Ghana. Dialogue and debates occurring during the development of this grant helped the authors think through some of the critical issues and dilemmas featured in this report.

Once this report made it to draft stage, we sought the support of peer reviewers from the academic and development partner communities. Peer reviewers offered valuable contributions, insights and critiques. We greatly appreciate contributions from Professor Jophus Anamuah-Mensah (ex-Vice Chancellor, University of Ghana), Professor J. S. Djangmah (ex-Director of Ghana Education Service, ex-Chairman of West African Examination Council), Hiroyuki Hattori (UNICEF), Nicole Goldstein (DfID-Ghana), Dr. Rachel Hinton (DfID), Ernesto Cuadra (World Bank), Sukhdeep Brar (World Bank), Marguerite Clarke (World Bank), Qaiser Khan (World Bank), Kafu Kofi Tsikata (World Bank) and Andrea Vermehren (World Bank). At various stages, we received welcome support from

Marisol Perez (USAID-Ghana), Eva Oberg (ODI Fellow MoE, PBME/DfID-Ghana), Kabira Namit (ODI Fellow GES, Financial Controllers Office), Harry Patrinos (World Bank), Deborah Mikesell (World Bank), Eunice Ackwerh (World Bank) and Robert West (Independent consultant). Ishaac Diwan (World Bank, recently Harvard University, Kennedy School of Government), Peter Materu (World Bank), Elizabeth King (World Bank), Ritva Reinikka (World Bank), and Yusupha Crookes (World Bank) offered invaluable guidance and support during various stages of production and review processes which we are greatly appreciative.

The germ of this book was planted during an event hosted by the Ghana Ministry of Education in April 2011. During the event, GES staff from districts and from headquarters (including the Director of Basic Education), education advocates from think tanks and development partner organizations and other concerned citizens gathered in Accra to discuss critical issues facing basic education in Ghana. We acknowledge the many, and varied advocates, policymakers and educators striving to improve basic education and build a better future for Ghana. Writing this report would not have been worth it were it not for the knowledge that others would carry this critical debate forward. Any errors or omissions of fact are the responsibility of the authors alone.

About the Authors

Peter Darvas has worked on basic, secondary, and higher education and training in Ghana since 2005. He also lived in Ghana between 2006 and 2009 where, as the education sector coordinator for the World Bank and as the sector leader for the development partners, he provided strategic support to the Government of Ghana in its effort to develop the Education Strategic Plan (2010–20) and led partnership in the annual sector performance reviews and in other multidonor partnerships. For the World Bank, Peter led various investment projects including the Education Sector Project, the Education For All—Fast Track Initiative, and the Ghana Skills and Technology Development Project. He also led a number of World Bank–sponsored sector analyses including the Demand and Supply for Technical and Vocational Skills and a study on education service delivery, which provided much of the data and analysis used in this book. Peter works with the World Bank Senior Education Economist at the Human Development Department of the Africa Region and is based in Washington, DC.

David Balwanz worked with the Ghana Ministry of Education (MoE) and the Ghana Education Service on basic and secondary education, education planning and policy analysis, and program design from 2010 to 2011. During this time, he was embedded in the MoE Planning, Budget, Monitoring and Evaluation Division (PBME), where, in collaboration with PBME colleagues, he completed financial modeling and operational planning exercises to support Ghana's application for Education For All—Fast Track Initiative funding. From 2011 to 2012, David worked with Department For International Development–Ghana to design programs supporting the expansion of complementary basic education and facilitating strategic planning to guide the reform and expansion of early childhood education in Ghana. David is an independent consultant based in South Africa. His experience includes program design and implementation, evaluation, and research on basic and secondary education programs in several countries, including Afghanistan, Jordan, Kenya, Malawi, Nigeria, South Africa, South Sudan, and Zambia.

Abbreviations

BECE	Basic Education Certificate Examination
CAGD	Controller and Accountant General Department
CBO	community-based organization
CCT	conditional cash transfer
CDD	Center for Democratic Development
CIDA	Canadian International Development Agency
COTVET	Council for TVET
CREATE	Consortium for Research on Educational Access, Transitions & Equity
CSA	Civil Service Agency
DACF	District Assembly Common Fund
DEO	District Education Office
DEOC	District Education Oversight Committees
DFID	Department for International Development
DP	development partner
DWAP	District-Wide Assistance Project
EDI	EFA Development Index
EFA	Education for All
EMIS	Education Management Information System
ERP	Economic Reform Program
ERRC	Education Reform Review Committee
ESP	Education Strategic Plan
ESPR	Education Sector Performance Report
FCUBE	free compulsory universal basic education
FTI	Fast-Track Initiative
GAR	gross admission rate
GDHS	Ghana Demographic and Health Survey
GDP	gross domestic product
GER	gross enrollment ratio

GES	Ghana Education Service
GETFund	Ghana Education Trust Fund
GLSS	Ghana Living Standards Survey
GNAT	Ghana National Association of Teachers
GNI	gross national income
GoG	Government of Ghana
GPI	Gender Parity Index
GPRS	Growth and Poverty Reduction Strategy
GRATIS	Ghana Regional Appropriate Technology Industrial Service
GSFP	Ghana School Feeding Program
GSS	Ghana Statistical Service
HDI	Human Development Index
HE	higher education
HEI	Higher Education Institute
HIPC	heavily indebted poor country
HIV & AIDS	human immunodeficiency virus and acquired immune deficiency syndrome
HND	Higher National Diploma
ICCES	Integrated Community Centers for Employable Skills
ICT	Information and Communication Technology
IMF	International Monetary Fund
IQR	interquartile range
JHS	junior high school
JICA	Japan International Cooperation Agency
KG	Kindergarten
KNUST	Kwame Nkrumah University of Science and Technology
LEAP	livelihood empowerment against poverty
LESs	less endowed schools
MDBS	multidonor budget support
MDG	millennium development goals
MDRI	multilateral debt relief initiative
MLGRD	Ministry of Local Government and Rural Development
MMDAs	Metropolitan, Municipal and District Assemblies
MoE	Ministry of Education
MOESS	Ministry of Education Science and Sport
MoFEP	Ministry of Finance and Economic Planning
LG	local government
MPs fund	Member of Parliament fund
MTEF	medium-term expenditure framework

NAB	National Accreditation Board
NAR	Net Admission Rate
NCTE	National Council for Tertiary Education
NDC	National Democratic Congress
NEA	National Education Assessment
NER	Net Enrolment Ratio
NERIC	National Education Reform Implementation Committee
NERP	National Education Reform Program
NESAR	National Education Sector Annual Report
NGO	nongovernmental organization
NPP	New Patriotic Party
NVTIs	National Vocation Training Institutes
OECD	Organization of Economic Cooperation and Development
PBME	Planning, Budgeting, Monitoring and Evaluation
PCE	per-child recurrent expenditure
PE	personnel emoluments
PER	Public Expenditure Review
PPP	Purchasing Power Parity
PRSCs	Poverty Reduction Strategy Credits
PRSP	Poverty Reduction Strategy Paper
PTA	parent teacher association
PTE	per teacher recurrent expenditure
PTR	pupil-teacher ratio
PTTR	pupil-trained teacher ratio
RFUF	residential facility user fees
SHS	senior high school
SIML	social impact mitigation levy
SMC	school management committee
SPAM	school performance assessment meeting
SSA	Sub-Saharan Africa
SSSCE	Senior Secondary School Certificate Examination
SSSS	Single-Spine Salary Structure
TED	Teacher Education Department
TIMSS	Trends in International Mathematics and Science Study
TTIs	Technical Training Institutes
TTL	task team leader
TVET	Technical and Vocational Education and Training
UBC	Universal Basic Completion
UBE	Universal Basic Education

UCC	University of Cape Coast
UNDP	United Nations Development Programme
UNESCO	United Nations Education, Scientific and Cultural Organization
UNICEF	United Nations Children's Fund
UPC	Universal Primary Completion
USAID	United States Agency for International Development
VAT	value-added tax
WAEC	West African Examination Council
WASSCE	West African Senior Secondary Certificate Examination
WB	World Bank
WDI	World Development Indicators

Overview

Today, more Ghanaian children have access to basic education and are entering upper secondary education than at any time in the history of Ghana. Education is about the future. Ghana's recent achievements in education indicate the possibility of more fully realizing the human potential of all individuals and of the country.

Recent progress inspires hope of further progress. At the same time, if the future is to be better than the past, we must also identify new and persistent challenges. For human development to contribute to national development, improving learning outcomes for the poorest half of Ghanaian children offers a key opportunity and challenge.

Now is a good time for reform. Ghana is on a strong trajectory toward solidifying its middle income status. Broadly sharing the benefits of growth requires taking aggressive steps toward realizing the vision of free, compulsory and universal quality basic education. We hope the content herein stimulates a lively and productive debate on the future of basic education in Ghana.

Inequity: The Central Challenge

Inequality in learning achievements is the central challenge facing basic education in Ghana and the contribution of basic education to furthering national development.

Promotion of equity is based on principles of fairness and justice. In an equitable society, an individual's life chances (for example, economic, social, health) should not be predetermined by his or her characteristics at birth (for example, gender, household wealth, ethnic/language group, geographic location, orphan status) or by his or her membership in particular groups (for example, groups defined by religious, ethno-linguistic, sexual orientation). To protect equity, societies may also "decide to intervene to protect the livelihoods of its neediest members [from absolute deprivation]…even if the equal opportunity principle has been upheld" (World Bank 2005, 19).

In Ghana, access to school, allocation of key education inputs and distribution of learning outcomes show persistent and significant inequities across different groups. Children from the northern regions, deprived districts, poor and rural households and ethnic and linguistic minorities are most disadvantaged by inequities in basic education service delivery. Existing inequities systematically disadvantage marginalized groups, denying their right to basic education; depresses overall system performance (for example, average learning outcomes) and compromise national progress toward post-basic education goals (for example, skills development and tertiary preparation) and broader goals of increasing economic competitiveness, nurturing democratic development and strengthening social cohesion.

Basic education is a right guaranteed by the Constitution of Ghana, and underpins other national development goals, including development of a more equitable society. Basic education promotes individual academic and nonacademic development and welfare, supports access to jobs and sustainable livelihoods and provides the cognitive skills and status needed for dignified and meaningful participation in a democratic society.

Reducing social and economic inequities can help Ghana make progress toward national goals including acceleration of economic growth, promotion of human rights and strengthening of social cohesion. Improving the quality of basic education services for all can play an important role in reducing these broader inequities. While Ghana has recently become classified as a lower-middle income country, widespread and deepening social and economic inequality is a critical challenge facing future development and stability. These challenges are compounded by the limited social protection measures in place to protect vulnerable populations, increasing urbanization and informal settlement without commensurate increases in employment and social services and underinvestment in rural and remote areas.

Several recent studies suggest that high levels of inequality can discourage development of accountable government, undermine civic and social life, which can lead to conflict in multiethnic settings, and increase risk of political and financial crisis—during which it is more difficult for individuals to invest in income-generating activities and their own education. Improving equitable access to quality basic education has been shown to promote economic growth and poverty reduction, improve public health and strengthen democratic participation (Berg and Ostry 2011; Hanushek and Wosserman 2008; OECD 2012; Palma 2011; UNESCO 2008).

Improving equity in basic education can greatly strengthen system performance. Students and populations who require the most support to meet learning outcomes receive, on average, disproportionately fewer resources from the government than their peers. These inequities significantly depress overall system performance. In the 2011 National Education Assessment (NEA), over 25 percent of P6 students did not attain minimum competency in English and nearly 40 percent of P6 students did not attain minimum competency in mathematics. Importantly, several studies suggest that students who demonstrate below-average learning outcomes in poorly resourced environments are likely to show the biggest gains in learning outcomes when provided additional support. More promising: there are already several small-scale initiatives in Ghana designed to improve equitable and efficient allocation of resources and provide additional instructional support to disadvantaged children and schools.

Meeting the challenge of inequity will take place in a complex and rapidly changing country context.

Ghana has realized rapid growth and change over the past two decades. Population growth, urbanization and significant GDP growth have changed the economic, political and social landscape of Ghana. In 20 years, the population in Ghana has increased by nearly 70 percent to 25 million people and the number of people living in urban areas has doubled. In 2010, buoyed by the discovery of oil, Ghana became classified as a lower-middle income country. In the past decade alone, GDP increased fivefold and incidence of extreme poverty has been cut in half.

Growth has brought about high expectations and new constituencies and influences... Growth has led to higher expectations for jobs, earnings and public services and fueled internal migration. Growth has also brought about new influences and constituencies. A new middle class accounts for nearly half of Ghana's population; district and regional branches of government, each with revenue generation and decision-making roles and responsibilities, influence public policy and service delivery priorities at their respective levels.

...and increased the complexity of the policy environment and service delivery. The above issues, among others, have made the politics and management of public service delivery more complex: there are more interests involved in influencing policy, more layers of management and more institutions and agencies involved in key service delivery decisions (for example, financing and distribution of key inputs).

Change in basic education mirror recent growth and change seen in Ghana. Implementation of Free, Compulsory, Universal Basic Education (FCUBE), introduction of Kindergarten into basic education and increased transition to JHS have supported a near doubling of basic education enrollment (to 7 million pupils in 2011) in the past 15 years. Government expenditure on basic education in the past decade has more than tripled in real terms. *However, widespread and equitable improvements in basic education quality have lagged behind access gains.*

The past decade has seen increased public debate on issues of equity and education. Citizens' increased expectations of government have been revealed in recent political debates and media coverage on issues related to national health insurance, civil service salary reform (for example, the single-spine salary system), free senior high school and support for accelerated development of economically marginalized regions (for example, the Savannah Accelerated Development Authority). In 2003, the Education Strategic Plan (ESP) 2003–15 set the strategic direction for country attainment of EFA goals. In 2010, the Ministry of Education developed a new ESP for the period of 2010–20, which promotes accelerated development of basic and post-basic education.

Many inequities associated with powerful constituencies appear resistant to change. Specifically, many inequities, such as the allocation of trained teachers and the insufficient provision of support to deprived districts and populations, appear perpetuated by interests associated with powerful constituencies such as teachers unions, the upper middle class and government decision-makers responsible for allocation and management of public resources. Further, as more families enter the middle class and urbanize, many pupils are exiting the public system and paying for elite private schools. The influence of powerful interests and the exit of influential constituencies from public schools each reduce pressure on government to reform basic education and leaves poorer families worse off. This dynamic presents important public policy choices: Do the people of Ghana want to support strong public basic schools or will the education landscape in Ghana continue to follow the current trajectory of a highly unequal two tiered system?

This report emphasizes the need to develop a post-MDG strategic agenda in Ghana that focuses on equity and quality and is supported by improvements in efficiency and accountability.

Basic Education in Ghana draws on an extensive body of new data and analysis to explain the relationship between persistent inequities and poor system performance, discuss equity in relationship to quality, efficiency, finance and management/accountability goals and situate basic education within the broader social and political context of national development. In doing so, this report points to the possibilities and challenges facing promising interventions, outlines strategic issues and critical dilemmas facing education planners in Ghana and sets the stage for a lively and productive debate around the development of a post-MDG strategic agenda.[1]

Improving equity and quality in basic education is related to progress toward efficiency and accountability goals and requires consideration of education expenditure, finance and management. As such, the report includes separate chapters on Equity, Quality and Efficiency and extensive discussion on accountability. Since equity-improving efforts take place in an organizational context, this report also provides data and discussion on education expenditure, finance and management.

The Ghanaian experience is applicable to other countries in Sub-Saharan Africa which have realized similar change and challenge in basic education. As a new lower middle income country, Ghana's experience offers important lessons for other countries in the region. Indeed, many countries are already seeing expectations of and pressures on government increase following significant progress toward meeting the Education MDGs. Report findings and recommendations are presented below.

Basic Education in Ghana: Main Findings

Equity Findings

Children in Ghana come from highly diverse and unequal backgrounds. Levels of adult literacy and educational attainment and household socioeconomic status vary greatly across Ghana. Regional differences in geography, economic conditions and social and cultural practices across Ghana add to the diverse and unequal backgrounds of children. The three northern regions account for the majority of households in the poorest two wealth quintiles.

Ghana has seen huge gains in access to basic education in all regions, among the poor, by gender and by urban and rural status in the past decade. In less than 15 years, enrollment in basic education has nearly doubled, from around 3.5 million pupils enrolled in 1999/2000 to nearly 7 million pupils enrolled in 2010/11 (see Table 0.1, MoE 2008 and MoE 2012). Enrollment gains have been made in all regions with the Upper East and Upper West Regions experiencing the greatest percentage gains in attendance. By 2011, enrollment in Kindergarten had grown to 1.5 million pupils, up from 700,000 in 2004. *Even with these gains, recent estimates place between 300,000–800,000 children of primary school age as not in school* (MoE 2012; UNICEF 2012). Children from poor households, children living in the Northern regions and children who are orphaned or living with a relative or guardian, are the most likely to be out of school (UNICEF 2010).

Even with significant access gains, pupil attendance at primary and secondary schools vary greatly by household wealth and urban-rural status. Figure 0.1 shows primary and secondary school net attendance ratio (NAR), by wealth quintile and urban-rural status (GSS 2011). Primary NAR for pupils from the

Table 0.1 Enrollment and NER in KG, Primary, and JHS 1990–2011/12

Basic subsector	1999/2000	2003/04	2006/07	2011/12
KG enrollment	—	.69m	1.10m	1.54m
KG NER	—	—	56%	64%
Primary	2.5m	2.96m	3.37m	4.45m
Primary NER	—	58% (est.)	79%	82%
JHS	.80m	.98m	1.13m	1.43m
JHS NER	—	—	51%	46%

Source: MoE Education Sector Performance Report 2008 and 2012, and MoE EMIS (qtd. in Akeyampong, 2007).
Note: — = not available.

Figure 0.1 Primary and Secondary School Net Attendance Ratio, by Wealth Quintile and Urban-Rural Status, 2011

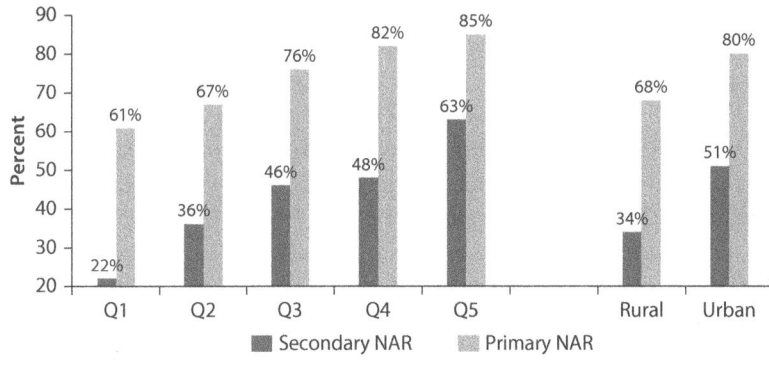

Source: GSS 2011.

Figure 0.2 Primary Net Attendance Ratio, by Region, 2011

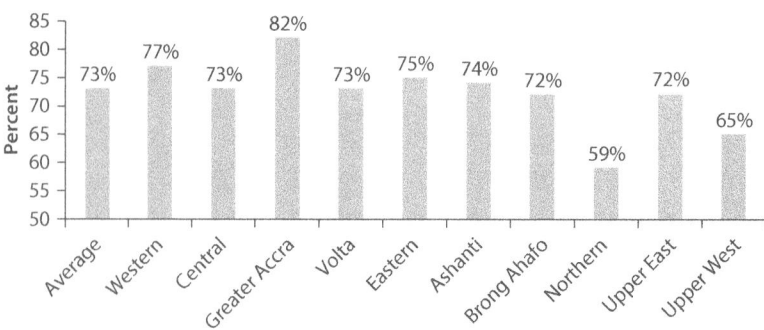

Source: GSS 2011.

wealthiest households (Quintile 5) is 85 percent, compared to a primary NER of 61 percent for students coming from the poorest households (Quintile 1). Difference in NAR by wealth quintile is more pronounced in SHS: students from wealthiest households are nearly three times as likely to have access to senior high school compared to peers in the lowest wealth quintiles (63 percent vs. 22 percent). Similar disparities are evident when comparing access by urban-rural status. Figure 0.2 shows primary net attendance ratio by region (2011). While pupil primary school attendance varies by region, all regions face access challenges. By region, excepting Greater Accra, primary net attendance in Ghana is less than 80 percent.

As with access, distribution of key inputs (for example, trained teachers, textbooks), is also highly inequitable. Urban and wealthy districts in Ghana have larger numbers of trained teachers per student in comparison to poor, rural and northern districts. This inequity is important because trained teachers are recognized as one of the most critical factors in improving student learning. At a national level, 66 percent of the primary teaching force is made up of trained teachers. Map 0.1 shows the percent of Trained Primary Teachers by region for 2011/12. Note the highly unequal distribution of teachers. In four regions, Western, Upper East, Northern and Brong Ahafo, 40–50 percent of the teaching force is made up of untrained teachers. In four other regions, Ashanti, Volta, Eastern and Greater Accra, 70–90 percent of the teaching force is comprised of trained teachers.

Figure 0.3 shows district-level primary PTTR by SES (each box represents one district). Districts in the poorest wealth quintile (Q1) have on average 126 primary students per trained teacher while districts in the highest two wealth quintiles have a primary PTTR of nearly half this amount (67 for Q5 and 58 for Q4).

Instead of compensating for deprivation, public expenditure exacerbates inequality by allocating fewer resources per child to regions where the majority of deprived districts are located. Table 0.2 shows the Per Child Expenditure (PCE) in 2008 GHc measured at district level for KG, Primary and JHS.[2] PCE is the GoG district-level recurrent expenditure divided by the number of enrolled children in the district. The table shows the average PCE by district and the average PCE for the

Map 0.1 Percentage of Trained Primary Teachers, by Region, 2011/12

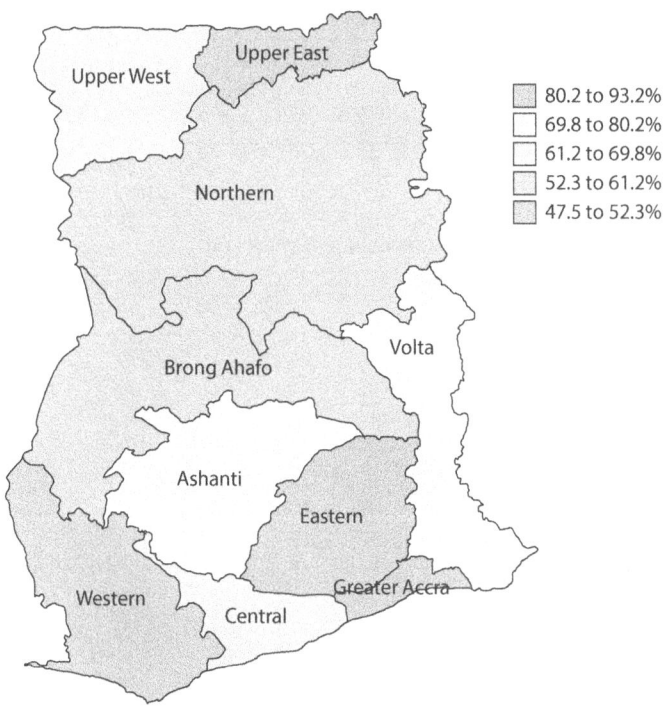

Source: ESPR 2012.

Figure 0.3 Primary PTTR, by SES, 2008/09

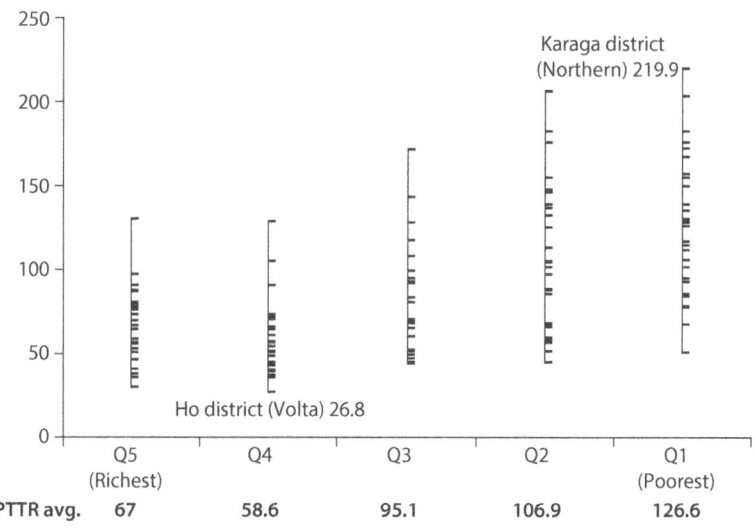

Source: World Bank 2010. Based on EMIS. Estimates based on GLSS 2005/06 and EMIS 2008/09.
Note: PTTR = pupil trained teacher ratio.

Basic Education beyond the Millennium Development Goals in Ghana
http://dx.doi.org/10.1596/978-1-4648-0098-6

Table 0.2 Per-Child Expenditure in 2008 GHc Measured at District Level

	KG	Primary	JHS
Average (all districts)	47	125	196
Average (bottom third of districts)	23	90	134
Bottom third PCE (% of avg. PCE)	50%	72%	68%

Source: World Bank 2010.

Figure 0.4 Percentage of P6 Pupils Attaining Proficiency in English and Maths, by Urban-Rural Status

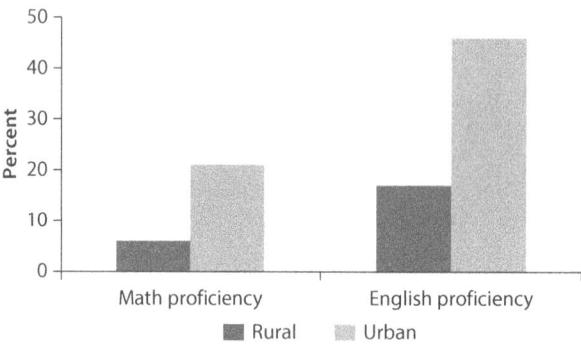

Source: MoE 2012.

bottom third of districts. In 2008, the PCE in primary school was 125GHc and the average PCE in districts comprising the bottom third was 90GHc. Districts in the bottom third received, on average, 28 percent less per child than the average PCE. Similar trends are evident in KG and JHS PCE analysis. Since personnel emoluments (that is salaries) account for a majority of MoE recurrent expenditure in primary education, variation in PCE largely reflects the disparity in teacher allocation across districts.

Basic education outcomes—primary completion rates, learning in English and mathematics and BECE pass rates—are also unequally distributed by region, urban-rural status and household socioeconomic status. P3 and P6 proficiency in English and mathematics has been measured by the National Education Assessment (NEA) on a biannual basis since 2005. Reports on NEA assessments from 2005 as well as other analyses indicate that inequality in learning outcomes is largely explained by differences (i) between major population center districts (for example, Accra, Tema, Kumasi, and Shama-Ahanta East (Takoradi)) and the rest of the country, (ii) urban-rural status and (iii) regional status (Joseph and Wodon 2012; MoE 2012; USAID 2009).

Figure 0.4 shows the percent of P6 pupils attaining proficiency in English and mathematics by urban-rural status. In English, 46 percent of urban pupils attain a proficiency score compared to 17 percent of rural pupils. Mathematics scores follow a similar trend with 21 percent of urban pupils attaining a proficiency

Figure 0.5 Percentage of P3 and P6 Students Achieving Proficiency in English, by Region

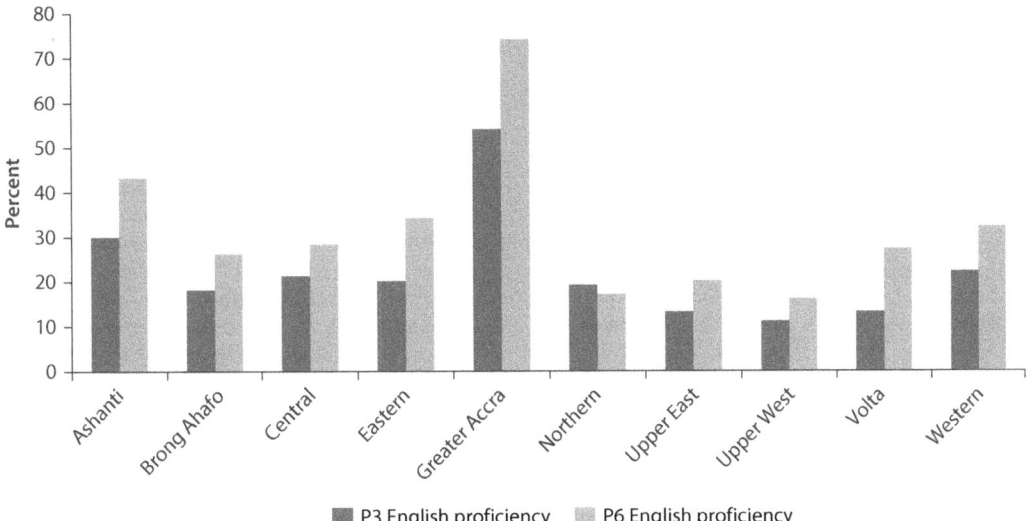

Source: MoE 2012.

score compared to 6 percent of rural pupils. Regional variation is also very high (see figure 0.5). MoE (2012, xiv) notes:

> P6 and P3 students in Greater Accra outperformed their peers in other regions and in both subject areas by a wide margin. For example, the ratio of Greater Accra students achieving proficiency compared to students in the lowest-performing regions ranged from 4.9 on the P3 English test to 9.5 on the P6 maths test. In other words, in comparing students from Greater Accra to those from the lowest-performing regions, between nearly 5 and 10 times more students from Greater Accra were able to achieve proficiency-level scores than students from lower-performing regions.

In the past decade, Ghana has implemented several equity-improving measures designed to improve basic education access and quality with varying degrees of success. Several of the programs listed in Table 0.3, including the Capitation Grant Scheme and the Livelihood Empowerment Against Poverty (LEAP) program show promise, but face critical targeting, implementation and cost-effectiveness challenges. Notably, most inputs-focused initiatives respond to part of the "access challenge," however these programs do not address other issues (for example, age of initial enrollment, household expectations of child labor, school culture) that also act as access-barriers. Further, none of these programs directly address the structural inequities in the current system, including getting trained teachers to pupils with the greatest need.

Data from this section show that students and populations who may require the most support to meet expected outcomes (for example, learning, primary

Table 0.3 Overview of Selected Equity Improving Programs

Intervention	Description	Results	Challenges
Capitation Grant	Grant of 4.5GHc per child enrolled sent to every basic education school	Initially supported NER increase	Amount is seen as insufficient, management issues (funding delay and leakage), funding does not target the poorest
LEAP	Monthly cash transfer to poor families of 8–15 GHc	Increase nutrition and education access to vulnerable populations	Targeting needs strengthening, program management issues, high implementation cost
Ghana School Feeding Program	Provision of breakfast or lunch during the school day	Increase school access and child nutrition	Targeting very poor, many program management issues, high implementation cost
Complementary Basic Education	Initiative to mainstream rural, overage, vulnerable children into GES schools	Majority of participants get functional literacy and are mainstreamed; cost-effective	Currently outside of MoE/GES system, operates only in northern regions
Grants to Deprived Districts (for example, PPS)	Provision of block grants to "deprived districts"	District capacity development, support to flexible, district-led interventions	Delay in funding to districts, difficult to measure targeting and specific impact of funding

Sources: Various evaluation documents, including World Bank 2011.

completion, access to secondary), receive, on average, disproportionately fewer resources (for example, trained teachers, textbooks) from the government than their peers. *Inequitable distribution of inputs creates a negatively reinforcing loop where children with the greatest need receive the fewest resources and opportunities, thereby reproducing cycles of poverty and inequality.*

Quality Findings

Linked to inequity is the challenge of quality: Learning outcomes of P3 and P6 students in English and mathematics results remain low and the supply of qualified teachers has regularly been at least 50,000 below then number required. In the 2011 National Education Assessment (NEA), 35 percent of P6 students tested at proficiency level in English and 16 percent tested at proficiency level in Maths (see Figure 0.6). Outside of Greater Accra, fewer than 25 percent of students in attain proficiency in P3 Maths, P3 English or P6 Maths (excepting Ashanti Region for P3 English). NEA scores, in corroboration with other information included in this report, indicate that the majority of P6 students who complete primary school are doing so without having attained proficiency in core subject areas.

Score patterns on several assessments suggest the presence of a "missing middle." Many students score well on the NEA, but an even larger number of students do not attain a minimum competency level (except in the case of P6 English result). In a different assessment, in 2009, the World Bank implemented an English exam to test P3 and P5 student fluency in naming letters, reading words and

Figure 0.6 Percentage of P3 and P6 Students Attaining Proficiency in English and Maths, 2011

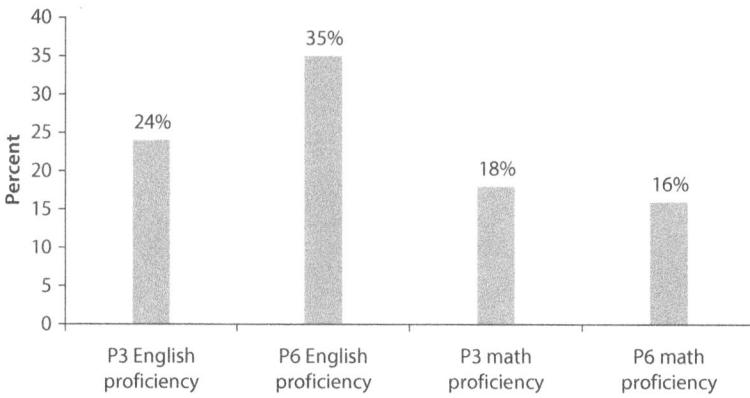

Source: MoE 2012.

Figure 0.7 Percentage of P3 and P5 Students, by Reading Comprehension Score

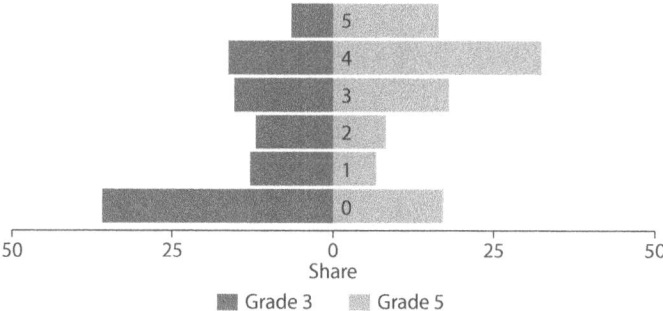

Source: Cloutier 2010.

reading comprehension. Figure 0.7 shows the percentage of P3 and P5 students by reading comprehension score. The data show a large number of students with zero scores, a slim middle and a moderate number of students with high scores. On the World Bank English assessment, 35 percent of 3rd graders and more than 15 percent of 5th graders received zero scores in reading comprehension exercises. This finding has some alignment with NEA results, where, in the reading comprehension portion of the English exam, 42 percent of P3 students had a 0 of 1 score (out of six questions). *Zero score results on this exam and the NEA indicate that large numbers of children have passed through three or six grades of school having learned little to no English.*

This report presents analysis on factors positively and negatively associated with learning outcomes. School level factors associated with a positive effect on NEA scores include the proportion of trained teachers, availability of textbooks and the proportion of female teachers.[3] Factors negatively associated with NEA achievement included presence of high repetition and dropout, multigrade classrooms and a high percentage of orphans (MoE, 2012).[4] Language spoken at home (if it

Figure 0.8 Percentage of Trained Teachers in Primary School and JHS, 1987/88–2009/10

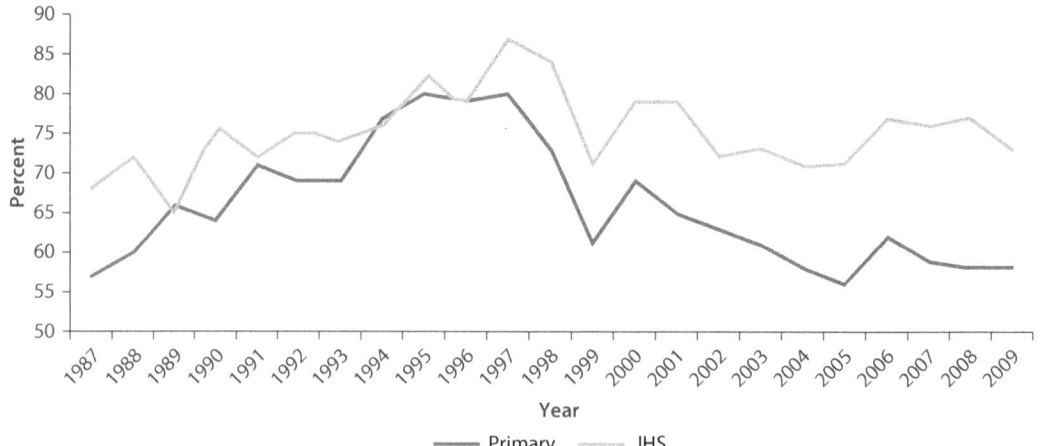

Source: Thompson and Casely-Hayford 2008; ESPR 2011 (2006/07–2010/11); ESPR 2008 (2003/04–2005/06). Public school only.

is not English) may also explain low exam scores. Inequality in NEA learning outcomes is largely explained by differences between (i) major population center districts—Accra, Tema, Kumasi, and Shama-Ahanta East (Takoradi)—and the rest of the country, (ii) urban-rural status and (iii) regional status. *These differences are also associated with inequitable distribution of inputs, including trained teachers.*

Insufficient numbers of qualified teachers are a critical barrier to improving equity and quality. Meeting the MoE target of 95 percent qualified teachers requires the addition of over 50,000 qualified teachers in basic schools. Figure 0.8 shows the percentage of trained public primary and JHS teachers from 1987 to 2010 (MoE EMIS). In the past 5 years, the percentage of trained primary teachers has been nearly flat (between 58 percent and 62 percent); between 30 percent and 40 percent of the KG teaching force has been comprised of trained teachers while 70–80 percent of JHS teachers hold a Diploma in Basic Education. Like the primary subsector, in both KG and JHS subsectors, deprived districts are substantially worse off than nondeprived districts with respect to the percentage of "trained teachers" (ESPR 2011). From an equity standpoint, the high percentage of untrained teachers working in KG and lower primary is highly disadvantageous to poorer students—who require strong instruction in early years.

Several recent studies argue that additional support should be given to improving learning in multigrade multilevel (MGML) schools. There are more than 5,000 schools with MGML classrooms in Ghana. The majority of teachers in MGML schools (64 percent) do not have relevant training. Figure 0.9 shows that pupils in multigrade classrooms perform significantly worse in language learning that counter-parts in non-multigrade classrooms. According to MoE (2012, 38), "Teaching in multigrade classrooms presents particular challenges as the teachers must prepare multiple lessons to be able to teach students learning at different grade level."

Figure 0.9 Percentage of Students Reaching Minimum Competency and Proficiency, by Classroom Type, P3 English, 2011

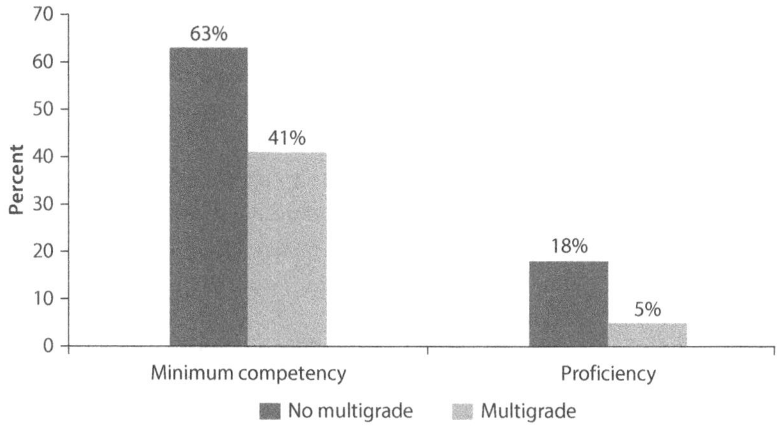

[Bar chart: Minimum competency — No multigrade 63%, Multigrade 41%; Proficiency — No multigrade 18%, Multigrade 5%]

Source: OLE 2011.

A study by Open Learning Institute and GES/TED (2011) recommends that meeting basic education learning objectives will requires giving more attention to MGML classrooms and providing additional support MGML classroom teachers though initial preparation and continuous professional development.

Improving broad-based acquisition of literacy in basic education requires policymakers and other education stakeholders to critically review policy and implementation issues related to the National Literacy Accelerated Programme (NALAP). NALAP is a transitional bilingual literacy program in 11 Ghanaian languages for implementation in grades KG-P3. NALAP curriculum and materials focus on improving literacy learning through mother tongue instruction in Kindergarten through third grade with an early transition to English. NALAP pilot schools outperformed public schools in English on the NEA in 2009 and 2011. However, transition to NALAP has been a contentious issue between policymakers, education experts, and the MoE, and NALAP training and implementation has been riddled with challenges.

Efficiency Findings

Inefficient allocation of qualified teachers, teacher absenteeism and loss of instructional time during the school day are three of the greatest inefficiencies in the current system. Teachers are inefficiently allocated by region, district and deprived district status. As noted earlier, student achievement is higher in schools with more qualified teachers. A more equitable distribution of these teachers would likely support improved overall learning. Regarding teacher absenteeism, a 20 percent reduction in teacher absenteeism would be the equivalent of hiring 5,200 additional new teachers. Efficiency improvements in the use of money, human and physical resources and time could help Ghana realize improved learning outcomes within the same budget envelope.

Inefficiencies at the school level, led by teacher absenteeism and teacher delay, may account for the loss of more than 50 percent of available instructional time in many primary schools. Several studies point to a teacher absenteeism rate of between 20 percent and 30 percent in Ghana—the equivalent of more than one day per week. While evidence is not conclusive, Abadzi (2007) suggests that there is poorer use of instructional time in the northern regions and in rural schools. Figure 0.10 presents data from studies on "instructional time use" in four countries. In Ghana, out of 197 school days, teachers were, on average, absent for 43 days and delayed for 40 days. Other factors, including student absence (11 days) and student delay (9 days) and poor use of instructional time led to the finding that, out of the 197 day school year in Ghana, students were engaged in learning activities for only 76 days.

Several factors contribute to absenteeism, including illness, participation in official teaching related duties, administrative matters (for example, salary collection, HR issue), funeral attendance, religious practices, farming activities (rural teachers) and participation in continuing education courses (Table 0.4). Absenteeism is not

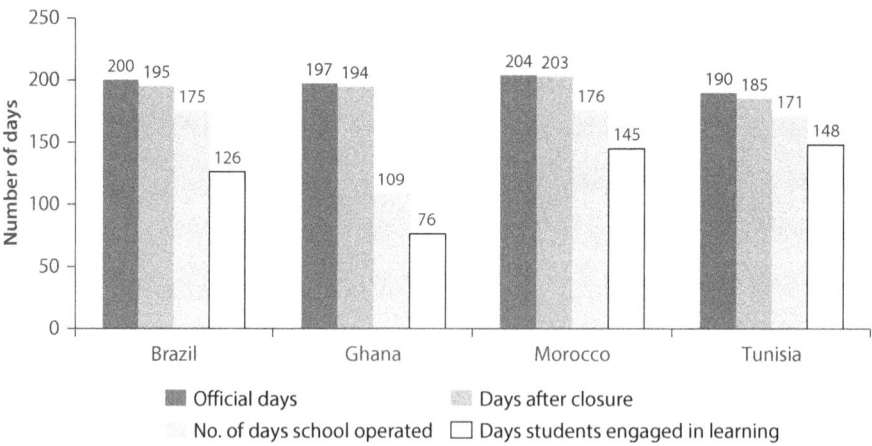

Figure 0.10 Instructional Time in Basic Schools in Four Countries

Source: Abadzi 2007.

Table 0.4 Factors Explaining Teacher Absenteeism

- Teacher illness/health clinic visits***
- Official teaching duties (for example, in-service training/workshop)**
- Funeral attendance**
- Religious practices (for example, Friday prayers for Muslim teachers)**
- Farming activities
- Continuing education (Study Leave, Sandwich course)
- Official nonteaching duty

Sources: Abadzi 2007; EARC 2003; CDD 2008; Transparency International 2009a.
** Indicates a frequently cited reason
***Maternity leave is included in "health"

necessarily a reflection on teachers' commitment to work. High absenteeism also reflects a policy and management environment challenged by salary delays, lack of supervision, distance from teachers' homes to schools and from schools to health care and banking facilities and, in many cases, poor working conditions. Factors which appear to reduce absenteeism include improving teacher work conditions, the presence of "dedicated and disciplined" school leadership, increasing circuit supervisor visits, preparedness to sanction recalcitrant staff (from the head-teacher, circuit supervisor, or DEM), altering the academic schedule of DBE and sandwich courses and increasing parental involvement (Abadzi 2007; CDD 2008; PDA-PPVA 2011; World Bank 2010).

Pupil enrollment explains less than 50 percent of the distribution of classrooms in basic schools pointing to large inefficiencies in infrastructure investment. These inefficiencies are likely encouraged by the complex environment in which infrastructure planning, procurement and financing takes place. Increasing enrollment means that there will be a need to continue expanding (and rehabilitating) infrastructure (for example, classrooms, libraries, staff rooms, toilets, water points). *While comprehensive data are not available, analysis included in this report suggests that a close review of infrastructure investments could identify areas for efficiency gains.*

Finance, Management, and Accountability Findings

In the past decade, public finance of and expenditure on education in Ghana has demonstrated four characteristics.

1. A lot of money is spent on education in Ghana: education accounts for 18–27 percent of public expenditure, equal to 5–6 percent of Ghana's GDP.
2. Personal emoluments have accounted for more than 97 percent of government expenditure in basic education over the past 5 years. PE expenditure does not appear constrained by Ministry of Finance budget ceilings and annually crowds out expenditures in other budget categories (for example, service and investment).
3. Education financing is fragmented among a number of sources and among an even larger number of flows of funds. Basic schools in Ghana have little say over the resources needed to deliver quality basic education: teachers and resources generally flow from the center.
4. The complexity of education finance sources and delivery systems complicate efforts to improve accountability.

In the 2013 budget, wages, salaries, and allowances accounted for 99 percent of the GoG basic education budget.[5] *Expenditure in 2013 is expected to be 3,700 million Ghana cedis, or 179 percent, of the budgeted amount.* The trend in the wage bill poses two critical challenges:

1. *The wage bill crowds out expenditures in other critical areas.* In 2012, GES received just over a third of their goods and services budget allocation. Consequently, districts were heavily dependent on non-GoG funds to manage their day to day expenses.

2. *Increasing the percentage of trained teachers will require the wage bill grow faster than GDP in the medium term.* Increasing the number of trained teachers is important for improving equity and quality; however, given the size of the 2013 wage bill and the higher cost of trained teachers, it is unclear if there is room for such growth absent salary reform.

Table 0.5 shows budget category share of GoG expenditure and execution as a percentage of the amount budgeted for the 2009, 2010, and 2011 fiscal years. In the past 5 years, expenditures in PE have come in at 15–78 percent *above* the budget ceiling given by the Ministry of Finance. According to the Ministry of Education, Education Sector Performance Report (2012, 53), in 2011, the MoE's total PE expenditure "was GH¢ 2.45 billion against a budget of GH¢ 1.42 billion creating a budget overrun of GH¢ 1.03 billion. The PE execution rate of 172 percent can be attributed to two major factors namely: The low level of PE ceiling given to the sector by MOFEP [and]... implementation of the Single Spine Salary Scheme."

Annual wage bill overruns are a result of a planning system with no hard budget constraint. Specifically, the financial ceiling determined by the MoFNP for basic education wages and salaries is not based on the actual number of teachers on GES payroll. The budget estimate for the past 5 years has systematically undercounted the number of staff on GES payroll, creating the annual overrun and crowding out of expenditures in other categories. The migration to the Single Spine Salary Scheme has not addressed this issue.

Education financing is fragmented among a number of sources and among an even larger number of flows of funds. Figure 0.11 shows sources and flows of funding and resources for a government primary school in Ghana. The authority to allocate the key resources is divided among four agencies: The Ministry of Finance is responsible for setting the overall budget and determining Civil Service Agency (CSA) remunerations; the Ghana Education Trust Fund (GETFund) is responsible for investments; Ghana Education Service (GES) is responsible for allocating recurrent expenditure and to set teacher numbers; and the Ministry of Education (MOE) is responsible for allocating donor funds and proposing the annual budget to the Government. This fragmentation of budgetary responsibilities and the lack of a hard constraint on the wage bill are, perhaps, the main reason why planned and executed budgets differ.

Table 0.5 GoG Budget Share, by Budget Category and Execution in Relation to Budget Amount

	2009		2010		2011	
GoG budget category	Share (%)	Execution (%)	Share (%)	Execution (%)	Share (%)	Execution (%)
PE	97	136	97	147	97	172
Admin	2.1	130	1.9	101	1.6	137
Service	0.7	31	0.7	52	0.7	83
Investment	0.1	56	0.1	58	2.1	105

Source: ESPR 2010, 2011.

Figure 0.11 Sources and Flows of Funding and Resources for a Primary School in Ghana

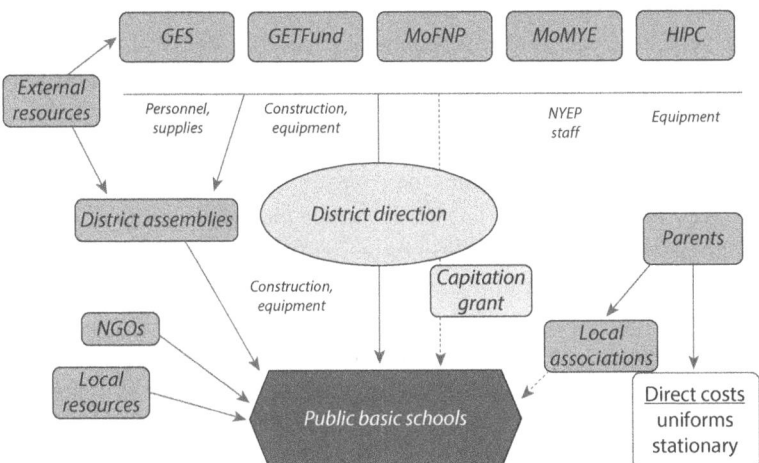

Source: Adapted from UIS 2011.

Many key decisions affecting education service delivery (for example, teacher salary negotiations, recruitment, and posting of NYEP teachers) are made outside of the MoE and GES. To adequately plan for and finance core education costs (for example, teachers, infrastructure and textbooks), MoE must negotiate with several other institutions on an annual basis. In 2011, GETFund resources were used to fund infrastructure, textbooks, the capitation grant and NYEP teachers. MoFNP plays a critical role in deciding annual changes in the salary grille. MoPDC arranges implementation of the Ghana School Feeding Program through district assemblies. MoE also works with development partners to provide resources for items such as grants to deprived districts, sector budget support and project support to purchase textbooks and infrastructure and train head-teachers.

The fragmented and decentralized nature of education finance and management compromises national-level accountability efforts. Most effective "accountability" exercises have originated from outside of the education sector—either led by civil society organizations or development partner efforts to track public funding of education. Absent efforts from these organizations, evidence of fund leakage in the Capitation Grant scheme and school books expenditures and anomalies in District Assembly Common Fund (DCAF) fund use may not have come to light.

At the district level, accountability for service delivery is further compromised by the limited authority of and resources available to basic schools and districts. At present most MMDAs are not fully autonomous in expenditure decisions, especially in the areas of teacher management, remuneration (salaries and allowances), investment budget (classroom, school buildings, teachers' houses, etc.) and textbooks provision (Steffensen 2006).

Ongoing decentralization poses a great opportunity and a great challenge. Decentralization promises to provide district authorities, with more authority and capacity to supervise and manage service delivery and resource allocation activities.

Even so, several factors, including lack of resources and insufficient professional development hinder their successful execution of job responsibilities. Basic schools in Ghana have very little say over the resources needed to deliver quality basic education and limited management support. Teachers and resources generally flow from centralized structures. While districts have some responsibility for infrastructure and textbook provision, they often have insufficient resources.

Circuit supervisors and head-teachers can play important management and accountability roles; however several factors, including lack of resources and insufficient professional development hinder their successful fulfillment of job responsibilities. The limited authority and training of circuit supervisors and head-teachers mean that they are often not seen as figures of authority at the school. Studies have shown that rigorous and frequent school visits by circuit supervisors, though uncommon, can play an essential management role. Improving the teacher supervision structures and offering incentives tend to decrease teacher absenteeism and lateness (Akyeampong et al. 2007).

The role of PTAs and SMCs in improving "social accountability" at the school level is mixed. Recent efforts to implement School Report Cards, School Performance Improvement Plans (SPIPs) and School Performance Assessment Meetings (SPAMs) show promise, but evaluation of the effectiveness of these interventions is not yet been completed.

Teacher Policy Dilemmas

Effective management of teachers is hampered by several factors. While GES has the mandate to assure that schools have enough teachers, it does not have effective tools to ensure that teachers remain in the school or district to which they are assigned. Factors contributing to excused and unexcused teacher absenteeism can greatly frustrate efforts by head-teachers, circuit supervisors and DEOs to effectively manage teachers. Many head-teachers and circuit supervisors have limited job-specific training and in most cases have limited authority to address teacher work performance and disciplinary issues.

Education planners face several genuine policy dilemmas when it comes to teacher policy and management.

1. Basic schools require more than 50,000 qualified basic education teachers, but GES does not appear to have sufficient resources to finance salaries of this many more qualified teachers.
2. Placing less qualified staff into primary teaching vacancies does not appear to improve quality. Specifically, utilization of 70,000 untrained teachers (including National Youth Employment Program [NYEP] and the National Service Scheme [NSS] staff) has reduced primary PTR at a limited cost to GES but does not appear to have had a measurable impact on quality.
3. The majority of teachers are not satisfied with the conditions of service—however, most changes to conditions of service require more resources. Taking away costly benefits (for example, Study Leave) may have negative political implications.

4. Posting teachers to rural and deprived areas continues to be especially challenging. Teacher preference for employment in urban areas, and modern amenities, is understandable. However these preferences are also a powerful counterweight to equity-improving policies. Unfortunately, the posting process for new teachers appears to reproduce the unequal distribution of qualified teachers instead of serving as a mechanism to address this issue.

Basic Education in Ghana: Recommendations

Recommendations

Implicit in the basic education strategic goal (in the ESP 2010–20) is Government commitment to full implementation of FCUBE and that, at a minimum, all pupils should leave primary schools with proficiency in numeracy and literacy.[6] Recommendations included below seek to support national progress toward the basic education strategic goal, prioritizing improvements in quality and equity. These recommendations offer a prioritized list of strategic areas for reform, priority interventions and provocative ideas which we hope stimulate a lively and productive debate on basic education reform in Ghana. Many of these recommendations are drawn from ESP 2010–20, Volume 2 and the experience of GES pilot programs and interventions.

1. *Improve the equitable allocation and increase the number of qualified teachers.* Accelerating progress toward learning goals requires addressing the national shortage and inequitable distribution of qualified teachers. *Some strategies to consider:*

   - *Reform the teacher deployment system.* Centralized recruitment and deployment of teachers has not managed to address persistent inequities in teacher allocation. As long as this system remains in place, poorer and more rural schools and districts will not have equitable access to qualified teachers.
   - *Introduce location-specific recruitment of teachers and ensure teachers' language skills match school needs.* In location-specific recruitment, newly qualified teachers would compete for positions posted by schools or districts. Providing schools more choice in hiring decisions and teachers' more choice in deployment can help fill unpopular posts and improve retention and gender balance.[7] Furthermore, Ghana has more than 5,000 multigrade, multilevel basic schools. Recruitment and deployment should ensure teachers' language skills match school needs.
   - *Upgrade qualifications and strengthen professional support for underqualified teachers.* Ghana's basic schools are likely to rely on a large number of unqualified teachers over the next two decades. The Untrained Teachers Diploma in Basic Education (UTDBE) offers a cost-effective way to upgrade the skills/qualifications of underqualified teachers. Attention should be paid to ensuring the quality of the UTDBE program to ensure it produces effective teachers.

- *Provide incentives for teachers and head-teachers in deprived areas.* Newly qualified teachers are attracted to the amenities and incentives in urban districts. To help schools in deprived areas compete, positions at these schools could be linked to benefits, such as accelerated promotion, salary top-up, study leave with pay, transport or accommodation allowances or loan forgiveness. Pilot studies should be used to determine how to best target benefits and which benefits offer the best value for money.
- *Improve transition rate of CoE and university graduates into the teaching profession; improve retention; reduce attrition. Aggressively recruit SHS graduates for CoE studies.* Every year, a large number of CoE, UEW and UCC graduates do not enter the teaching profession and 10,000 teachers leave basic education. *On these issues, this report has more questions than answers especially since the causes and remedies likely point beyond education policy and education reform.*
- *Deploy more qualified teachers to KG1-P3 classes.* Anecdotal evidence suggests that qualified teachers are more likely to teach upper primary and JHS classes and that KG and lower primary classes are likely to have high pupil-teacher ratios. Learning in early grades provides the foundation for future learning. School leaders should be encouraged to direct appropriately qualified teachers to teach KG1-P3 classes and lower PTRs in early grades.
- *Eliminate study leave.* If wage bill reductions are not considered politically feasible, GES could access the equivalent of 3.4 percent and 3.8 percent of the total annual education budget by eliminating paid study leave and eliminating allowances to trainee teachers. More than 3,000 teachers take paid study leave on an annual basis and do not return to the classroom.

2. *Strengthen instructional support for children in early grades and for children who need it most.* The Government of Ghana made a positive step toward improving equity and quality by adding Kindergarten to basic education. More can be done to improve early grades learning. *The following are some strategies to consider:*
    - *Provide additional instruction to children with low learning outcomes.* There is an increasing body of evidence about which schools fall behind in performance, what the reasons are and what can be done to improve learning outcomes of students who falling behind. One example: A study implemented by the Teacher Community Assistant Initiative shows that providing after-school numeracy and literacy instruction using a trained teacher-community assistant has a positive impact on literacy and numeracy skills of lowest level learners in deprived schools (TCAI 2012).[8] Performance data and information on promising practices should be brought into the annual performance reporting system to support discussion on mainstreaming and scale-up.
    - *Further strengthen national literacy efforts.* The National Accelerated Literacy Program (NALAP) shows promise, however to sustain progress, KG1-P3

teachers needs more guidance, skills and resources to effectively teach literacy in multilingual environments.
- *Ensure the provision of sufficient teaching and learning materials.* In the past 5 years, the pupil-textbook ratio has declined to one (of three required) core textbooks per primary and JHS pupil. ESPR (2012) identifies lack of textbook provision to basic schools over the past 4 years as a critical failure in GES service delivery. This situation leaves children from low literacy environments and poor households at a disadvantage to their peers.

3. *Improve equitable access, demand for schooling and funding for basic education through existing programs.* In the past decade, GES has piloted several innovative programs which have helped children from vulnerable households attend school. The second generation of programs should seek to address critical targeting, implementation and cost-effectiveness challenges. *Some strategies to consider include the following:*
   - *Strengthen equity of the capitation grant scheme and the resource allocation model.* GES introduction of the Resource Allocation Model, which provides additional funding to schools in deprived districts, shows great promise. Reforming the capitation grant scheme along the same lines (e.g. providing a base grant for all schools or providing additional money to schools in deprived areas or with insufficient teachers) could support equitable progress toward learning goals in small schools and schools in deprived districts.
   - *Strengthen demand-side interventions, especially LEAP.* Livelihood Empowerment Against Poverty (LEAP), a conditional cash transfer program, supported increased access to basic schools. However, the program has high implementation costs and does not reach children from the most vulnerable households. The Ghana School Feeding Program and the Take Home Rations program face similar issues. Ghana could provide a continent-leading example of improving social protection and interministerial collaboration by significantly strengthening design, targeting and cost-effectiveness of these programs.
   - *Continue efforts to support out-of school children, children from marginalized and disadvantaged groups and children with disabilities.* GES partnerships with School for Life, IBIS and others have made a large impact in improving school access to children from disadvantaged and marginalized populations, especially in the three northern regions. Growing informal settlements in urban areas point to new challenges and the need to continue creative access-promoting interventions.[9] GES can build on partnerships with CAMFED, USAID-TAP, UNICEF and PAGE to continue to address challenges facing girls and children with disabilities.

4. *Strengthen management accountability for results, transparency and democratic participation at all levels.* Education accounts for 20 percent of government expenditures and reaches over 7 million children in basic schools. Yet, the use

and distribution of resources is often unclear to the public. Action on several fronts—in civil society, within MoE and GES, in communities, and with the newly established National Inspectorate Board—can improve transparency and accountability. *Some strategies to consider include the following:*

- *Give local authorities power and develop local capacity to supervise and manage service delivery.* District authorities should be given authority to hire, dismiss and deploy teachers and more resources to support professional development and supervise teacher performance. The current, fractured, system for teacher management allows for high absenteeism and leaves districts with no power to enforce professional standards of conduct.
- *Professionalize school management and strengthen instructional leadership.* Head-teachers and circuit supervisors should have the educative, management and leadership capacities, the authority and sufficient resources to execute the managerial and instructional leadership responsibilities of their position.[10] GES-led training of head-teachers and circuit supervisors should be complemented with increased responsibilities and resources for school and circuit leaders.[11]
- *Reduce teacher absenteeism and teacher delay.* A 20 percent reduction in teacher absenteeism would have the equivalent effect of hiring an additional 5,200 teachers. Policymakers in Ghana are discussing options for reducing high absenteeism, including reducing the number of days allowed for "unexcused absence" or due to participation in teacher education courses and allowing district officers to freeze teacher pay. In rural areas, targeted provision of a transportation allowance may reduce absenteeism and delay of teachers living off-site.
- *Increase time on task.* Increasing the amount of time in the school day spent on learning activities will likely improve learning outcomes with minimal cost to government. Supporting this effort may require guidance and supervision from the National Inspectorate Board and buy-in and capacity development of circuit supervisors, head-teachers and classroom teachers.
- *Increase support to civil society stakeholders and the media.* Civil society actors such as the Center for Democracy and Development and the Ghana National Education Campaign Coalition have provoked important debate on critical issues, including inequities and leakages in public expenditures and inequities between urban and rural areas and in teacher allocation.
- *Implement the School Report Card, the School Performance Improvement Plan and the School Performance Appraisal Meeting.* Implementation of the SRC, SPIP, and the SPAM can strengthen accountability for results, transparency and community participation. These tools provide access to *comparative* data on school quality and public resources (for example, trained teachers, textbooks, capitation grant) and create a space for community dialogue on education.[12]

- *Fully back the National Inspectorate Board (NIB).* The NIB requires full funding and independent exercise of its authority in setting and overseeing educational attainment and performance standards and oversight of district inspection and supervision.

5. *Improve efficiency of PE and infrastructure expenditure.* PE and infrastructure costs account for the vast majority of public expenditures on basic education. Improving value for money would release resources which could be directed toward equity and quality goals. *Some strategies to consider include the following:*

    - *Enforce a hard budget constraint on the GES wage bill. The wage bill presents a true dilemma: balancing the priority for more trained teachers (who have higher recurrent costs) with efforts to manage public expenditure.* In 2013, the wage bill accounted for 99 percent of the GoG basic education budget; wage bill expenditures regularly crowd out expenditure on other education priorities. Setting targets for the overall composition of spending (that is the ratio of PE to other recurrent funding in the final approved budget), ring-fencing critical admin and service items, or rationing the number of centrally-paid teachers per school are possibilities worth exploring.

    - *Strengthen district procurement and infrastructure project management.* Infrastructure costs in Ghana are high in comparison to other countries in West Africa. Basic education infrastructure responsibilities (for example, classrooms, water points, toilets) has been decentralized to the districts, however, capacity to plan for, procure (for example, transparent and competitive bidding) and oversee infrastructure projects varies greatly by district.

6. *Foster a culture of innovation and collaborative learning, everywhere.* In education, "learning is the work" (Fullan 2011). Just as people, cities and nations grow and change, so to must education. For Ghana to meet the possibilities and challenges of the twenty-first century, a *learning culture* should be fostered. Characteristics of such a culture could include the following: collaboration and shared learning; seeking out and funding promising ideas for pilot programs; developing habits of collecting and using relevant data and evaluation at the school level (for example, so teachers are continuously learning about themselves and their pupils) and system level (for example, to consider policy relevance and scale-up potential of promising programs) and encouraging local innovation (since different contexts may require different education interventions). If change is the only constant, change-orientation and learning must be built into the DNA of the education sector.

Authors' Note: This book does not include content on several important issues. First, while this book focuses on basic education, some issues and challenges specific to KG and JHS education and curriculum, are not discussed. The ESP 2010–20 covers adult education, nonformal education and education for children with disabilities (CWD). Making progress toward these EFA goals would result in improvements in equity and social inclusion; however, space did not allow for extensive discussion on these important issues. Last, there are a large number of Islamic Schools in Ghana, many of which are supported by the GES Islamic Education Division. EDC (2007) offers a useful overview of the Islamic education sector.

Notes

1. This report draws on important new education data and analysis on access, equity, learning outcomes, expenditure and management in Ghana and recently completed evaluations of equity-improving programs and public expenditure. New data include the following: National Education Assessment 2011 (MoE 2012); Education Sector Performance Reports 2010, 2011, 2012 (MoE); Tackling Poverty in Northern Ghana (World Bank 2011); Public Expenditure Review 2011 (MoE 2011); An analysis of out of school children in Ghana (UNICEF 2010); EdSEP Implementation Completion Report (World Bank 2012); TIMSS 2007 Ghana Report (Anamuah-Mensah 2009).
2. PCE includes budget categories PE, admin, and service, but not investment.
3. USAID 2009 analyzed 2005 and 2007 NEA scores against EMIS. An earlier evaluation found that increasing textbook access contributed to improvement in English and Maths scores (World Bank 2004).
4. Multigrade classrooms should not be seen as a "cause" of low quality. The social/rural conditions that may lead to the use of a multigrade classroom may offer more power in explaining low NEA scores.
5. Total 2013 GoG basic education budget: 2,070 million cedi; Budget for wages, salaries and allowances: 2,051 million cedi. In the 2012 budget, wage bill expenditure was 3,471 million against 1,279 million allocation: a difference of 2.192 million. Budgets for 2014 and 2015 are expected to follow a similar trajectory (GES 2013).
6. The basic education strategic goal is to "provide equitable access to good-quality child-friendly universal basic education, by improving opportunities for all children in the first cycle of education at Kindergarten, primary and junior high school levels" (MoE ESP 2010–20, 2010).
7. Evidence is based on (Mulkeen 2010, on location specific recruitment in Lesotho, Uganda and Zambia). Implementation of location-specific recruitment may not work by itself. This policy option may also need to include introduction of local incentives and equity-protecting safeguards overseen by NIB.
8. In TCAI, a trained Teacher-Community Assistant from the NYEP supported the program. Untrained NYEP teachers should not take the place of a qualified teacher, however with sufficient training, NYEP staff can provide effective tutoring support.
9. Notably, girls' access, especially in the three northern regions, and girls' drop-out in upper primary and JHS, remain critical challenges.
10. Prominent educators in Ghana contend that nothing less than a change in the organizational culture and attitudes of the education bureaucracy and school leadership is required. Elaborating and providing recommendations on this critique is beyond the scope of this report, but an important consideration in further public debate. [This footnote references the important work of Prof. Jophus Anamuah-Mensah, ex-Vice Chancellor, University of Education, Winneba and Chairman of National Council for Curriculum and Assessment and Prof. J.S. Djangmah, ex-Director of Ghana Education Service, ex Chairman of West African Examination Council.]

11. Responsibilities include, circuit supervisor visits, in-service professional development, supervisory and disciplinary actions. The teacher education universities (UCC & UEW) could be approached to support such training.
12. Providing democratic space and information will allow community members to ask important questions: Why does school X have more qualified teachers? Why does school Y have higher BECE scores? Are we being short-changed by the school, district, or national government? However, we should also add a note of caution against an overreliance on community participation as a "solution" to low quality in poor or marginalized areas. Participation efforts, in the absence of increased professional development and resources and professional support for teachers and deprived schools, is not sufficient.

CHAPTER 1

Introduction—Why Focus on Inequity?

Inequity in learning achievements is the central challenge facing national development and the development of basic education in Ghana. Within basic education, existing inequities in service delivery disadvantage marginalized groups, depress overall system performance (for example, average learning outcomes) and weaken efforts to meet quality, efficiency, and accountability goals. Inequitable service delivery undermines public trust in government and supports the reproduction of existing social and economic inequalities. The effects of this inequity are realized beyond basic education in compromising progress toward post-basic education goals (for example, skills development and tertiary preparation) and broader national goals of increasing economic competitiveness, nurturing democratic development and strengthening social cohesion.

Promotion of equity is a social and political choice and is based on principles of fairness, justice and equal treatment under the law. Equity is a central tenant of most social, political and religious philosophies and the legal framework of most nations. Simply put, people want to live in societies where principles of fairness and justice are protected. These conceptions of equity recognize that people are born into different life circumstances, have different talents and abilities and are affected by different experiences (for example, drought, conflict) as well as by historical prejudices and deprivations (World Bank 2005).

In an equitable society, an individual's life chances (for example, economic, social, health) are not predetermined by his or her birth circumstances or membership in particular groups. Equity can be defined using two concepts: *equal opportunity* and *avoidance of absolute deprivation*. Equal opportunity means that the outcome of an individual's life should not be predetermined by his or her characteristics at birth (for example, gender, household wealth, ethnic/language group, geographic location, orphan status) nor by his or her membership in particular groups (for example, groups defined by religious, ethno-linguistic, sexual orientation). Avoidance of absolute deprivation means that "societies may decide to intervene to protect the livelihoods of its neediest members…even if the equal opportunity principle has been upheld" (World Bank 2005, 19).[1]

Implementation of Free, Compulsory Universal Basic Education (FCUBE) shows the aspiration of Ghana to create a more equitable society. However, despite this aspiration, basic education service delivery in Ghana remains highly inequitable. In Ghana, access to school, distribution of inputs (for example, teachers, textbooks) and learning outcomes and advancement to senior high school show persistent and significant differences across different groups. Populations from the northern regions, deprived districts, poor households and ethnic and linguistic minorities are most disadvantaged in the current system. Figure 1.1 shows three facets of the equity challenge in Ghana: gender, poverty and region. Girls from the poorest households in Ghana's Northern Region are twice as likely to not attend school when compared to the national average (UNICEF 2010). Data on NEA and BECE performance and access to senior high schools show similar disparities by wealth, region and urban-rural status. Children from higher wealth households and from urban areas are more likely to access the best senior high schools, attend university and secure wage employment (Djangmah 2011). *For Ghana to meet the promise of FCUBE and accelerate progress toward national human, social and economic development goals, the government should prioritize improving equity in basic education.*

The critical importance of improving equity in basic education in Ghana is based on three rationales:

1. *Basic education for all is a, yet unrealized, right guaranteed by the Constitution of Ghana.*
2. *Quality basic education for all can play a critical role in addressing broader social and economic inequities and stimulate progress toward broader national development goals.*
3. *Improving equity in basic education service delivery can greatly strengthen system performance in terms of quality and efficiency.*

Figure 1.1 Attendance Rates, Ages 6–14 Years, by Poverty, Gender, and Region, 2003–08

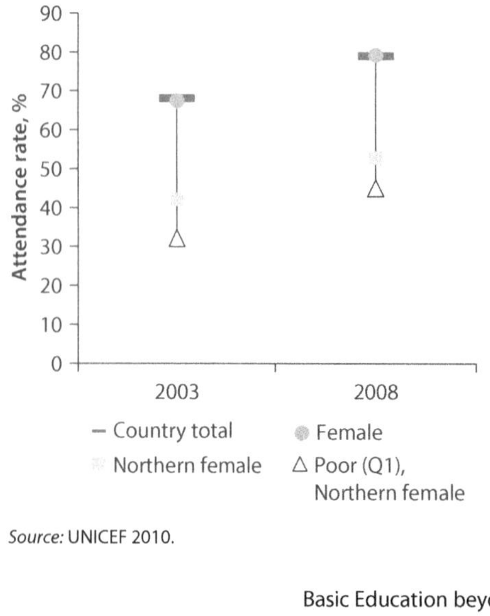

Source: UNICEF 2010.

Basic education is a right guaranteed by the Constitution. The right to basic education is laid out in Article 25 of the Constitution (1992), which states "Basic education shall be free, compulsory and available to all." The Constitution further specifies that citizens' acquisition of functional literacy should be "encouraged or intensified" to the extent possible. The right to basic education underpins other national development goals, including development of a more equitable society. Basic education promotes individual academic and nonacademic development and welfare, supports access to jobs and sustainable livelihoods and provides the cognitive skills and status needed for dignified and meaningful participation in a democratic society. Ensuring the right to basic education for all promotes both facets of equity: equal opportunity and avoidance of absolute deprivation.

Quality basic education for all can help address broader inequity. While Ghana has realized strong economic growth in the past decade, wide-spread and deepening social and economic inequality is a critical challenge facing future development and stability. In 2010, Ghana became classified as a lower-middle-income country and was identified as having a rapidly expanding middle class. However, even with recent growth, there are worrying trends in disparities across regions and socioeconomic groups in terms of poverty incidence and the depth of poverty. These challenges are compounded by the limited social protection measures in place to protect vulnerable populations, increasing urbanization and informal settlement without commensurate increases in employment and social services and underinvestment in rural and remote areas.

Reducing social and economic inequities can help Ghana make progress toward national development goals including acceleration of economic growth, promotion of human rights and strengthening of social cohesion. Available research does not demonstrate a straightforward, causal relationship between inequality reduction and economic growth. However, several recent studies suggests that high levels of inequality can discourage development of accountable government, undermine civic and social life, which can lead to conflict in multiethnic settings, and increase risk of political and financial crisis—during which it is more difficult for individuals to invest in income-generating activities and their own education. Each one of these issues compromise country efforts to sustain and share economic growth (Berg and Ostry 2011; Palma 2011; OECD 2012; UNESCO 2008).

Improving the quality of basic education services for all can play an important role in reducing broader social inequity and reducing extreme poverty and vulnerability. Improving equitable access to quality basic education has been shown to promote economic growth and poverty reduction, improve public health and strengthen democratic participation (OECD 2012; Hanushek and Wosserman 2008; UNESCO 2008).

Improving equity can greatly strengthen system performance. **Existing inequities in basic education significantly depress overall system performance.** The majority of children in Ghana leave primary school without having attained proficiency in core subject areas. More troubling is that a large segment of P3 and P6 students show negligible learning in mathematics and English.[2] Inequitable distribution of inputs (for example, qualified teachers, textbooks) by region and urban-rural status tally closely with observed differences in learning outcomes and test scores (for example, NEA scores and BECE pass rates). This report shows that students and populations who require the most support to meet expected outcomes (for example, learning targets, access to secondary) receive, on average, disproportionately fewer resources (for example, trained teachers, textbooks) from the government than their peers. These disparities show up as a "missing middle" on graphs of assessment results: some pupils do really well, many pupils perform poorly and there is no one in the middle.

Improving equity in service delivery can greatly strengthen system performance in terms of quality and efficiency. A study by McKinsey and Company (2010) argues that an important step in sustained system improvement is to bring all schools and students to a "minimum quality threshold." Meeting this threshold requires providing additional resources to support children and schools which are falling behind. Importantly, students who demonstrate below-average learning outcomes in poorly resourced environments are likely to show the biggest gains in learning outcomes when provided additional support. As this report shows, there are already several small-scale initiatives in Ghana designed to improve equitable and efficient allocation of resources and provide additional support (for example, learning materials, instructional time) to disadvantaged children and schools.

Report Framework

Improving equity in basic education is the central theme of this report. However, issues of equity are strongly related to quality, efficiency, and accountability. Further, since service delivery is organized through community and national institutions, this report provides discussion on education management, finance and expenditure and the politics of education reform. Key concepts are defined in box 1.1.

Box 1.1 Definitions of Key Themes

Equity: This report uses two concepts to define equity: *equal opportunity* and *avoidance of absolute deprivation*. Equal opportunity means that the outcome of an individual's life should neither be predetermined by his or her characteristics at birth (for example, gender, household wealth, ethnic/language group, geographic location, orphan status) nor by his or her membership in particular groups (for example, religious, ethno-linguistic, sexual orientation). Avoidance of absolute deprivation means that, "societies may decide to intervene to protect the livelihoods of its neediest members…even if the equal opportunity principle has been upheld" (World Bank 2005, 19).

---

box continues next page

Box 1.1 Definitions of Key Themes *(continued)*

Quality: This report recognizes the complexity of defining quality. Basic education has multiple objectives (for example, development of pupil cognitive, noncognitive and technical skills and delivery of content on civic issues such as safety, the environment and citizenship) and service delivery is expected to meet certain quality assurance standards (for example, teacher certifications and professional standards; access to teaching and learning materials; safe and secure infrastructure and learning environment; adequate supervisory support and professional development; capacity to support to children with special needs).

This report argues that all schools should be brought to a minimum-quality threshold: pupils should leave primary schools with proficiency in numeracy and literacy, teachers should have the knowledge, skills and institutional support to effectively instruct students, schools should be equitably resourced and supported and children who require additional support to access school and to learn should have access to it.

Efficiency: Efficiency in education is making the best use of available resources to meet basic education objectives. In education, efficiency is often measured by comparing education inputs with education outputs and outcomes. Efficiency analyses can help policymakers improve utilization of available resources such as money, human and physical resources and time. Given the definition of equity—it follows that some pupils may require more resources than others to meet learning outcomes and other basic education objectives.

Accountability: Accountability exists when the performance of tasks or functions by an individual or institution are subject to the oversight of another individual or institution. Simply put, accountability requires that one institution "answer to" another and, should a task or function not be met, that the second institution must be able to enforce a penalty or remediating action on the first. *For example, if a school or district is accountable to a community, then if the school fails to provide adequate textbooks, ensure that teachers present during the school day, or support pupil progress toward numeracy and literacy attainment, then the community should have the power to force the school to address these deficiencies.*

Management: Management is a process or set of actions through which organizations define objectives and marshal and utilize resources to achieve them.

Figure 1.2 shows the conceptual framework for this report. Education goals are dialectically related to the system context. Equity improvements and mindfulness of equity considerations can support progress toward education goals and strengthen system context.

This report promotes a vision of equity wherein all schools and students are brought to a "minimum quality threshold." Objectives of basic education in Ghana include development of cognitive skills (for example, numeracy, literacy, scientific reasoning), noncognitive and social skills (for example, teamwork, communication) and delivery of content on civic issues such as safety, the environment and citizenship.[3] The chapter on quality recognizes the complexity of defining quality. Basic education has multiple objectives and service delivery is expected

Figure 1.2 Conceptual Framework for Basic Education in Ghana

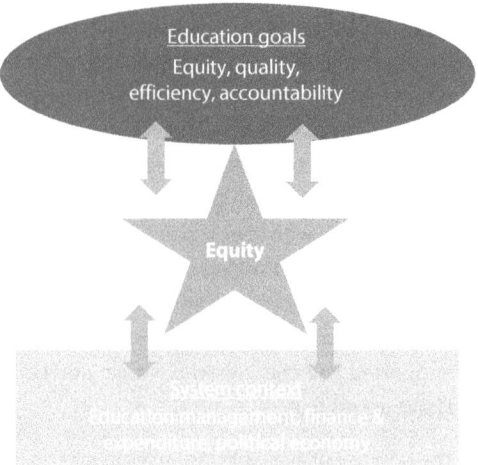

to meet certain quality assurance standards (for example, teacher certifications and professional standards; access to teaching and learning materials; safe and secure infrastructure and learning environment; adequate supervisory support and professional development; capacity to support to children with special needs). *This report argues that, at a minimum, pupils should leave primary schools with proficiency in numeracy and literacy, teachers should have the knowledge, skills, and institutional support to effectively instruct students, schools should be equitably resourced and supported and children who require additional support to access school and to learn should have access to it.*

To discuss this vision of equity, we recognize equity, quality, efficiency, and accountability in basic education as distinct and interrelated issues. Equity, quality, efficiency, and accountability represent distinct priorities in basic education. However, there is also a strong relationship between these themes. Efforts to meet efficiency or quality goals can positively or negatively reinforce progress toward other goals while patterns of inequity can contribute to low quality and may perpetuate accountability issues. Efficiency and accountability challenges include inefficient allocation of money, learning materials and trained teachers, inefficient use of instructional time, high rates of teacher absenteeism, absence or mis-procurement of textbooks and leakage of capitation grant funding, to name a few. This report includes separate chapters on equity, quality, and efficiency to discuss each theme in detail and interrelationships between themes.

Equity-improving efforts must also consider organizational context. In this report, we consider education management, finance and expenditure and the politics of education reform. Managing nationwide delivery of basic education services and supporting progress toward the basic education objectives is a large and complex task. Service delivery of basic education takes places through 20,000 schools and 250,000 teachers supported by district, regional and national offices, accounts for more nearly 10 percent of annual government expenditure and reaches more than 7 million pupils. The national system reaches a broad and highly diverse population and geography. While pupil learning takes place at the school level, many decisions supporting or constraining the opportunity to learn are made at circuit, district, or national levels.

Efforts to improve equity, quality, and efficiency must intersect with efforts to improve accountability and reform education management, finance and expenditure. Recent reform efforts also evidence the politics of education reform. This intersection is evidenced in the Education Strategic Plan 2010–20, which notes the need to reduce recurrent expenditures that "appear to reward a relative few at the expense of a relatively deprived majority" (ESP Vol. 1, 2010, 29). Reforms in management, accountability, finance and expenditure (for example, professionalizing school management, decentralization, strengthening social accountability) often have a political aspect which chapters on Expenditure and Management, Finance and Accountability discuss.

When we consider the politics of reform, we also return to the importance of equity. Is an individual disadvantaged by his or her birth circumstance or group membership? If so, what is it in the structure, management or politics of basic education service delivery which contribute to or perpetuate this inequity? More importantly, how can such issues be resolved?

Now is a good time to address inequity in basic education in Ghana. Projected future economic growth and political stability place Ghana on a strong trajectory toward solidifying its middle-income status and creates the possibility more broadly sharing the benefits of growth. Available resources can be used to mitigate the effects of extreme poverty now and to move Ghana closer to realizing its vision to provision of free, compulsory, universal (quality) basic education.

McKinsey and Company (2010) offers a framework, informed by the experience in Ghana, which shows a series of interventions designed to improve education equity and quality in basic education. Figure 1.3 shows the framework developed based on research in Brazil, Chile, Ghana, India, and South Africa. While this framework should not be seen as a prescription for education reform in Ghana, it does show how a set of access and learning interventions can come together in a coherent "reform package." The expected outcomes of interventions in figure 1.3 are (i) increase access to learning and (ii) reduce the variance in practices across low-performing schools and classrooms. Some interventions in the figure are already being implemented in Ghana (for example, expanding seats, implementing national assessments); others (for example, providing support to low-performing schools and improving time on task) are included in the ESP 2010–20; and still others (for example, use of scripted lessons) may be rejected or considered not feasible in Ghana.

A first caveat: education cannot address broader social inequality by itself. Education is not a silver bullet for reducing inequality. Pupils come from highly unequal family, social and economic backgrounds. While implementing measures to increase access and learning among disadvantaged groups can make an

Figure 1.3 Themes and Interventions System Improvements in Literacy and Numeracy

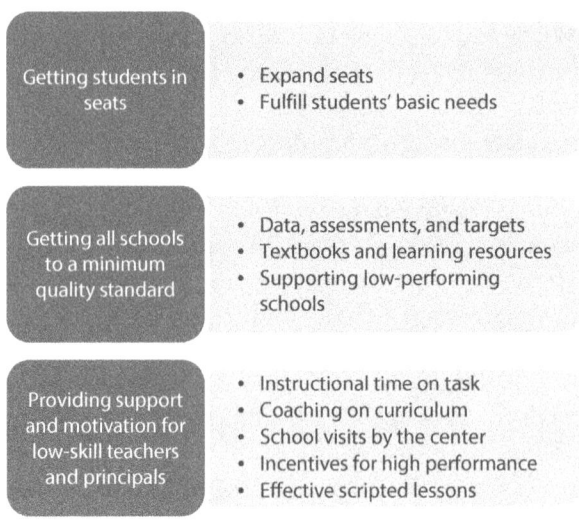

Source: Adapted from McKinsey and Company 2010; Chijioke 2012.

important difference, policymakers should not look to education alone to attain broader equity goals. Further, education can just as easily reproduce inequality if negative gender or ethno-linguistic stereotypes are perpetuated through classroom practices or learning materials.

A second caveat: equity-improving policies and programs, if poorly designed or implemented, can waste scarce resources. Some of the most economically efficient equity-improving policies involve the direct transfer of resources to beneficiaries demonstrating great need. In Ghana this could mean transfer of financial resources or improving the equitable distribution of teachers, textbooks and inputs to basic education. Equity-improving programs in which a high percentage of resources are consumed by program management and implementation costs may not provide the "value for money" sought by the Government of Ghana.

Before providing in-depth discussion on issues of Equity, Quality and Efficiency, it is important to provide some background on the country context and education reform history in Ghana. The next two chapters provide this background.

Notes

1. In *Educational finance: An economic approach* (1990), Monk provides detailed discussion on different definitions of equity in education. Equity has many interpretations, including equal treatment of equals (for example, equal inputs) and unequal treatment of unequals (for example, providing additional support to disadvantaged populations or support to gifted and talented children), among them. Recent discourse on equity in education argues for an "adequacy" approach. An adequacy approach

specifies that there be sufficient resources and support to ensure students an effective opportunity to acquire specified knowledge and skills. Adequacy analysis can link outcomes among different populations with resources required to meet those outcomes. For example, learners in a nondominant mother tongue or in a rural area may require more resources to become proficient in English.

2. Results of the 2011 National Education Assessment show that 65 percent of P6 students score below proficiency in English and 84 percent of P6 students score below proficiency in Math. A small number of high scores and large number of low scores contribute to a missing middle in Ghana: for example, 43 percent of P3 students scored a 0 or 1 (out of six) on the reading comprehension section on the 2011 NEA English exam.

3. The basic education strategic goal as identified in the ESP 2010–20 is to "provide equitable access to good-quality child-friendly universal basic education, by improving opportunities for all children in the first cycle of education at Kindergarten, primary and junior high school levels."

CHAPTER 2

Country Context

In the past 15 years, Ghana has realized dramatic success and persistent challenges in the areas of equity, quality, efficiency and education finance and management. Ghana is expected to continue to have a dynamic economic, social and political environment in the medium term. In the context of these disruptive and potentially dividing forces, government education policy can play an important role in mitigating system inequalities and strengthening education sector performance.

Rapid Growth and Change

Ghana has realized significant economic growth and poverty reduction in the past 15 years. Living standards in Ghana have increased in terms of both key human development indicators and levels of income. Gross National Income (GNI) per capita has increased from US$1,200 (using PPP) in 1995 to US$2,700 (using PPP) by 2010. Since 1995, gross domestic product has grown on average by 5.4 percent annually, reaching 7.7 percent in 2010. Oil production is expected to push GDP growth into double digits in 2011 and in the 8 percent range in 2012 (IMF 2011). The incidence of extreme poverty was cut in half from 36.5 percent to 18.2 percent between 1991 and 2006. During the same period, the percentage of the population living below upper poverty line fell from 51.7 percent to 28.5 percent (NDPC 2012).

Ghana is now classified as a lower-middle-income country with an expanding middle class. AfDB (2011) identifies 20 percent of the population in Ghana as middle class and 26 percent of the population as members of a "floating" class. The floating class (individuals who live on between US$2 and US$4 per day) dominates the middle-class structure in Ghana and remains at risk of relapsing into poverty. The growth of the middle class poses opportunities and risks. Urbanization, economic growth, increased labor mobility and growth of the middle class suggest that demands for infrastructure and social services in urban areas will continue to grow. Increases in levels of education absent corresponding increases in employment growth or reductions in inequality threaten growth, stability and social cohesion.

In spite of recent growth, there are worrying trends in disparities across regions and socioeconomic groups in terms of poverty incidence and the depth of poverty. Poverty incidence still remains quite high among rural dwellers and in the three northern regions. About a quarter of the poor in Ghana in 2006 are estimated to come from the Northern Region. Upper East and Upper West Regions include about 30 percent of Ghana's households living in poverty. NDPC (2012) notes,

> The high incidence of poverty in the three northern regions and among food crop farmers as well as high depth of poverty and inequality in spite of remarkable reduction of poverty at the national level and in rural areas should engage attention of policymakers and relevant stakeholders. (NDPC 2012, 17)

Income inequality has increased between 1991 and 2006. The poorest quintiles share of national wealth has declined from 6.8 percent to 5.6 percent over this period. This pattern is observed in both the rural and urban areas and in seven regions.

The depth of poverty is measured by poverty gap ratio. The poverty gap ratio expresses the total amount of money required to raise the poor from their present income to the poverty line as a proportion of the poverty line and averaged over the total population. At the regional level, excepting Greater Accra, Upper East and Upper West regions, poverty depth is calculated to have surged in Ghana between 1991 and 2006. The depth of poverty is still highest in the three northern savannah regions with poverty gap ratio of over 40 percent (NDPC 2012).

While the population is expected to grow at a modest rate over the next decade, urban areas are expected to continue to grow at high rate during the same period. Population projections suggest that the population in Ghana will rise from 25 million people in 2010 to nearly 30 million by 2020. United Nations Population Division estimates place Ghana's population at 45 million in 2050. Over the next decade, urban areas are expected to grow at an annual rate of 3.5 percent. The population living in urban areas grew from 40 percent in 1995 to 50 percent in 2010. Between 2010 and 2025, the population living in urban areas is expected to grow by another 10 percent (UNESA 2013).

Middle-income countries now account for most of the world's population living in absolute poverty. This evidence suggests that economic growth does not necessarily equate to reductions in absolute poverty. Kenny (2011) argues that increasing levels of domestic resources mean that reduction in poverty and inequality will become increasingly determined by domestic politics. Palma (2011) argues that the political influence of a growing middle class means that politics will increasingly be a fight between the richest 10 percent and poorest 40 percent for public resources not captured by the middle classes. Both analyses suggest that development and education policy that emerges in new middle-income countries may in some respects be affected by the politics of the new middle class.

Recent Progress in Education

Ghana has seen huge gains in access to basic education in all regions, among the poor, by gender and by urban and rural status in the past decade. In less than 15 years, enrollment in basic education has nearly doubled, from around 3.5 million pupils enrolled in 1999/2000 to nearly 7 million pupils enrolled in 2010/11. Enrollment gains have been made in all regions with the Upper East and Upper West Regions experiencing the greatest percentage gains in attendance. By 2011, KG enrollment had grown to 1.5 million pupils, up from 700,000 in 2004.

MoE and GES support several innovative programs and policies which show promise in helping the sector address a number of critical education sector needs. Innovations and new programs piloted include the capitation grant, grants to deprived districts, LEAP, NALAP (mother tongue instruction), TCAI, the NEA, the SRCs and SPIPs, UTDBE, GSFP and introduction of head-teacher and circuit supervisor training, among others. Several of the programs have been shown to improve equity, quality and efficiency.

Education has secured a large share of government resources since the late 1990s. High levels of education finance have been maintained across political administrations. In 2011, education expenditure in Ghana as a share of GDP stood at 6.3 percent—close to the UNESCO and the African Union target of 6 percent of GDP for a middle-income country. Over the past 6 years, education expenditure as a percentage of total GoG expenditure has ranged from 18 percent to 25 percent. Basic education expenditure as a share of total sector expenditure ranged from 45 percent to 55 percent during the same period (ESPR 2008, 2011).

Persistent Challenges

Access to education, distribution of critical educational inputs (for example, teachers) and education outcomes remain highly unequal. At a national level, access to basic education and key public sector inputs are generally more accessible to wealthier children and children in urban areas. Learners living in low population density and language minority areas and pupils requiring targeted economic support or remedial learning assistance (including poor, orphaned, foster-children or otherwise disadvantaged learners) have proportionately lower access to core education inputs. There are also challenges to access among the urban poor. Akyeampong (2009b) using GLSS IV and GLSS V data finds that school attendance among urban boys coming from the lowest wealth quintile dropped by 27 percent between 1998/99 and 2005/06. Inequity in primary completion and learning outcomes by region, wealth quintile and urban/rural status roughly track distribution of education inputs and household socioeconomic status. Expansion of the current model for delivery of basic education may not be the best way to provide appropriate and equitable support to the diversity of learners it serves.

Education quality as measured by the NEA falls far below system expectations and remains highly unequally distributed. The 2011 NEA found 35 percent of

P6 students to be "proficient" in English. Sixteen percent of P6 students were classified as "proficient" in Math. ESP targets for proficiency in English and mathematics are set at 60 percent for 2012. Consistent with inequity in inputs, the three northern regions lagged behind the rest of the country in terms of NEA performance among P3 and P6 pupils. However, it is important to recognize that even as the education system experienced large increases in enrollment of pupils from lower SES households, average NEA scores did not decline.

Broad-based improvements in learning outcomes in KG and early primary grades is desirable for several reasons including the expected effect of literacy on learning in later grades and improved life chances for children for whom JHS is the terminal step in their formal education. In addition to a robust formal sector, Ghana has a growing entrepreneurial and informal economy in which many JHS and second cycle leavers are employed. Individuals with strong foundational skills are more likely to be successful in this environment than peers without these skills.

Core inputs comprising the majority of basic education expenditure (teachers, infrastructure, textbooks) could be deployed and utilized with greater efficiency. Specifically, efficiency gains in deployment of qualified teachers, reduced absenteeism and an increase in the amount of time students spend learning would mitigate some of the most critical system equity and quality challenges.

Challenges facing education management and finance hinder MoE and GES efforts to achieve timely and effective delivery of basic education services. Education financing is fragmented among a number of sources and among an even larger number of flows of funds. Education management at the central level (planning, securing resources, oversight, evaluation) and the district level (administration and service delivery) takes place in a complex environment where many institutions are involved in key decisions affecting service delivery. This interdependence and complexity increases the uncertainty of realizing annual operational plans and budget targets. Limited powers of MMDAs and district officers in the administration and management of key basic education inputs undermine their capacity to effectively deliver services in response to district needs.

CHAPTER 3

Education Reform History

Education Reform: 1951–2008

From 1951 to 2005, enactment of fee-free, compulsory basic education was on the agenda of most governments. Up until 1987, these efforts were punctuated by periods of economic and political distress resulting in setbacks in basic education financing, quality and access. In 1952, the Ghanaian government announced the introduction of fee-free primary education under an Accelerated Development Plan for Education. The 1961 Education Act was introduced to reinforce the commitment to free primary education. During this period and related to these initiatives, primary enrollment increased sevenfold, growing from 153,360 (1951) to 1,137,495 (1966) primary school students over a 15-year time span (Foobih and Koomson 1998).

However, in the late 1970s, the Ghanaian economy and consequently the education system retracted due to institutional mismanagement and poor economic policy (Akyeampong et al. 2006). From 1976 to 1983, the proportion of GDP allocated to the education sector sank from 6.4 percent to about 1.5 percent (World Bank 2004). As a result of scarce financial resources, textbooks and other school materials became in short supply, school infrastructure deteriorated and the necessary data for strategy, planning and policy purposes were not compiled anymore (Akyeampong et al. 2006). In the years following 1975, when over 2.3 million children attended primary schooling, sectorwide deterioration led to a decline in enrollment of over one million children by the early eighties (World Bank 2004). Thompson and Casely-Hayford (2008, 10) note:

> As government funding plummeted, the sector was also weakened by the brain-drain that had hit the rest of the economy as a result of the deteriorating social and economic conditions in the country. By 1983, approximately 50 percent of trained primary school teachers had left the country. (Ahadzie 2000, 20, qtd. in Thompson and Casely-Hayford)

To address teacher shortages, the government began hiring large numbers of underqualified teachers. Foobih and Koomson (1998, 166) add, "The state of Ghana's education system by 1985 was aptly described as clinically dead."

A white paper issued by the government in 1974 shows the ongoing debates over equity, quality and efficiency in the public arena. In an effort to reverse educational decline following the overthrow of the Nkrumah government in 1966, the Acheampong Government appointed N.K. Dzobo, Dean of the Faculty of Education, University of Cape Coast, to head a committee to produce a report that would form the basis of the 1974 White Paper, *New Structure and Content of Education for Ghana*. Though recommendations of the Dzobo committee were only partially implemented (largely due to changes in national leadership and continued economic decline), Fobih and Koomson (1998) argue that recommendations from the report significantly influenced the structure of the 1987 economic reforms. Key observations from the Dzobo Committee include the need to reduce pretertiary education from 17 years to 12–13 years (to align with international norms), that disadvantaged students were disproportionately denied access to secondary school (which affected their later success in life) and that the current system "fostered the development of unhealthy attitudes towards manual work and non-academic occupations." Thompson and Casely-Hayford (2008, 9) add:

> The thrust of the ensuing report of the Dzobo Committee was that the existing system, especially the preparatory schools and experimental schools, was not adequately addressing the manpower needs of the economy but was instead serving as the "training grounds of the elite and ruling class."

Observations by the Dzobo committee are echoed in other academic work (Foster 1965; Weis 1979) which found that the structure of the secondary system served to reproduce social inequality as opposed to enhancing social mobility.

The 1987 Education Reforms were undertaken as a part of a broader effort to stabilize and grow the provision of education after a long period of decline. The reforms followed many of the suggestions of the Dzobo Committee. The length of pretertiary education was reduced from 17 years to 12 years (primary: 6 years; JHS: 3 years; SHS: 3 years) with primary and JHS defined as basic education. An emphasis on improving access and rehabilitation resulted in the massive increase of education finance and material inputs into the sector. The priority of improving teaching and learning, with an emphasis on increasing the number of qualified teachers, led to new standards for teacher trainees and the introduction of allowances for teacher trainees attending Teacher Training Colleges.

The period of the 1987 Education Reforms also marked a new beginning for large-scale involvement of external funding agencies in education sector financing and reform projects. The 1987 Education Reforms are closely linked to the broader Economic Reform Program (ERP), supported by the World Bank and the International Monetary Fund (IMF), which began in 1983. It was through the ERP that the World Bank supported activities which would help prepare for the 1987 reforms. Given the huge task of changing the system, the 1987 reforms were implemented over 6 years (Thompson and Casely-Hayford 2008; World Bank 2010). Led by the World Bank, external agencies began to contribute more resources to basic education in Ghana (Thompson and Casely-Hayford 2008; World Bank 2010).

Over the 15-year period from 1987 to 2002, the World Bank and other donors provided close to US$600 million in soft loan and grant financing to support a series of education reform programs. In the mid-1990s, the IMF and the World Bank designated Ghana as a heavily indebted poor country (HIPC). This gave Ghana access to special assistance to foster economic growth and reduce poverty by means of channeling debt repayment to key development sectors including education and health. To qualify for assistance, each HIPC country needed to prepare a Poverty Reduction Strategy Paper (PRSP). Ghana submitted its "Growth and Poverty Reduction Strategy" (GPRS), updated 4 years later as GPRS-II, and began receiving HIPC funding in 2003 through a series of 1-year projects (Poverty Reduction Strategy Credits, or PRSCs) from the World Bank. Starting in 2007, HIPC funding started being phased out, and a new modality for debt relief, the multilateral debt relief initiative (MDRI), replaced HIPC funding.

In 1995, the "free compulsory universal basic education" (FCUBE) reform was introduced. Several factors influenced the declaration of FCUBE, including the 1992 Constitution, which required that FCUBE be provided for every Ghanaian child over a 10-year period following the return to civilian rule in 1993; Ghana's participation in the World Conference on Education for all in Jomtien, Thailand in 1990 and increased financing and influence by external donors (Nishimura, Ogawa, and Ampiah 2009).

Development of the MTEF, MDBS, FTI funding and the Education Strategic Plan 2003–15. Introduction of the PRSP corresponded with an effort by external funding agencies to move away from project support to program and budget support. Budget support was framed within a rolling medium-term expenditure framework (MTEF). Ghana's MTEF is updated annually to cover the 3-year planning periods. Through an instrument known as multidonor budget support (MDBS), participating donors release funds once key development indicators ("triggers") have been met. Budget support of this kind is intended to lower transaction costs by eliminating the need for multiple reporting requirements by the government and duplicative supervision activities by the donors.[1] Several donors still provide financing and technical assistance through project-based support—which suggests that transaction costs have probably not realized intended reductions.

The other new development of particular relevance for Ghana's education sector has been the Catalytic Fund of the EFA Fast-Track Initiative (FTI). To qualify for FTI funds, a country has to prepare a credible strategy for achieving EFA goals by 2015 and demonstrate the existence of a funding gap. Ghana prepared its Education Strategic Plan (ESP) 2003–15 in 2003. The local donors endorsed the plan and made a recommendation to the FTI partners for funding. Ghana was given an initial grant of US$33.2 million. Disbursement began in 2005 and reached a cumulative total of US$19 million by 2008. As part of the ESP, Ghana established the National Education Sector Annual Review (NESAR), a regularly scheduled meeting to review performance in the sector. The Department of Planning, Budgeting, Monitoring and Evaluation (PBME) in the MoE compiles an annual Education Sector Performance Report (ESPR) which is presented to other staff in the Ministry and the Ghana Education Service (GES), as well as to education donors and other stakeholders, for discussion on priorities for the coming year. *From 2006–11, the share of external agencies in the expenditures in Ghana's education sector ranged from 3.6 percent to 6.8 percent.*

Progress following the 1987 Reforms saw large increases in enrollment but limited improvements in quality. Implementation of the capitation grant in 2005 resulted in a significant spike in enrollment nationwide. Importantly, regions with the lowest net enrollment realized the greatest gains. However, during this same period, data on the supply of qualified teachers offer a very different story for quality. Between 1987 and 1997, the proportion of trained teachers in the teaching force gradually increased by about 20 percentage points for primary as well as for JHS. Since 1997, the share of qualified teachers has followed a consistent downward trend. *A graph is included in the chapter on Quality.* One explanation of this trend is that the supply of qualified teachers could not keep up with the growth in student numbers. To address this issue, as in the period from 1974 to 1987, the government substituted unqualified teachers for qualified ones, with negative impacts on equity and quality. Underqualified teachers are disproportionately sent to schools reaching poor, remote or otherwise marginalized populations.

External agency involvement in education reform in Ghana has been subject to criticism from several quarters. Involvement of external agency financing and technical support to basic education worldwide and in Ghana has received extensive criticism. External agency funding in support to EFA and MDG goals has fallen far short of the resources required, an evaluation by the IEG/World Bank identified several challenges with World Bank support to Primary Education following the EFA declaration in 1990, and, some interpretations of SWAPs and PRSPs argue that these modalities' emphasis on "partnership" and a "shared development agenda" in fact masks ongoing power inequalities between rich and poor countries and do little to strengthen donor agency accountability (Klees 2002; Thompson and Casely-Hayford 2008; World Bank 2005).[2] Education budget share accounted for by external agency resources has been declining over the past decade.

Recent Policy Initiatives

The National Education Reform Program (2007), the Education Act (2008) and the Education Strategic Plan 2010–20. In 2001 the new government (after the elections in 2000) constituted the Education Reform Review Committee (ERRC) to re-examine the "goals and philosophy" of Ghana's education system. In late 2002, the Committee released its report, "Meeting the Challenges of Education in the Twenty-First Century." This led to the issuance of the "White Paper of the Report of the Education Reform Review Committee" in 2004, to the establishment of the National Education Reform Implementation Committee (NERIC) in early 2007, and to the launch of the National Education Reform Program (NERP) later in 2007.

These efforts led to the Education Act (2008). Key features of the Act include confirmation of state responsibility for implementation of FCUBE, inclusion of 2 years of Kindergarten as part of basic education and provision of a framework for decentralization wherein several responsibilities for the provision, finance and infrastructure for basic education have been shifted (as yet, incompletely) from the center to MMDAs (District Assemblies) and District Education Oversight Committees. To improve quality, efficiency, and better management of the system, the Act created the National Teaching Council (NTC), the National Inspectorate Board (NIB), and the National Council for Curriculum and Assessment (NCCA). The Act also provides a framework for formal recognition of private education institutions which realized strong enrollment growth in the first decade of the 2000s and the expansion of Second Cycle education from 3 to 4 years. Second Cycle education has since been changed back to having a duration of 3 years.

Other recent initiatives include implementation of several pro-poor interventions including provision of free school uniforms and exercise books, implementation of the single spine salary structure, drafting an (yet to be passed) act which would upgrade Teacher Training Colleges into College of Education, and creation of the Education Strategic Plan 2010–20, which provides strategic objectives, outline strategies, and a financing plan for meeting education sector goals. Development partner engagement in basic education in Ghana continues with several external agencies providing financing and technical support in various areas and the MoE working with the Global Partnership for Education (GPE) to secure additional funding to address basic education policy priorities. GPE was formed to carry forward the mission of the EFA-Fast-Track Initiative.

The next five chapters provide data and analysis on the state of basic education equity, quality, efficiency, expenditure, management, finance and accountability in Ghana. Like the proposed package of reforms in the McKinsey framework, it is likely that continued progress in basic education will require a set of reforms and programs targeting access, equity and quality objectives. The final chapter outlines some of the dilemmas facing basic education reform in Ghana and outlines some ways forward for consideration by policymakers.

Notes

1. About 20 percent of the external funds flowing to the Government via HIPC, MDRI and MDBS funding are earmarked for education. When one of the 2007 MDBS triggers (primary education's share of the education budget) had not been met, DFID temporarily suspended its disbursements to GoG through MDBS.
2. Further criticism of World Bank policies and strategies is included in "The World Bank and Education: Critiques and Alternatives," authored by Steven Klees, Joel Samoff and Nelly Stromquist (Sense Publishers 2012).

CHAPTER 4

Equity

The Constitution of Ghana and the Education Act (2008) commit the government to improving equitable access to basic education. This chapter outlines progress made in reducing inequity and documents inequities which persist in access to education, distribution of educational inputs and education outcomes. The chapter also discusses several equity-improving initiatives, which unfortunately, often end up disproportionately benefiting individuals from wealthier populations. A growing body of research suggests that improving educational equity should be an integral part of any economic growth program.

Overview

As noted in chapter 1, in an equitable society, an individual's life chances (for example, economic, social, health) are not predetermined by his or her birth circumstances or membership in particular groups. Equity can be defined using two concepts: *equal opportunity* and *avoidance of absolute deprivation*. Equal opportunity means that the outcome of an individual's life should be predetermined neither by his or her characteristics at birth (for example, gender, household wealth, ethnic/language group, geographic location, orphan status) nor by his or her membership in particular groups (for example, groups defined by religious, ethno-linguistic, sexual orientation). Avoidance of absolute deprivation means that "societies may decide to intervene to protect the livelihoods of its neediest members...even if the equal opportunity principle has been upheld" (World Bank 2005, 19).

This report identified three rationales for improving equity in basic education in Ghana.

1. *Basic education for all is a yet-unrealized right guaranteed by the Constitution of Ghana.*
2. *Quality basic education for all can play a critical role in addressing broader social and economic inequities and stimulate progress toward broader national development goals.*

3. *Improving equity in basic education service delivery can greatly strengthen system performance in terms of quality and efficiency.*

Government commitment to equity is a central feature of the legal and policy framework guiding education in Ghana. Article 25 of the Constitution of Ghana (1992) states: "Basic education shall be free, compulsory and available to all." NERIC (2007) and the Education Act (2008) confirm this commitment. The first policy objective of the Education Sector Plan (ESP) 2010–20 commits the MoE to "Improve equitable access to and participation in quality education at all levels." Elaborating on this objective, the ESP adds that education should play a critical role in eliminating gender and other disparities that arise from exclusion and poverty and that MoE should reach out to excluded children and mainstream them into the public system whenever possible.[1] A growing body of research suggests that investments to improve equity in education should be an integral part of any economic growth program.

While education alone cannot be expected to resolve this issue, improving equity in education has long been recognized one of the best strategies for improving equality in society. As this chapter will show, unfortunately, students and populations who may require the most support to meet expected comes (for example, learning, primary completion, access to secondary), receive, on average, disproportionately fewer resources (for example, trained teachers, textbooks) from the government than their peers. *Inequitable distribution of inputs creates a negatively reinforcing loop where children with the greatest need receive the fewest resources and opportunities, thereby reproducing cycles of poverty and inequality.*

School-age children in Ghana come from highly diverse and unequal backgrounds. Levels of youth and adult literacy and educational attainment and household socio-economic status vary greatly across Ghana. Each of these characteristics has an effect on access to school, persistence in school and learning. The majority (74 percent) of the population (11 years and older) is literate and a large proportion (67 percent) of the population can read and write in English. However, a large portion of Ghanaian children come from literacy-poor home environments: Literacy levels in the three northern regions is below 50 percent (of the population aged 11 years and older) while in other regions at least 69 percent of the population is literate (GSS 2011). Youth literacy rates vary greatly across Ghana. GSS (2011, 234) notes, "Young women's literacy varies from 44 percent in the Northern region to 81 percent in Greater Accra, and young men's literacy varies from 47 percent in the Upper East region to 84 percent in the Western region." Nearly one third of adults in Ghana have never been to school while 40 percent hold a BECE, MSLC, or vocational certificate as their highest qualification.[2] Less than 15 percent of the Ghanaians possess a secondary or higher qualification (GLSS 2008, iv).

The three northern regions account for the vast majority of households in the poorest two wealth quintiles. Brong Ahafo, Volta and Eastern Regions also have household incomes below the national average. GLSS V notes:

> Average annual household expenditure in Ghana is GH¢1,918.00 whilst the mean annual per capita consumption expenditure in Ghana is GH¢644.00. Regional differences exist with Greater Accra Region having the highest per capita expenditure of GH¢1,050.00 whilst Upper West has the lowest of GH¢166.00. (GLSS 2008, vii)

The report goes on to note that annual household expenditure is about 1.6 times higher in urban localities (GH¢2,449) than in rural localities (GH¢1,514). In five regions, Ashanti, Greater Accra and Western, Eastern and Central, nearly 60 percent of households fall within the upper two wealth quintiles.

Regional differences in geography, economic conditions and social and cultural practices across Ghana add to the diverse and unequal backgrounds of children. Akyeampong (2011, 31; GSS 2003) notes, "Ghana has characteristically three different ecological zones—a sandy coastline backed by a coastal plain; a middle belt and western parts heavily forested, and an undulating savannah to the North." Each region faces particular access challenges with "economic pull factors that make sustained access difficult."

Equitable Access

Ghana has seen huge gains in access to basic education in all regions, among the poor, by gender and by urban and rural status in the past decade. Table 4.1 shows enrollment and NER for KG, Primary and JHS over the past 15 years. In less than 15 years, enrollment in basic education has nearly doubled, from around 3.5 million pupils enrolled in 1999/2000 to over 7 million pupils enrolled in 2011/12 (see Table 4.1, MoE 2008 and MoE 2012). Enrollment gains have been made in all regions with the Upper East and Upper West Regions experiencing the greatest percentage gains in attendance between 2003 and 2008 (UNICEF 2010).

Despite recent gains in access, different estimates place the number of out-of school primary school–aged children in Ghana between 300,000 and 800,000. GSS

Table 4.1 Enrollment and NER in KG, Primary, and JHS, 1990–2011/12

Basic subsector	1999/2000	2003/04	2006/07	2011/12
KG enrollment	—	.69m	1.10m	1.54m
KG NER	—	—	56%	64%
Primary	2.5m	2.96m	3.37m	4.45m
Primary NER	—	58% (est.)	79%	82%
JHS	.80m	.98m	1.13m	1.43m
JHS NER	—	—	51%	46%

Source: MoE Education Sector Performance Report 2008 and 2012, and MoE EMIS (qtd. In Akyeampong 2007).
Note: — = not available.

Figure 4.1 Primary and Secondary School Net Attendance Rate by Wealth Quintile and Urban-Rural Status, 2011

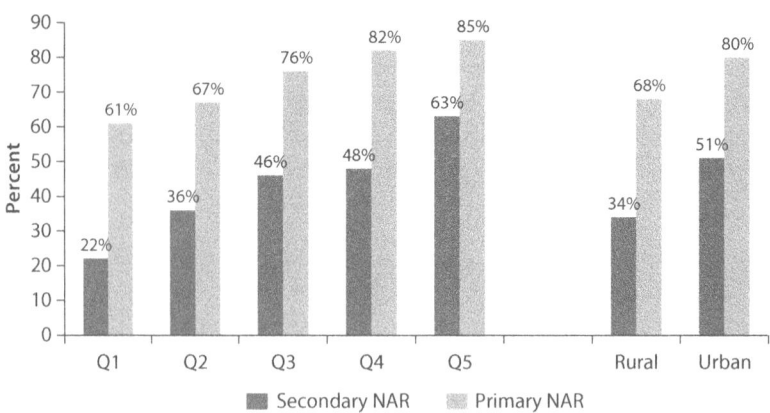

Source: GSS 2011.

(2011) finds that the national primary Net Attendance Rate (NAR) is 73 percent, suggesting that more than a quarter of primary school–aged children are not in primary school.[3] The reason for the broad estimate for the number of out-of-school children is because many 6–11-year-old children are attending Kindergarten instead of primary school. GSS (2011) suggests that as many as 20 percent of 6–11-year-olds are attending Kindergarten or preschool. MoE EMIS data (NER) and the primary NAR indicator regard these children as "out of school." However, if we take these children into account, the school attendance rate among 6–11-year-old children could be above 90 percent (GSS 2011),[4]

Even with significant access gains, pupil attendance at primary and secondary schools varies greatly by household wealth and urban-rural status. Figure 4.1 shows primary and secondary school net attendance rate (NAR) by wealth quintile and urban-rural status (GSS 2011). Primary NAR for pupils from the wealthiest households (Quintile 5) is 85 percent, compared to a primary NAR of 61 percent for students from the poorest households (Quintile 1). Difference in NAR by wealth quintile is more pronounced in SHS where students from wealthiest households are nearly three times as likely to have access to senior high school compared to peers in the lowest wealth quintiles (63 percent vs. 22 percent). Similar disparities are evident when comparing access by urban-rural status.

Primary and Secondary NAR also vary by region. Figure 4.2 shows primary net attendance rate by region (2011). Excepting Greater Accra, primary NAR in Ghana is below 80 percent. Primary NAR in Upper West and Northern Regions is 65 percent and 59 percent, respectively. Secondary NAR shows great range as well. Secondary NAR in all three northern regions is below 30 percent while in Greater Accra and Ashanti regions, it comes in at 51 percent and 49 percent, respectively. Notably, female children of secondary school age (44 percent) are more likely than males (40 percent) to attend secondary school.

Equity 51

Figure 4.2 Primary and Secondary Net Attendance Rate by Region, 2011

Source: GSS 2011.

Figure 4.3 Primary and JHS NER by Wealth Quintile

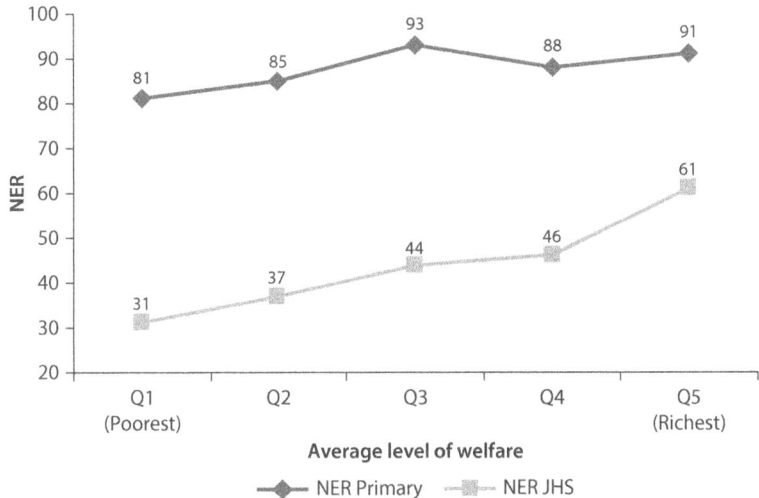

Source: World Bank 2010. Estimates based on GLSS 2005/06 and EMIS 2008/09.

Recent primary attendance gains have been realized by rich and poor alike (with the poorest households realizing the greatest gains) and across ethnic groups. Between 2003 and 2008 the number of children attending school increased by 11 percent. Children from the poorest households (wealth quintiles 1 and 2) realized gains of 17.3 percent and 12.8 percent, respectively. School attendance increased for all ethnic groups; however, Gruma and Mole-Dagbani groups (with attendance rates of around 60 percent in 2008) lag behind counterpart groups (with attendance rates of around 80 percent in 2008) (UNICEF 2010). Figure 4.3 shows NER by wealth quintile. Primary NER for pupils from the wealthiest households (Quintile 5) is 91 percent, compared to a primary NER of 81 percent for students coming from the poorest households (Quintile 1). Difference in NER by wealth quintile is more pronounced in JHS, indicating that poorer students are less likely to make the transition to JHS.[5] Gender parity in primary enrollment has been nearly achieved.

While significant gains have been made, late initial attendance in primary school, especially in rural areas, continues to be a challenge. The official primary school entrance age in Ghana (P1) is 6 years old. However, almost 60 percent of age 6 children in rural areas are not in school and just under 40 percent of age 7 children in rural areas are not in school (UNICEF 2010). In urban areas, over 45 percent of age 6 children are not in school while 25 percent of age 7 children are not in school.[6] Children who enroll late are more likely to be from poor families and are more likely to demonstrate lower learning achievement and have a higher rate of primary drop out. GSS (2011, 236) notes, "A positive correlation between six year olds entering grade one and socio-economic status is observed. In richest households, the proportion is 43 percent, while it is 24 percent among children living in the poorest households." This finding suggests a need to reach out to poorer households and encourage on-time enrollment. Improving *age-in-grade* has a significant effect on primary completion and learning (Akyeampong 2007; Lewin 2011).

Children from poor households, children living in the Northern regions and children who are orphaned or living with a relative or guardian are the most likely to be out of school (UNICEF 2010). Poverty often leads parents to prioritize child labor or income-generating activities over schooling, especially in areas with high levels of food insecurity (PDA-PPVA 2011). Costs associated with school, including materials and school uniforms, are a significant access barrier to children from poorer families. "Distance to the nearest school," is one of the major barriers to access in rural areas. Eleven percent of primary school–aged children in Ghana do not have physical access to a primary school; this figure rises to 30 percent in the Northern regions (UIS/UNICEF 2005; UNICEF 2010).

While the northern regions have low levels of access, nearly every region in Ghana has a large population of out-of-school children. Children for poor households in urban areas also have disproportionately low access (Akyeampong 2009a; UNICEF 2010). Additional reasons for nonattendance including the low value some households place on education; practices of fosterage and early marriage and the exclusion of children who have disabilities or who are from minority ethnic groups or migrant families. Nationally, around 10 percent of all school-age children are living in fosterage (CREATE 2010). The MoE draft Complementary Basic Education policy adds that child labor in rural areas (farming, fishing, cocoa farming) and urban areas (street hawking and working on tro-tros) contributes to the number of out-of-school children (MoE 2009b). An increasing awareness by parents of poor school quality in some schools also contributes to nonattendance.

The three northern regions are much more reliant on the public primary schools than other regions. Figure 4.4 shows private enrollment as a percentage of total enrollment in primary schools by region. Private primary enrollment has seen significant growth in the past decade. In 2010/11, 768,036 children were

Equity

Figure 4.4 Private Enrollment as a Percentage of Total Enrollment in Primary Schools, 2010/11

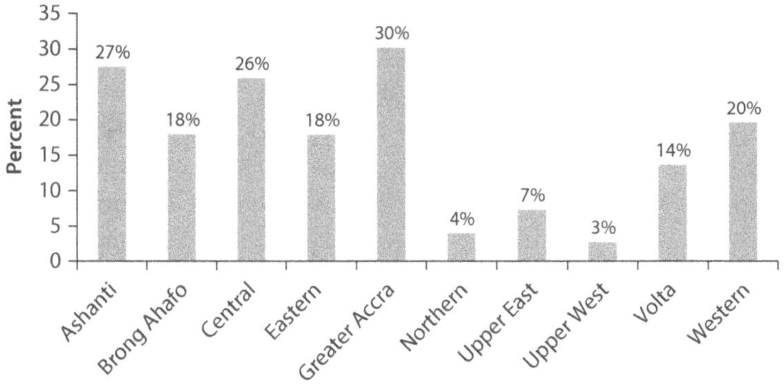

A bar chart showing private enrollment percentages by region: Ashanti 27%, Brong Ahafo 18%, Central 26%, Eastern 18%, Greater Accra 30%, Northern 4%, Upper East 7%, Upper West 3%, Volta 14%, Western 20%.

Source: MoE EMIS 2011.

enrolled in private schools accounting for 20 percent of total primary enrollment. Figure 4.4 shows private enrollment as a share of total enrollment stood at 30 percent and 27 percent in Greater Accra and Ashanti regions, respectively. In contrast, share of private school enrollment in the each of the three northern regions stood at less than 7 percent. In gross terms, Ashanti and Greater Accra, account for 45 percent of private school enrollment (350,892 pupils). In contrast, enrollment in private primary schools in the three northern regions stood at 35,519 pupils—*about ten times less than the Ashanti/Greater Accra figure*. There is a much greater reliance on the public school system in the three northern regions than in Ashanti and Greater Accra Regions. The ESPR (2012) notes that private sector share of enrollment in KG, primary, and JHS schools in deprived districts is half the national average.

Box 4.1 Providing Basic Education for Children with Disabilities

Children with disabilities are one of the most disadvantaged and marginalized populations in Ghana. Persons with disabilities account for 3 percent of the total population (a total of 737,743 individuals) in Ghana. GSS (2012) notes that "visual or sight impairment (40.1%) is the most common disability, followed by physical challenges (25.4%), emotional/behavioral problems (18.6%) and intellectual (15.2%)." Speech, hearing and other disabilities are also identified by the survey.

Recent analysis by the Ghana Statistical Service (GSS) of Children with Disabilities (CWD) shows that 20 percent of primary school age children with a disability are not attending school while only 10 percent of children without disabilities are out of school. This same analysis indicates as many as 27 percent each of children with intellectual disabilities and children with physical disabilities are not attending school.

The ESP 2010–20 Volume II offers several strategies for improving basic education for children with disabilities. Detailed analysis is currently underway by the GSS with support from UNICEF on the schooling status of CWDs. (Contribution: UNICEF, Ghana)

Equal Distribution of Inputs

Government-financed education inputs, especially trained teachers, are highly unequally distributed across Ghana. In the past decade, GoG education expenditure as a percentage of GDP has grown from 4 percent to 5 percent of GDP in the early 2000s to 6 percent of GDP in the past 5 years (ESPR 2008, 2012). In basic education, the MoE budget pays for inputs such as teachers, school infrastructure, textbooks, teacher education and MoE and GES operations. While GoG expenditure in education (as a percentage of GDP) is aligned with country targets and international norms, inputs are not equally distributed across Ghana.

Urban and wealthy districts in Ghana have larger numbers of trained teachers per student in comparison to poor, rural and northern districts. This inequity is important because trained teachers are recognized as one of the most critical factors in improving student learning. At a national level, 66 percent of the primary teaching force is made up of trained teachers. Map 4.1 shows the percent of Trained Primary Teachers by region for 2011/12. Note the highly unequal distribution of teachers. In four regions, Western, Upper East, Northern and Brong Ahafo, 40–50 percent of the teaching force is made up of untrained teachers. In four other regions, Ashanti, Volta, Eastern and Greater Accra, 70–90 percent of the teaching force comprises trained teachers.

Map 4.1 Percentage of Trained Primary Teachers, by Region, 2011/12

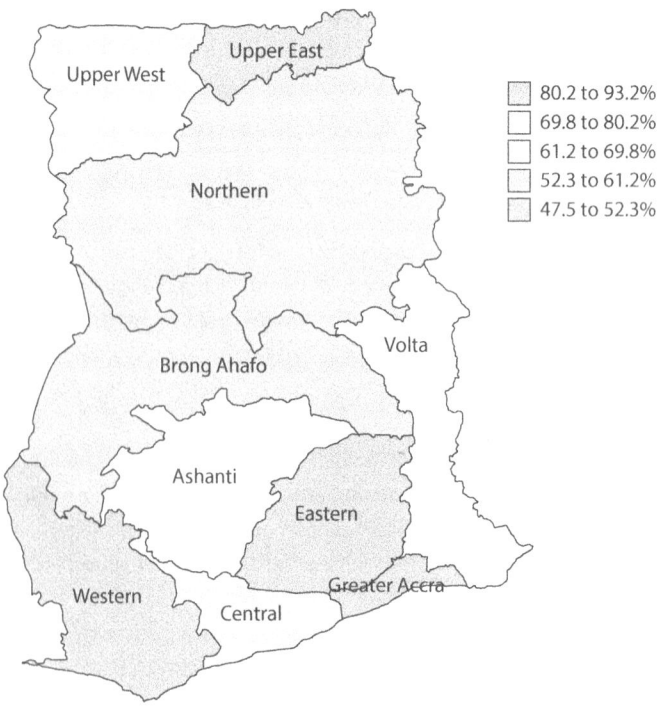

Source: ESPR 2012.

Equity

Figures 4.5 and 4.6 show (i) the proportion of trained primary teachers by region and district and (ii) district-level primary PTTR by SES. Each box represents one district in the region or wealth quintile. In figure 4.5, one can see that in Greater Accra, the district (lowest box) with the lowest proportion of

Figure 4.5 Proportion of Primary Teachers with Training, by Region/District, 2008/09

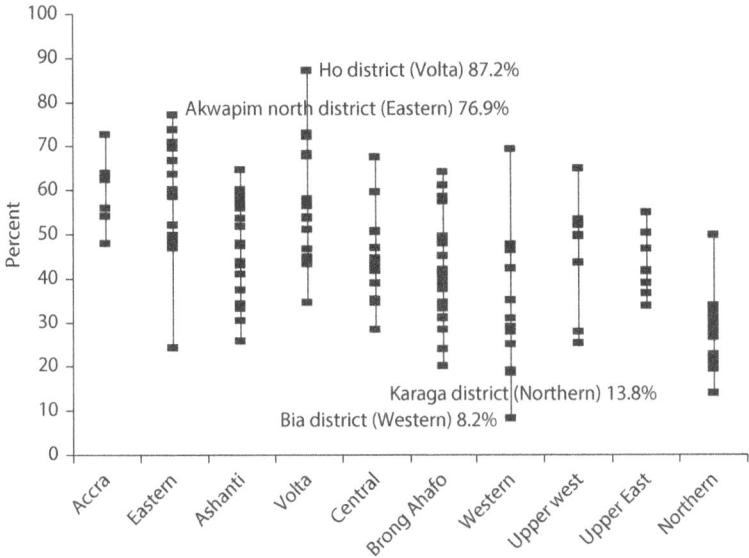

Source: World Bank data.

Figure 4.6 Primary PTTR, by SES, 2008/09

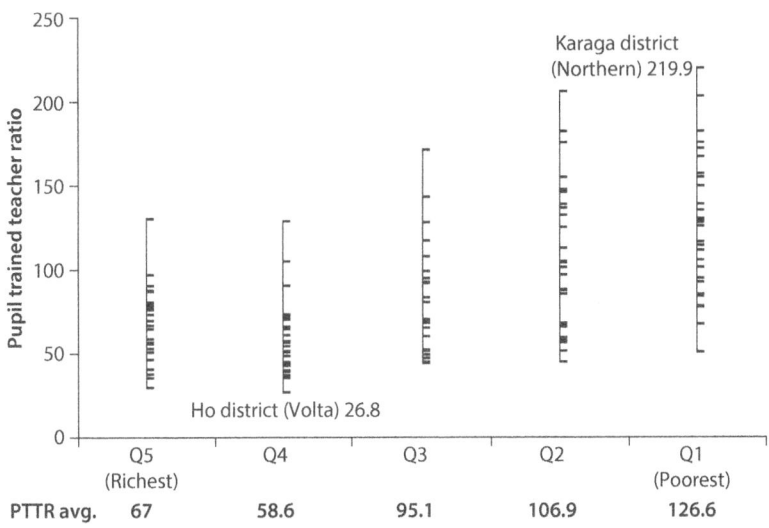

Source: World Bank 2010. Based on EMIS. Estimates based on GLSS 2005/06 and EMIS 2008/09.
Note: PTTR = pupil trained teacher ratio.

Map 4.2 Poverty Headcount, 2003–06, and Average PTR, by District, 2006/07

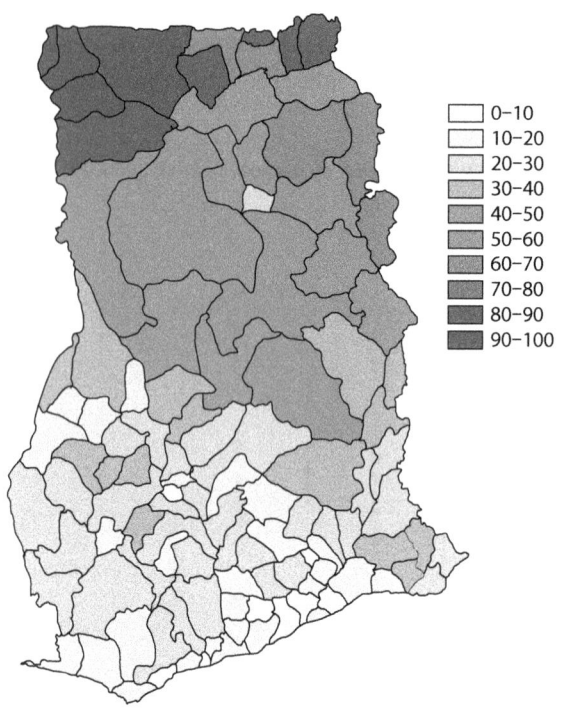

0–10
10–20
20–30
30–40
40–50
50–60
60–70
70–80
80–90
90–100

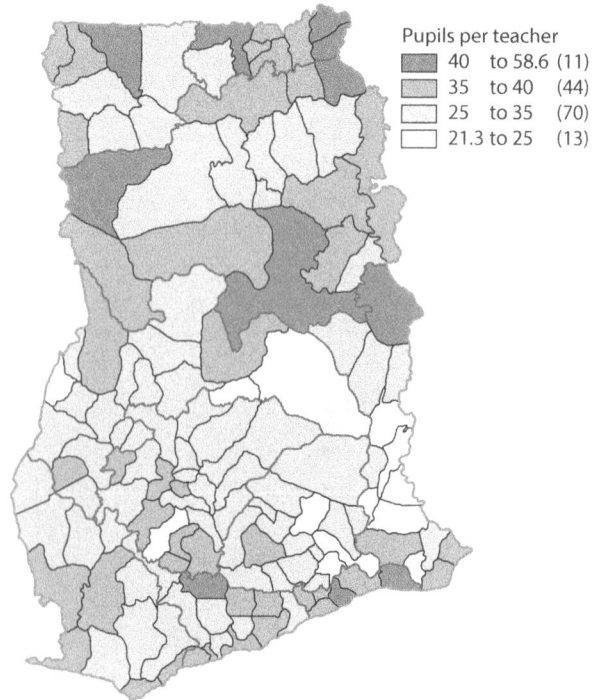

Pupils per teacher
40 to 58.6 (11)
35 to 40 (44)
25 to 35 (70)
21.3 to 25 (13)

Source: Bank 2010, based on MoE EMIS.

trained teachers is at the same level as the district with the highest proportion of trained teachers in the Northern Region. Figure 4.6 shows that districts in the poorest wealth quintile (Q1) have on average 126.6 primary students per trained teacher. Districts in the highest two wealth quintiles have a primary PTTR of nearly half this amount (67 for Q5 and 58.6 for Q4).

Instead of compensating for deprivation, public expenditure appears to exacerbate inequality by allocating fewer resources per child to regions where the majority of deprived districts are located. Map 4.2 shows district-level poverty count (top map) and the district-level average pupil-teacher ratio (PTR) for primary schools (bottom map). Darker districts indicate higher poverty count and higher PTR. Again, across Ghana, teachers are more likely to be located in wealthier districts than in poorer districts. As teacher salaries make up the bulk of public education expenditure, the figures show that poorer districts receive disproportionately low levels of public education expenditure. *It is important to note that many large, urban schools also face challenges finding sufficient staff. Even so, at the country level, it is the rural areas which face the greatest shortages of trained teachers.*

In the past 6 years, distribution of primary teachers appears to have become less equitable in Ghana. In comparison to neighboring countries, Ghana's allocation of teachers is one of the least equitable. An analysis of EMIS data (World Bank 2011) indicates that efficiency in teacher allocation generally decreased between 2005/06 and 2008/09 and seems to have further worsened by 2011. Figure 4.7 shows the extent to which allocation of teachers cannot be explained by student enrollment in public primary schools. In Ghana, 56 percent of teacher allocation cannot be explained by student enrollment. In comparison to other countries in Sub-Saharan Africa, only Liberia and South Sudan have a more "random" teacher allocation across their public primary schools.

Figure 4.7 Degree of Randomness of Teacher Allocation

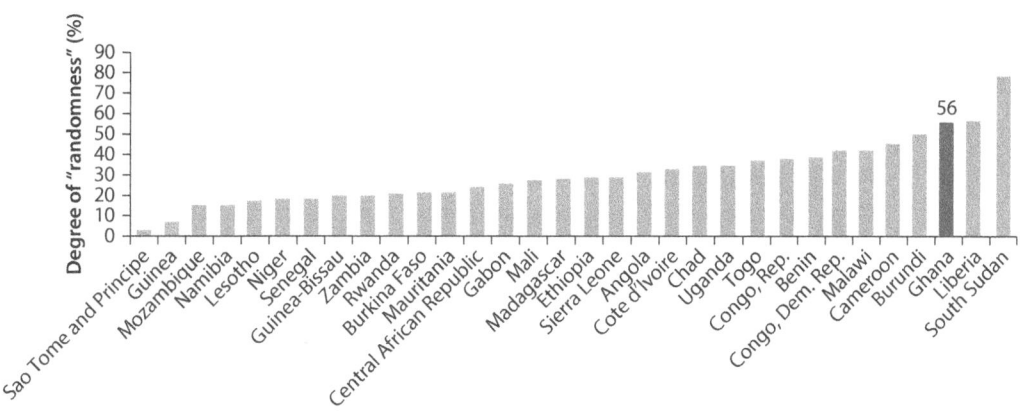

Source: World Bank 2011.

Table 4.2 Per-Child Expenditure in 2008 GHc Measured at District Level

	KG	Primary	JHS
Average	47	125	196
Median	37	118	172
Bottom third	23	90	134
Bottom third (avg.)	50%	72%	68%
Standard deviation	39	67	120
Min	5	12	20
Max	224	396	590

Source: World Bank 2010.

An analysis of per-child expenditure in primary school indicates that a key source of deprivation for deprived districts is the allocation of public expenditures itself. As background, one way to understand differences in inputs is to look at the GoG per-child recurrent expenditure (PCE) by district.[7] In one analysis PCE was calculated by dividing annual district recurrent expenditures by subsector by district enrollment in that subsector (World Bank 2010). Table 4.2 shows the PCE in 2008 GHc measured at district level.

Of note, median PCEs are consistently lower than the average PCE, indicating that more than half of the districts spend less than the average PCE. The high standard deviation indicates a substantial amount of variation in PCE across districts. Table 4.2 also shows the amount that demarcates the bottom third of the distribution of PCEs in 2008. In 2008, the PCE in primary school was 125GHc, the median PCE was 118 GHc, and the average PCE in districts comprising the bottom third was 90GHc. Districts in the bottom third received, on average, 28 percent less per child than the mean PCE.[8] Since personnel emoluments (that is salaries) account for a majority of MoE recurrent expenditure in primary education, variation in PCE largely reflects the disparity in teacher allocation across districts.

More than 50 percent of children in the three northern regions attend KG, Primary and JHS schools in districts where the PCE is below the bottom third of the nation. Figure 4.8 offers another way to look at PCE. In this figure, PCEs are plotted by district (each line represents one district). The vertical line cutting across the horizontal lines marks the bottom third of the PCE (equaling 90 GHc). Any district on the left of the horizontal line falls within the bottom third. It is important to note that (i) nearly all districts in the three northern regions are to the left of the horizontal line and (ii) in all other regions there is a wide variation in district PCE. A similar analysis using GES payroll data show that average per teacher expenditure in Greater Accra is 28 percent above the national average, while in three northern regions, average per teacher expenditure comes in at 4–10 percent below the national average (World Bank 2010).

Supply of primary textbooks and classrooms, key inputs to basic education, has not kept pace with enrollment growth. In KG, Primary and JHS subsectors, schools

Figure 4.8 PCE, by District, 2008

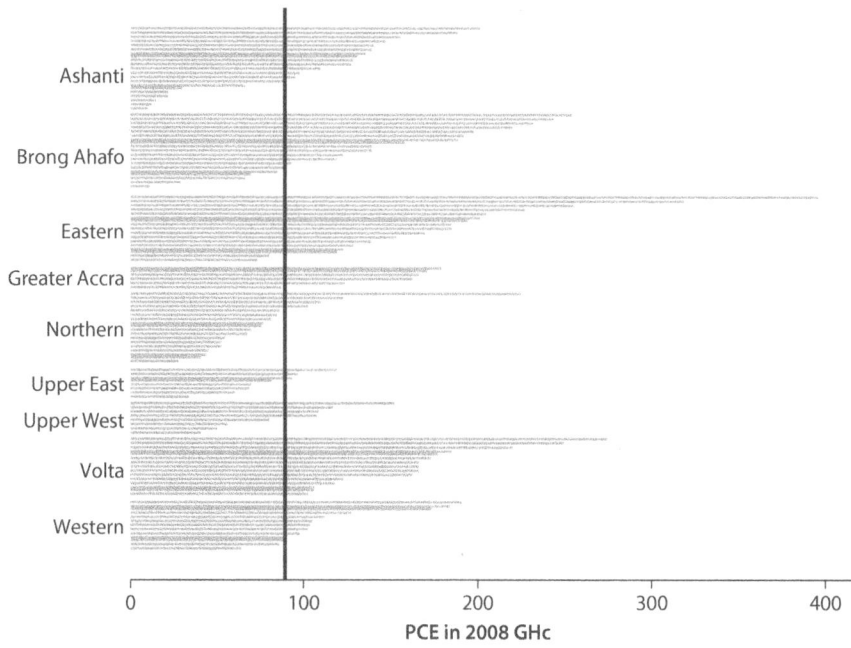

Source: World Bank 2010.
Note: Central region is not included in this figure.

in deprived districts have fewer of these inputs than nondeprived districts (ESPR 2011). The schools under trees program and EMIS data evidence the large number of primary classrooms needing major repair. EMIS 2008 data show the need for major repairs or new classrooms at over 20,000 basic schools. According to EMIS 2010, over 30 percent of basic schools are insufficiently equipped with water points and toilets (which are especially important for girls' health in upper primary).

Equitable Outcomes

Basic education outcomes, including primary completion rates, learning in English and mathematics and BECE pass rates as also unequally distributed by region, urban-rural status and household socioeconomic status. P3 and P6 proficiency in English and mathematics has been measured by the National Education Assessment (NEA) on a biannual basis since 2005. Reports on NEA assessments from 2005 as well as other analyses indicate that inequality in learning outcomes is largely explained by differences (i) between major population center districts (for example, Accra, Tema, Kumasi, and Shama-Ahanta East (Takoradi)) and the rest of the country, (ii) urban-rural status and (iii) regional status (Joseph and Wodon 2012; MoE 2012; USAID 2009). Figure 4.9 shows the percentage of P6 pupils attaining proficiency in English and mathematics

Box 4.2 GES Experimentation with a Resource Allocation Model

The Ghana Education Service (GES) is using a Resource Allocation Model (RAM) to support the more equitable allocation of basic education resources to the 170 districts and 10 regional education offices in Ghana. Priority is given to districts that lack sufficient infrastructure and which perform relatively poorly in education indicators. The RAM is being piloted in 2012 using government, DP and Global Partnership for Education resources.

The RAM provides two separate funding streams: one for goods and services (associated with recurrent expenditure) and one for assets (associated with capital expenditure). The RAM uses variables and data from the Education Management Information System (EMIS) collected by the Ministry of Education on an annual basis to determine "goods and services" and "assets" allocations.

The **Goods and Services** allocation is determined by the following variables aggregated at the district level: enrollment (35 percent); number of teachers (5 percent); number of schools (10 percent); base grant (10 percent) and district deprivation (40 percent). Districts with high enrollment, large number of schools and a high degree of deprivation will receive additional resources. District deprivation is assessed by measuring girls' enrollment (percent), untrained teachers (share), pupils with core textbooks (percent), GER, PTR, and BECE English and Maths pass rates. For district deprivation, each variable is given a score of 1–4 to reflect the extent of the disadvantage. Category 1 reflects the least disadvantaged and category 4 indicates the most disadvantaged. Each variable is assigned a score; the average score across all categories indicates the total deprivation sore.

The **Assets** allocation is determined by the following factors: enrollment (10 percent), number of schools (30 percent) and district deprivation (60 percent). Deprivation is determined by number of schools needing major repair, pupils having desks, schools with toilets, and schools with urinals. At the time of publication the total funding amount and the funding amount as a percentage of the total budget for basic education has not been determined.

Source: Ghana Education Service, 2012. Correspondence with Office of the Financial Controller.

---

by urban-rural status. In English, 46 percent of urban pupils attain a proficiency score compared to 17 percent of rural pupils. Mathematics scores follow a similar trend with 21 percent of urban pupils attaining a proficiency score compared to 6 percent of rural pupils. P3 student scores in mathematics and English follow the same pattern. *The NEA is explained in detail in the chapter on Quality.*

Regional variation is also very high. MoE (2012, xiv) notes:

> P6 and P3 students in Greater Accra outperformed their peers in other regions and in both subject areas by a wide margin. For example, the ratio of Greater Accra students achieving proficiency compared to students in the lowest-performing regions ranged from 4.9 on the P3 English test to 9.5 on the P6 maths test. In other words, in comparing students from Greater Accra to those from the

Figure 4.9 Percentage of P6 Pupils Attaining Proficiency in English and Maths, by Urban-Rural Status

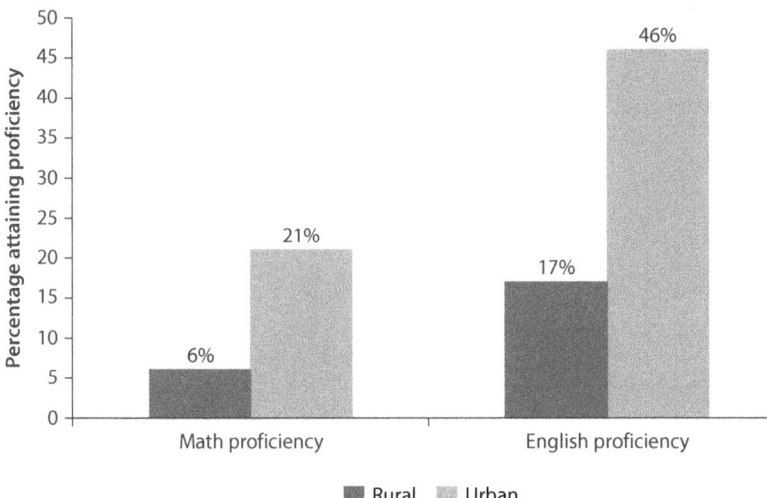

Source: MoE 2012.

lowest-performing regions, between nearly 5 and 10 times more students from Greater Accra were able to achieve proficiency-level scores than students from lower-performing regions.

The Quality chapter offers more data on regional variation. The variation in NEA scores by region persists over time (for example, NEA assessments conducted in 2005, 2007, 2009 and 2011) with the three northern regions consistently having the lowest percentages of pupils attaining proficiency in mathematics and English at both the P3 and P6 levels. The 2011 NEA results show a slight gender gap in mathematics but not in English.

A separate analysis reviewed district average NEA scores (by P6 students on the 2007 exam) against the district average household income (World Bank 2010). Figure 4.10 plots districts by average English and Math NEA scores and organizes districts by wealth quintile. The bold numbers at the top of the figure show the average score on the English and mathematics assessments for each quintile. Each box on the vertical lines represents one district. The figure shows the range of scores in each wealth quintile and shows the downward trend in test scores from wealthy to poor quintiles.

Chapter 5 ("Quality") will provide further analysis of NEA scores. The chapter identifies selected inputs which explain some of the variation in NEA performance (including trained teachers, textbook availability and proportion of female teachers) and which are identified in this chapter as inequitably distributed.

BECE pass rates in English and Math vary greatly by region and by gender. As shown in figure 4.11, in 2010/11, BECE pass rates for English and mathematics were highest in Greater Accra, Ashanti, Brong Ahafo, and Western Regions. At the national level, the mean pass rate was 61 percent and 59 percent for English and maths, respectively. Regional disparities are large. The Northern region had

Figure 4.10 NEA 2007 Scores (P6), by District Average and Wealth Quintile

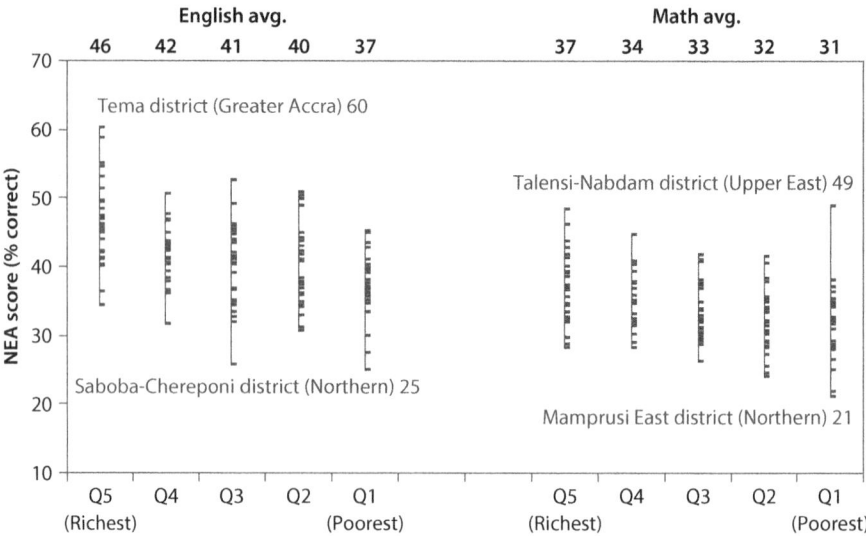

Source: World Bank 2010, Estimates based on GLSS 2005/06 and NEA 2007.

the lowest English pass rate (39.7 percent), while the Volta region had the lowest math pass rate (40.1 percent). The regional trend evident in figure 4.10 is consistent with the trend in regional pass rates on the 2008/09 BECE. *Of note, while NEA scores showed minimal gender disparity, there is a significant gender effect seen in the BECE.* In most regions (excepting Greater Accra), BECE pass rates for girls were 15–25 percent below that for boys. At the national level, 38 percent of girls received an aggregate 6–30, compared to 62 percent of boys (World Bank 2010).

At the district level, higher household income is associated with an increase in the pass rate on the BECE English exam. In the 2008/09 exam, differences in learning achievement were significant across wealth quintiles. On average, about 63 percent of students going to schools located in districts of the top quintile passed the BECE exams in 2008/09, whereas only 40 percent of students who resided in the districts of the poorest quintile passed. Figure 4.12 shows BECE English Pass Rate (2008/09) in Districts, by income. The regression shows a trend where districts with higher levels of average household income have higher BECE pass rates in English.

Girls, children in lower wealth quintiles and children living in the three northern regions and in deprived districts are less likely than comparison groups to complete primary school. In 2010/11, 94 percent of boys and 90 percent of girls completed primary school. The gender gap in primary completion has been consistent at about 4–5 percent over the past 5 years (ESPR 2012). Figure 4.13 shows completion rate by household SES. Students from districts with higher levels of average welfare are more likely to complete basic education. On average, students attending school in the poorest 20 percent of the

Equity

Figure 4.11 BECE English and Mathematics Pass Rates, by Region, 2010/11

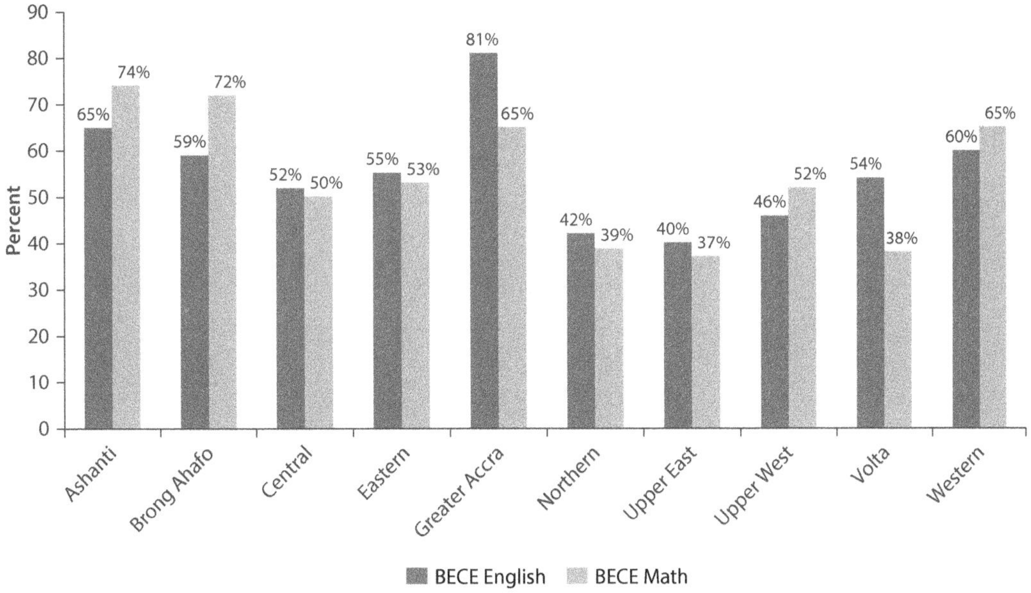

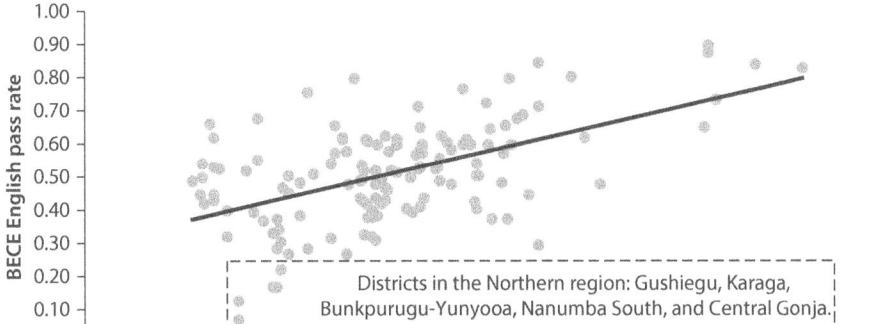

Source: EMIS 2011.

Figure 4.12 BECE English Pass Rate (2008/09) in Districts, by Income

Source: World Bank 2010, Based on data from GLSS, 2005/06; EMIS, 2008/09.

districts have a completion rate of 81 percent. Gaps between wealth quintiles are larger in JHS. Districts in the bottom wealth quintile (all located in the three Northern regions of Ghana) posted student JHS completion rates of 58 percent. This is about 20 percent below JHS completion rates posted by districts in the top three quintiles.

Figure 4.13 Primary and JHS Completion Rate by Wealth Quintile

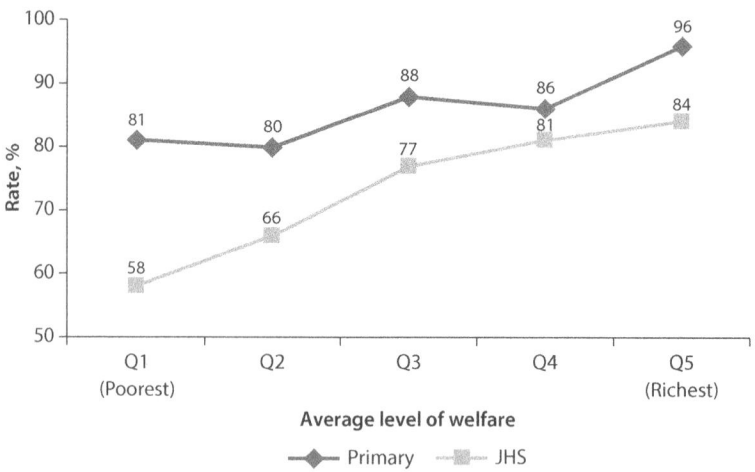

Source: World Bank 2010; estimates based on GLSS 2005/06 and EMIS 2008/09.

Social Mobility and Reproduction of Inequality

Education system inequalities hinder social mobility of the poorest and support the reproduction of social and economic inequality in Ghana. In a 2011 study of BECE and WASSCE scores by school type, Djangmah demonstrates how pupils' unequal opportunities in basic education explain subsequent access to high quality secondary schools and ultimately, tertiary study. Djangmah writes:

> The results show that ... secondary school education in Ghana is highly differentiated with regard to quality. The top schools which literally exclude public basic school pupils from admission on the basis of their weak BECE results grab the overwhelming proportion of tertiary education places. Considering that universities have more stringent requirements than non-university tertiary institutions university admissions must be almost the exclusive preserve of Ghanaian children who have attended fee-paying basic schools (2011, 13).

Like Addae-Mensa (2000), who showed that between 60 and 90 percent of students selected to various university degree programs came from the top 50 senior secondary schools, Djangmah shows that the top 20 percent of senior high schools in Ghana account for 75.7 percent of pupils with WASSCE scores which qualify them for tertiary education. Pupils from the next 20 percent of senior high schools account for 16.7 percent of qualifying WASSCE scores. The BECE and WASSCE act as "screens" which keep a large percentage of basic and SHS leavers, predominantly those from poorer households, from attending the next level of education.

Figure 4.14 shows the results of a model designed to predict students' access to SHS by wealth quintile. [*Note: This graph is meant to be illustrative. It is not a cohort analysis. Rather, it draws on household survey data showing access and*

Figure 4.14 Progression of Students to SHS, by Wealth Quintile

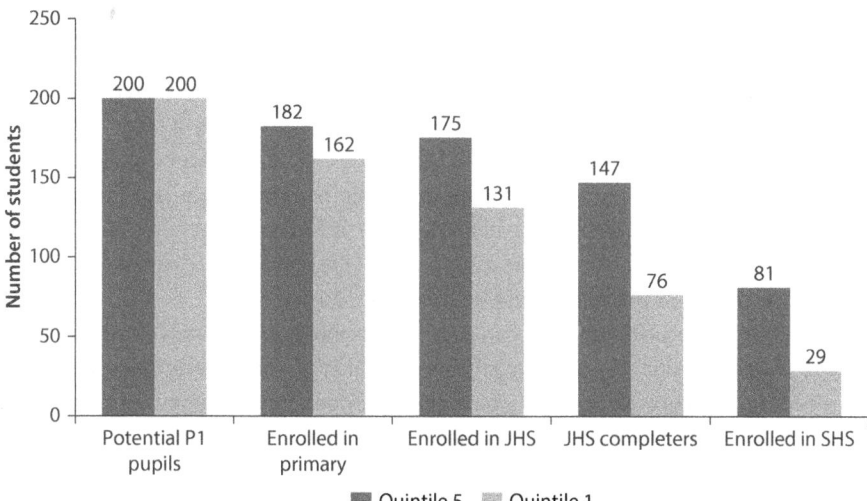

Source: Created by author using data from MoE EMIS 2011 and NER data from Casely-Hayford 2011.

completion by household wealth.] The model starts with 200 eligible P1 students in each wealth quintile (potential P1 pupils). Variation in primary access and primary and JHS completion rates by wealth quintile means that by the end of JHS, 147 students (of the original 200) from Quintile 5 would have completed JHS compared to 76 students from the poorest wealth quintile (Q1). The access gap between the two quintiles grows to a three to one difference in access to SHS. The figure shows only Quintile 5 and Quintile 1; however, the declining trend in access to upper levels of education is consistent from Q5 to Q1. Using 2008 data, Casely-Hayford (2011) notes that combined JHS and SHS NER for pupils for Q5 households is 61 percent, while that for pupils for Q3 and Q1 households is 42 percent and 22 percent, respectively.[9]

Identifying with the concerns raised by the Dzobo Committee (1974), Djangmah writes:

> Government is aware of the quality gap which is a mirror of the socio-economic gap in society between an affluent minority and a poorer majority. Children in public schools see themselves as unlucky to be receiving lower quality education in schools owned by the state. The inferiority complex generated by calling themselves *CYTO* meaning not in the main stream is evidence of how deeply the divide has grown. (2011, 15)

Results of Equity-Improving Policies and Programs

Equity measures are usually designed to improve the fairness and inclusivity of the education system. In the past decade, the Government of Ghana has initiated several programs designed to improve the lives of the poor and improve equity

Box 4.3 Improving Girls' Access to Secondary Schools in the Three Northern Regions

Girls from poor households in Ghana's three northern regions face multiple disadvantages in accessing and completing secondary education. At a national level, girls of secondary school age (44 percent) are more likely than males (40 percent) to attend secondary school (GSS 2011). However, in the three northern regions, female net attendance rate in secondary school is more 10 percent below the national average of 43 percent. In terms of household wealth, 3 percent of girls from the poorest 20 percent of the population complete Senior High School, compared to 88 percent of girls from the richest 20 percent.

To improve the participation of girls from poor households in the three northern regions, CAMFED and DfID Ghana are providing girls with scholarships which covers the cost of school fees, uniforms (made by local tailors which helps provide the community with work) and school supplies. The scholarship model engages communities in identifying scholarship recipients and also offers training to girls on financial literacy, business development and reproductive health.

While this initiative does not target basic education, the increased likelihood of access to secondary school may improve girls' JHS completion and break the cycle of inequality identified in this section.

---

in education. This section discusses supply-side and demand-side interventions and provides evidence on the impact of several recently implemented equity-improving programs.

The MoE has implemented several demand-side and supply-side measures to improve access to basic education. Patrinos (2007) writes:

> Demand-side financing is a way in which the government can finance private consumption of certain goods and services. In contrast to supply-side financing, where public funds go directly to suppliers, under demand-side financing consumers (or in the case of education, parents or students) receive a certain amount of money for specific expenditures. (Patrinos, 2007, 7)

Demand-side financing can include in-kind transfers, such as provision of school feeding or provision of school uniforms. The intended goal of such financing is to reduce barriers to educational access to disadvantaged children.

In Ghana, the Capitation Grant Scheme, the Ghana School Feeding Program (GSFP) and the Livelihood Empowerment Against Poverty (LEAP) are demand-side measures. Each program is based on the distribution of either money or food to support school attendance of children from disadvantaged backgrounds. Supply-side measures are programs or policies designed to expand supply of basic education. Such measures include the schools under trees program and implementation of complementary basic education in rural and marginalized areas and improving the quality of basic education (for example, by increasing the number of qualified teachers).

Table 4.3 Basic Education Demand- and Supply-Side Measures in Ghana

Demand-side measure	Supply-side measure
Conditional cash transfer/LEAP	Capitation grant scheme
School feeding	Expanding the system (establishing more schools near to communities)
Free uniforms/exercise books	Schools under trees program
	Complementary basic education
	Improving quality/increasing number of qualified teachers
	Grants to deprived districts (for example, Pilot Programmatic Scheme)

Table 4.3 shows some of the demand-side and supply-side initiatives being implemented in Ghana.

Following introduction of the capitation grant, primary NER (age-specific enrollment) realized some positive gains; however, following the initial capitation grant "bump," primary NER has leveled off at around 80 percent (ESPR 2012). Government of Ghana efforts to reach out-of-school children led to the implementation of the Capitation Grant (CG) scheme in 2004/05. The capitation grant is a GES-to-school cash transfer in which the school receives a small grant per child enrolled. The initial grant of 3.0 GHc per child was increased to 4.5GHc in 2008. Many studies attribute, in part, the increase in primary net enrollment rate (NER) from 59 percent in 2004/05 to 81 percent in 2005/06 to the replacement of school fees with Capitation Grants (UNICEF 2007).[10] However, other analysis (Akyeampong 2011; World Bank 2010) suggests that when impact of dropout is taken into account, the effect of the capitation grant on the increase in net enrollment is much smaller.

Recent policy dialogue suggests that the amount of the capitation grant has become insufficient to cover the tuition fees it was supposed to replace (MoE/PBME 2010). Recent MoE policy dialogue in the 2010 and 2011 NESAR has considered how the capitation grant policy can be strengthened. A study by MoE/PBME (2011, 23) suggests the grant may be more effective if "targeted to the poorest pupils, [and] providing a larger grant for those most in need." The study further suggests that to help small schools a minimum grant amount should be set so that each school, regardless of size, receives some basic funding. In the same study, "some evidence was found of the re-introduction of fees within sampled schools, which counters the initial aim of the [CG] intervention" (MoE PBME, 2010, 23). The study notes that further research is required to understand the extent to which the erosion of the economic value of the grant and/or delay or leakage in disbursements has "caused the return of fees in some schools." Limitations of demand-side interventions such as the Capitation Grant scheme are discussed at the end of this section.

Livelihood Empowerment Against Poverty (LEAP), a conditional cash transfer program, has been shown to benefit selected households primarily through increasing food consumption but also by helping households cover the costs of keeping children in school. However, implementation cost and poor targeting are causes for concern. LEAP targets orphans and vulnerable children through their caregivers and provides conditional and unconditional subsistence grants on a graduated payment scale of GH¢8-15 per month to beneficiaries. LEAP reaches poor households in districts considered poor by the NDPC with an estimated 57 percent share of outlays reaching the poor. However, there is concern that LEAP beneficiaries are not necessarily those occupying the bottom one-fifth of the poor. Issues with LEAP include delays in payment, local/elite capture and inequitable composition of Local Implementation Committees (PDA-PPVA 2011; World Bank 2011). PPVA (2011) suggests there is potential for communities to become more involved in implementation and better identify the poorest. LEAP impact on improving access to education has not been quantified and LEAP beneficiaries note that other fees associated with school attendance remain access barriers to access. On a broader economic and social note, PPVA finds that:

> While appreciating the grants they receive, many beneficiaries would rather have year-round, predictable livelihood sources than depend on handouts. Dignity is an issue for many beneficiaries and wherever it is possible to assist poor people to develop and utilize skills effectively, this should be seen as a credible alternative to long-term handouts. (PDA-PPVA, 54)

LEAP currently reaches 1 percent of the poor, and seeks to reach 10 percent. The cost-effectiveness of the program is a cause for concern: at present LEAP is incurring a cost of 1 GH¢ to provide 2 GH¢ of cash transfer.

The Ghana School Feeding Program (GSFP) is highly regarded by many beneficiary communities; however, only 21 percent of GSFP benefits go to children from the poorest two wealth quintiles. Several studies indicate that GSFP "is not particularly effective in targeting the poorest schools or the most food-insecure areas" and implementation favors regions in the south (PDA-PPVA, 2011, 58). Further, high implementation costs (54 GhC per child in 2008, an amount equal to over 40 percent of MoE per capita expenditure in basic education in that year) foreshadow sustainability problems. During initial implementation, "acts of corruption, inappropriate award of contracts, forged signatures and inflated school enrollment figures" along with lack of transparency gave the program a bad reputation (PWC cited in SEND). Several stakeholders have also voiced concern that time spent on feeding takes away from time on task during the school day. Nonetheless, many communities have strong positive feelings about the potential of such a program in high-poverty, food insecure and nutrition poor areas. PPVA notes that efforts have been made to strengthen local sourcing of food and local implementation of the program to improve program externalities and reduce costs.

Since 1995, more than 150,000 out-of-school children have completed a Complementary Basic Education (CBE) program. Seventy percent of graduates have mainstreamed into GES schools. Impact assessment findings suggest that CBE programs provide access to children who would otherwise not attend school; that CBE graduates (boys and girls) demonstrate primary retention and completion rates on par with non-CBE program participants and that the unit cost of CBE programs is below MoE unit costs (Casely-Hayford and Ghartey 2007; CREATE 2010). Through the program, 60–70 percent of CBE participants become functionally literate in their mother tongue. CBE implementers (usually NGOs) locate education centers near a "pocket" of out-of-school children and target poor, rural and "over-age" learners with a flexible, child-friendly learning program supported by community facilitators. After completing a fee-free 9-month CBE cycle, graduates have the opportunity to mainstream into the formal school system at the P3 or P4 level. In 2008, MoE drafted a CBE Policy outlining CBE as a national strategy for inclusion of out of school children into the formal system especially in communities where there are no schools (MoE CBE Policy, 2009). CBE implementation is included as a priority in the Education Strategic Plan 2010–2020. There are many differences between CBE centers and MoE schools with respect to school culture, management and institutional support which the MoE/GES will need to consider as it moves toward implementation of its draft CBE policy.

The Pilot Programmatic Scheme (PPS) provided direct budget support to deprived districts on a pilot scale for targeted operational activities. Using resources form PPS, deprived district DEOs articulated district strategic priorities in an Annual Program of Work (APoW) for subsequent local implementation and management. A sample analysis of 27 deprived district 2011 APoWs, across all 9 regions targeted by the PPS, showed that: (i) 52 percent of all investments were used for school rehabilitation and furniture, (ii) 33 percent of the investments were used to improve school-level sanitation (that is boreholes, water tanks and toilet facilities), and (iii) 12 percent on support to needy pupils.

The project completion report (World Bank 2012) recognized PPS as critical to (i) developing a mechanism for providing grants to deprived districts, (ii) supporting capacities of these districts to develop APOWs and (iii) supporting the piloting and nationwide roll-out of the capitation grants program. Notably, the largest share of PPS resources were directed to Ghana's three poorest regions—Northern, Upper East and Upper West.[11] The PPS led to GES development of a "Resource Allocation Model" (discussed earlier) which uses a formula that directs a greater share of central government resources to districts with the greatest need.

Evidence is either mixed or unavailable on the impact and implementation of other equity-improving programs. Other programs include the distribution of school uniforms and exercise books, the schools under trees program and girls' scholarship initiatives. School uniform, exercise book, and schools under trees initiatives have been criticized for poor targeting and lack of transparency (GNECC, 2010). Regarding the school uniform and exercise books initiatives, PBME (2011) notes, "in the absence of clear criteria, it is difficult to assess the success of targeting interventions." Table 4.4 offers an overview of selected equity-improving programs.

A review of program evaluation documents suggests three general lessons learned from implementation of equity-improving programs.

First, several inputs-focused programs, including the Capitation Grant Scheme, the Ghana School Feeding Program (GSFP) and the Livelihood Empowerment Against Poverty (LEAP) have improved equity in access to basic education. However,

Table 4.4 Overview of Selected Equity-Improving Programs

Intervention	Description	Results	Challenges
Capitation grant	Grant of 4.5GHc per child enrolled sent to every basic education school	Initially supported NER increase	Amount is seen as insufficient, management issues (funding delay and leakage), funding does not target the poorest
LEAP	Monthly cash transfer to poor families of 8–15 GHc	Increase nutrition and education access to vulnerable populations	Targeting needs strengthening, program management issues, high implementation cost
Ghana School Feeding Program	Provision of breakfast or lunch during the school day	Increase school access and child nutrition	Targeting very poor, many program management issues, high implementation cost
Complementary basic education	Initiative to mainstream rural, overage, vulnerable children into GES schools	Majority of participants get functional literacy and are mainstreamed; cost-effective	Currently outside of MoE/GES system, only operates in northern regions
Grants to deprived districts (for example, PPS)	Provision of block grants to "deprived districts"	District capacity development, support to flexible, district-led interventions	Delay in funding to districts, difficult to measure targeting and specific impact of funding

Sources: Various evaluation documents, including World Bank 2011.

it should be noted that while these programs have progressive possibilities, none of these programs directly address the structural inequalities in the current system, including getting trained teachers to pupils with the greatest need.

Second, as currently implemented, existing equity-improving programs disproportionally support students from higher wealth households. This highly problematic outcome of programs designe to reach those with the greatest need is worth emphasizing. *Program implementation requires significant strengthening, especially with respect to targeting of beneficiaries and management, if desired reductions in unequal access are to be realized.* Several programs have experienced leakage or mismanagement of resources and have a record of inconsistent and delayed distribution of resources. Table 4.5 shows the number of students (by wealth quintile) who receive the capitation grant and school meals. Children in the lowest two wealth quintiles receive disproportionally low shares of capitation grants and school meals. While both programs have improved primary access among the poorest children, it is noteworthy that implementation of these program mirrors the unequal distribution of inputs. Regarding leakage of funding, PBME (2011, 3) notes: "previous studies have found evidence of leakage and delays within the distribution channels for the interventions, especially for capitation grants (CDD 2010, GNECC, 2010) and School Uniforms."

Last, inputs-focused initiatives respond to part of the "access challenge"; however, these programs do not address other issues (for example, age of initial enrollment, household expectations of child labor, school culture) which also act as access barriers. Late initial enrollment and dropout in later grades (often related to overage

Equity

Table 4.5 Share of Students Receiving Capitation Grants and School Meals by Deprivation Index

	National	Q1	Q2	Q3	Q4	Q5	Poor
Total enrollment	2,606,512	344,942	436,174	512,147	577,893	735,356	522,736
Total students receiving school meals	372,372	26,484	48,832	63,116	74,583	159,357	45,791
Total students receiving capitation grants	2,273,722	289,647	377,870	455,176	508,159	642,870	443,828
Percentage of students receiving school meals	100	7.11	13.11	16.95	20.03	42.80	12.30
Percentage of students receiving capitation grants	100	12.74	16.62	20.02	22.35	28.27	19.52

Source: Wodon and Joseph 2010. Using school-level data *from EMIS, a school-level deprivation index is calculated using the following* variables: text book to pupil ratio, whether the school has classrooms that need major repairs, percentage of qualified teachers, student teacher ratio, pass rate in primary, and girls' enrollment rate.

enrollment, economic requirements, or concern with the quality/values of schooling) are two of many factors suggesting that focusing on initiatives such as the capitation grant or school feeding is an overly narrow way of considering how policy may be used to improve equity in access. While recognizing the value of the capitation grant in bringing out-of-school children into education, Akyeampong (2011) notes:

> The introduction of Capitation Grant as a demand-side intervention to improve access works up to a point—its success lies in pulling a large group of out of school children back into education. …the greater challenge is to eliminate dropout and [realizing] that the age of entry and regular attendance is at the heart of the challenge facing the achievement of sustainable access. (Akyeampong 2011, vii)

Box 4.4 and figure 4.15 show the Zones of Exclusions Framework, designed by the CREATE research project to identify "zones" in which particular subpopulations of students dropout or are at-risk of dropping out (Lewin 2007).

Box 4.4 Zones of Exclusion Framework

Zones of Exclusion is a framework developed through research from CREATE to identify "zones" in which particular subpopulations of students drop out or become at-risk of dropping out. The framework provides a useful map of different populations of "at-risk" pupils. As such, the framework can be used by policymakers to differentiate between these populations and better design interventions to support basic education completion and learning for all. The framework highlights seven zones of exclusion:

- Zone 0: Children who never attend KG
- Zone 1: Children who do not enroll in school
- Zone 2: Children who drop out of primary school or fail to complete a full primary cycle

box continues next page

Box 4.4 Zones of Exclusion Framework *(continued)*

- Zone 3: Children in school, but who are at risk of dropping out. These children, who are often overage or have low attendance, are considered "silently excluded."
- Zone 4: Children who fail to transition to JHS
- Zone 5: Children who drop out of JHS school or fail to complete a full cycle
- Zone 6: Children at risk of dropping out from JHS.

Figure 4.15 Access and Zones of Exclusion in Primary and JHS

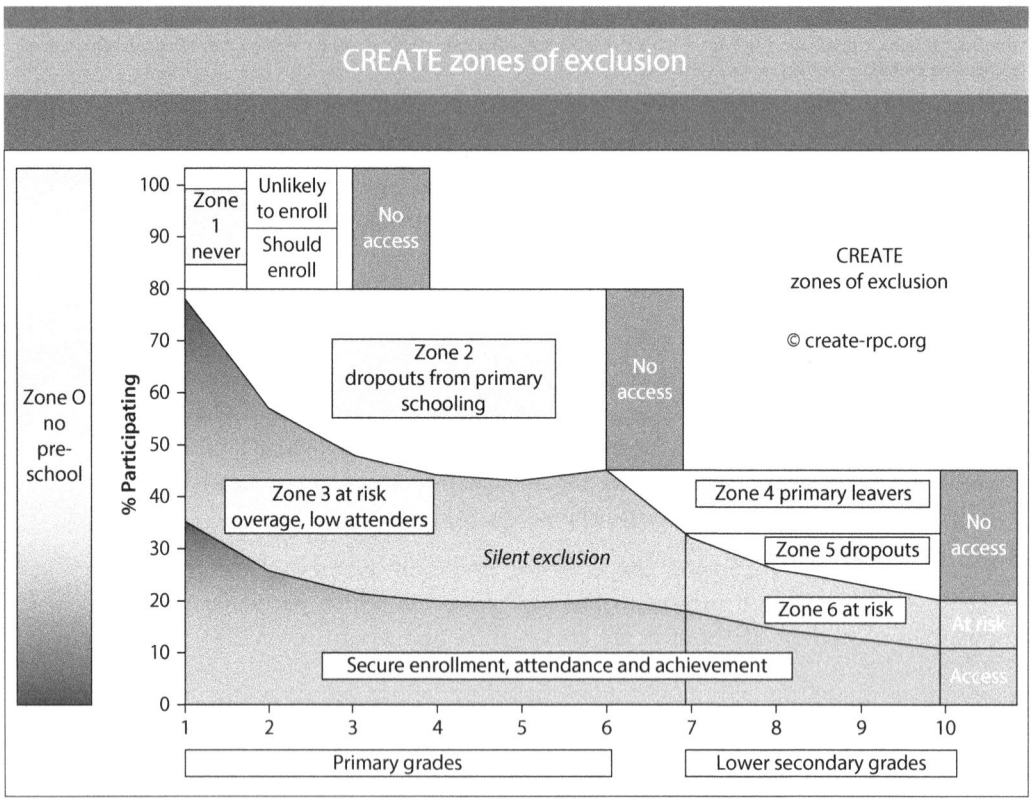

Source: Lewin 2007.

Box 4.5 Equity, Quality, Efficiency in Rural Schools

Challenges facing rural schools are different from those facing urban schools. Rural students are more likely to be engaged in seasonal work or pastoral responsibilities and live long distances from school. Teachers posted to rural areas often live in town and have difficulty

box continues next page

Box 4.5 Equity, Quality, Efficiency in Rural Schools *(continued)*

finding reliable transport to their post. Teachers often prefer to live in town because of the lack of amenities (for example, housing, electricity and safe water) in rural areas.

The distance of these schools from the DEO make it difficult and expensive for the circuit supervisor to visit schools and support teachers on a regular basis. Rural schools in minority language areas may find it difficult to secure a qualified teacher who is proficient in several mother tongues and in English. Further, low population density in rural areas means that under current policy, many of these schools should contain multigrade classrooms. Many teachers are not prepared to effectively teach in such environments. At the JHS level, securing a teaching staff with the required expertise required to teach a full range of subjects is especially challenging.

Rural school cannot operate on the scale economies of urban schools – therefore, unit costs may be higher in rural schools. It is not clear if there is infrastructure policy which takes into account the specific needs and constraints to infrastructure works (e.g. "new build" and rehabilitation) in low-population density areas. Private and NGO schools have experimented with renting space and using micro-loans (for rehabilitation of classrooms) to address space needs. (ESP 2010–2020; PDA-PPVA, 2011; Mingat, 2010).

Notes

1. ESP 2010–20, chapter 3 provides "outlines strategies" supporting this objective which include the following: (i) Make available public and private child-friendly basic education for all through the District Assemblies, the Private Sector, CBOs, NGOs and FBOs.; (ii) Ensure that no child is excluded from BE by virtue of disadvantage; (iii) Remove barriers to education by improving pupil welfare to motivate parents and learners to attend school. (iv) Ensure equal basic education opportunities for all.
2. Basic Education Certificate Examination (BCEC), Middle School Leaving Certificate (MSLC), VOC. Nearly 7 percent of households in Ghana are female-only-headed households (GLSS, 6).
3. Primary school net attendance rate (adjusted): Number of children of primary school age currently attending primary or secondary school.
4. There is some difference between "Net Enrollment Ratio" indicator, used by MOE during the school census, and the "Net Attendance Rate" used here, which comes from the GSS (2011) Multiple Indicator Cluster Household Survey. In this case, in 2011, the Primary NAR was 73 percent and the Primary NER was 82 percent. Both data sets show variation in access by region; however, GSS 2011 provides more detail on attendance by wealth quintile and urban-rural status.
5. Attendance data (from GDHS 2008, a household survey) and enrollment calculations (from EMIS and GLSS) come from different data sources. Household surveys are often considered more reliable than national EMIS systems. Even so, the trends (NER by wealth quintile) remain similar in both data sets.
6. GSS (2011, 236) provides more recent data noting "The proportion of children of primary school age who are attending primary school is directly related to age—the net attendance rate for children aged 6 years is only 34 percent." The figure increases to 57 percent at age 7 and 94 percent by age 11.

7. PCE includes budget categories PE, admin and service, but not investment.
8. First, World Bank 2010 analysis found substantial differences between district and national-level data. It is unclear why this is. At the national level, the MoE calculates "per child recurrent expenditure" on an annual basis. This figure is calculated by dividing the GoG subsector recurrent expenditure by the total subsector enrollment. In 2008/09, the figure was 188GHc. In 2010/11, the figure had risen to 224 GHc. Second, a deprived district is a district that falls below the national average on a number of MoE selected indicators. Roughly one-third of districts in Ghana are classified as "deprived." Refer to World Bank 2010 for further details.
9. This figure is not the result of a cohort analysis. Rather it uses currently available data to construct a model of progression to SHS. Data used to construct this graph include Primary NER by wealth quintile, primary and JHS completion rates by wealth quintile and transition rate (JHS to SHS) by wealth quintile. JHS and SHS NER by wealth quintile were used to triangulate calculations and analysis.
10. Notably, every region in the country experienced a rise in enrollment with the Northern regions experiencing the largest increase.
11. PPS was a component of EdSep, a project implemented by the World Bank form 2004–11 (World Bank 2012).

CHAPTER 5

Quality

This chapter shows a mixed picture in terms of quality improvement. While results on national and international assessments have realized some improvement over the past decade, learning outcomes in English and mathematics remain far below national targets and there remains a shortage of over 50,000 qualified teachers. Making sustained improvements in quality is a critical task facing education leaders and policymakers. This chapter provides information on learning outcomes, factors positively affecting learning and issues related to the supply and retention of qualified teachers.

Overview

In the past 15 years, in addition to expanding access and improving equity, Ghana has also committed to improving basic education quality. Ghana has had some success in meeting this challenge: In 15 years, basic education enrollment has increased by 2 million pupils and learning outcomes as measured by the National Education Assessment (2005–11) and the TIMSS have realized slight increases. Larger numbers of P6 pupils are gaining proficiency in English and mathematics and many of these pupils are transitioning to JHS and SHS. Further, a significant number of new classrooms, water points and sanitation facilities have been constructed creating safer and healthier learning environments. However, the state of quality in basic schools can also be interpreted differently. In the 2011 National Education Assessment (NEA), 35 percent of P6 students tested at the proficiency level in English and 16 percent tested at the proficiency level in mathematics. While these scores represent a slight upward trend, they fall far below MoE targets for P6 student numeracy and literacy.

Improving basic education quality is a central issue of education policy dialogue in Ghana. Recent lectures and papers from the academic community and annual conferences and reports facilitated by MoE highlight a growing and broad-based concern over the quality of basic education (Ampiah 2010; Anamuah-Mensah 2009; Akyeampong 2010; ESPR, 2012; MoE 2012). This debate has been informed by the growing availability of data on learning outcomes and reflects the long-standing commitment of MoE and GES to regularly measure and share results of learning assessments. This openness is no small matter: regular measurement and dissemination of assessment results reflect a transparency which carries political and reputational risk—especially given the large differences in regional BECE pass rates and NEA performance. Lackluster performance on the NEA or TIMSS provides critics with evidence to disparage a system which has also realized great successes and comprises tens of thousands of dedicated teachers and administrators.

A broad definition of quality is inclusive of basic educations' multiple objectives and service delivery standards. Basic education *objectives* include supporting development of pupil cognitive, noncognitive and technical skills and delivery of content on civic issues such as safety, the environment and citizenship. This development is usually guided by the curriculum. Quality includes the "relevance" of basic education to securing a livelihood and transitioning to adulthood. World Bank (2010) offers extensive back ground on the relevance of basic education to girls' health and well-being and supporting transition to the world of work. *Service delivery standards* include teacher certifications and professional standards, ensuring access to teaching and learning materials, providing safe and secure infrastructure and learning environments, offering adequate supervisory support and professional development and providing support to children with special needs. A safe environment, where a child is free from bullying or sexual harassment and where there is access to clean water and sanitation, is an environment where learning and social development can take place.

Stakeholders in Ghana have many and diverse understandings of "quality" in basic education. Parents often look to school BECE pass rates and transition to secondary selection as indicators of quality. Professional educators often highlight the importance of subject matter knowledge and cognitive skills (for example, critical thinking) while teachers, community leaders and traditional authorities may also prioritize pupils' social, moral, cultural or citizenship development. Recognizing this diversity, one author notes:

> The education agenda has expanded dramatically over the years as societies entrust more and more responsibilities to vast and complicated curricula. There are many different interest groups in a society that is concerned about education. They promote different educational priorities, and greater consultation does not result in clarity of intents but rather in compromises and complexities. (Snyder 1999, 1)[1]

This report argues that bringing all schools to a minimum quality threshold may be a critical step toward broad and sustained improvement in basic education quality. Such a threshold may require that pupils should leave primary schools with proficiency in numeracy and literacy, teachers should have the knowledge, skills and institutional support to effectively instruct students, schools should be equitably resourced and supported and children who require additional support to access school and to learn should have access to such support. While many pupils are highly successful in the current system, a larger number of pupils pass through primary school without having gained proficiency in numeracy and literacy. Many of these students are not provided adequate incentives, inputs (for example, qualified teachers) or sufficient time on task to develop these basic skills.

In this chapter, quality is discussed in terms of results on national and international assessments, factors affecting learning outcomes, provision of qualified teachers and debate over mother tongue and English language instruction.

Learning Outcomes

Recent upward trends in English and mathematics achievement on the NEA show improvement in learning outcomes. However, learning outcomes remain well shy of national targets. As background, the NEA is a biannual nationally and regionally representative measure of student proficiency in mathematics and English in primary grades 3 and 6. The 2011 assessment covered all 10 regions of Ghana including more than 580 schools and 60,000 students in the sample. The assessments include 40 to 60 multiple choice items and measures student performance through two cut-off scores. A *minimum-competency* score of 35 percent is defined as such because it is a 10 percent over a *chance* score of 25 percent and thereby suggests that some learning has taken place. Adu (2006, iii) notes, "the proficiency level of 55%... [shows] that the pupil has learned the curriculum for the grade level (class) to the degree necessary to work at the next grade level."[2] There is some debate on the use of "proficiency" in discussing NEA scores. The MoE 2011 report on the NEA indicates that "international standards generally classify students as proficient if they have achieved a minimum score of 70%."

In the 2011 National Education Assessment (NEA), 35 percent of P6 students tested at proficiency level in English and 16 percent tested at proficiency level in maths. Outside of Greater Accra, fewer than 25 percent of students in attain proficiency in P3 Maths, P3 English or P6 Maths (excepting Ashanti Region for P3 English). As noted in the Equity chapter, scores vary greatly across regions. In none of the three northern regions do more than 20 percent of students score at the proficiency level in English or maths. Figure 5.1 and figure 5.2 show the percentage of P3 and P6 students achieving proficiency in English and maths, by region. In only four regions out of 10 do more that 30 percent of pupils attain a proficiency score in P6 English. NEA scores, in corroboration with other information presented in this chapter, indicate that the majority of P6 students who complete primary school are doing so without having attained proficiency in core subject areas.

Pupils demonstrate relatively strong oral comprehension of English, but have great difficulties in reading and writing. The majority of P3 and P6 students have not mastered any of domains assessed in the NEA Maths exam. The NEA English exam is organized into four domains: Listening, Grammar, Reading and Writing. The percentage of P6 students achieving proficiency scores in the listening domain was 78 percent; students scoring at the proficiency level in the *reading* and *writing* domains were 37 percent and 19 percent, respectively. The NEA P6 Maths exam is also organized into four domains. Students testing at the proficiency level in

Figure 5.1 Percentage of P3 and P6 Students Achieving Proficiency in English, by Region

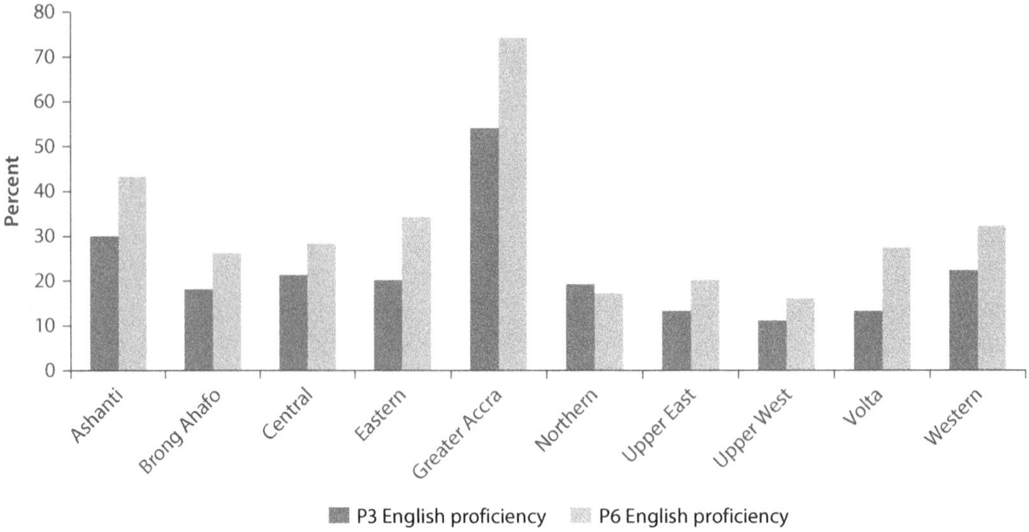

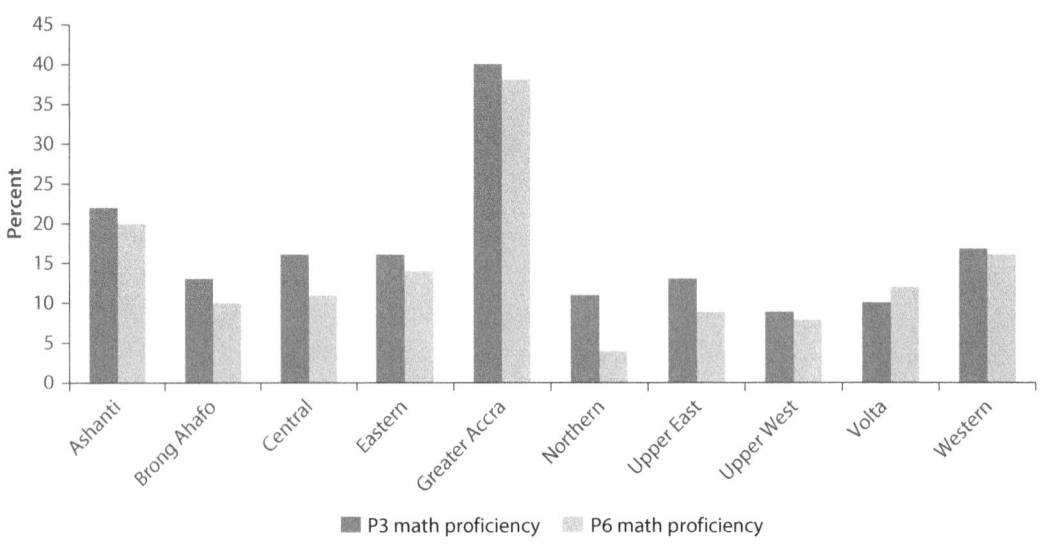

Source: MoE 2012.

Figure 5.2 Percentage of P3 and P6 Students Achieving Proficiency in Maths, by Region

Source: MoE 2012.

each domain is in parenthesis: Collecting and Handling Data (42 percent), Measurement of Shapes and Space(25 percent), Operations (18 percent) and Numbers (33 percent).

Figure 5.3 shows the percentage of P3 and P6 students attaining proficiency in English and maths during four separate administrations (2005–11) of the

http://dx.doi.org/10.1596/978-1-4648-0098-6

Figure 5.3 Percentage of P3 and P6 Students Attaining Proficiency in English and Maths

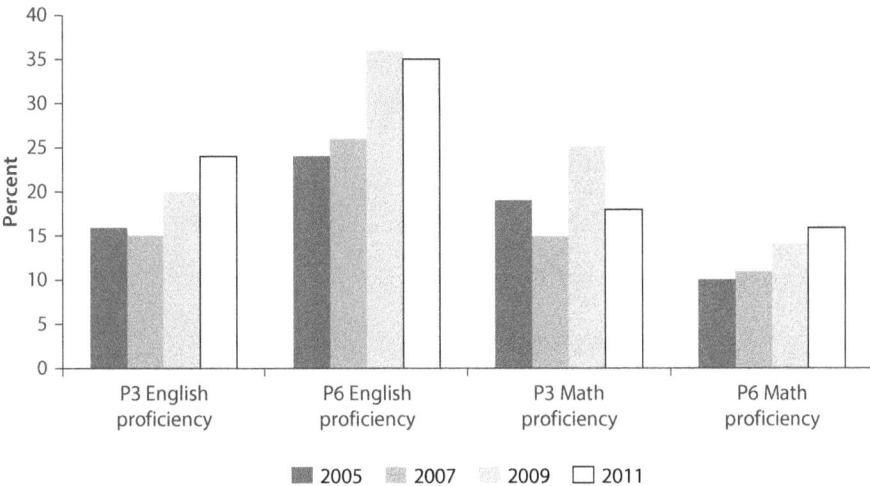

Source: MoE 2012.

NEA. MoE (2012, xi) notes, "Although the validity of comparing scores across years is limited…trend analysis still provides a sense of change in student performance over time." The percentage of P6 students achieving proficiency in English remains constant between 2009 and 2011, while the percentage of P3 students achieving minimum competency and proficiency in English has increased. In maths, 2011 scores saw a drop from 2009 scores, excepting the percentage of P6 student achieving proficiency. *Additional data are in MoE 2012 NEA report.*

Score patterns in the NEA and in a separately administered exam suggest the presence of a "missing middle." In the NEA, while many students are proficient, an even larger number of students do not attain a minimum competency level (except in the case of P6 English result). This finding is consistent with findings from a separate English assessment administered by the World Bank. In 2009, the World Bank implemented an English exam to test P3 and P5 student fluency in naming letters, reading words and reading comprehension. The exercise drew on a random sample of 50 schools and 1,700 children representing all regions. The test was tailored to what the students were supposed to know at 3rd grade.

Figure 5.4 shows the percentage of P3 and P5 students by reading comprehension score. The data show a large number of students with zero scores, a slim middle and a moderate number of students with high scores. On the World Bank English assessment, 35 percent of 3rd graders and over 15 percent of 5th graders received zero scores in reading comprehension exercises. This finding has some alignment with NEA results, where, in the reading comprehension portion of the English exam, 42 percent of P3 students (42 percent) had a 0 of 1 score (out of six questions).

Figure 5.5 shows the number of zero scores in reading words and reading comprehension by grade and by whether the pupil was underage, overage or age

Figure 5.4 Percentage of P3 and P5 Students by Reading Comprehension Score

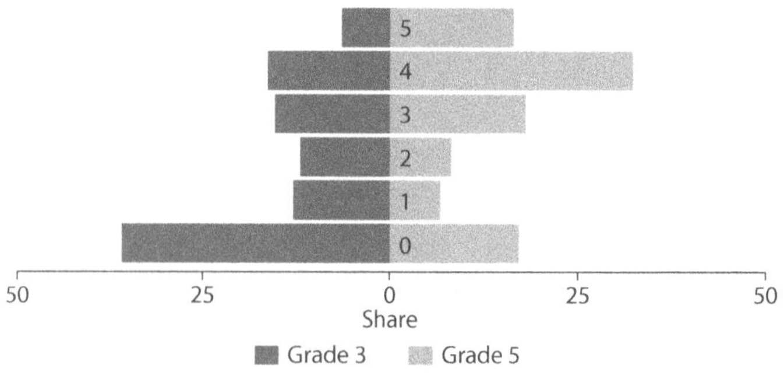

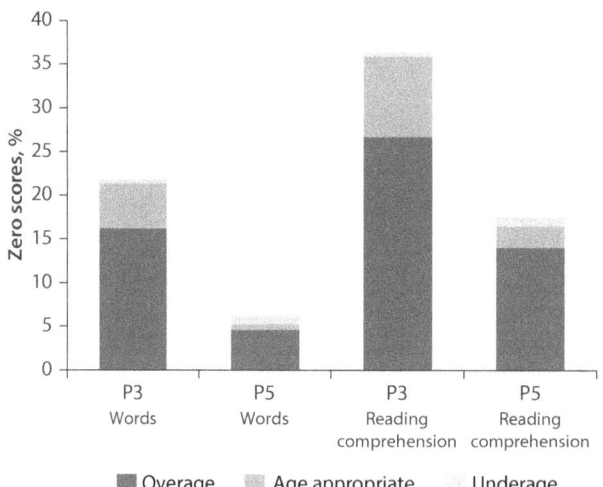

Source: Cloutier 2010/World Bank Ghana Survey 2010.

Figure 5.5 Zero Scores in Reading Words and Comprehension, by Grade and Age Group, 2009

Source: Cloutier/World Bank Ghana Survey 2010.

appropriate for the grade. Over 25 percent of third graders have difficulty naming letters (graph not shown) and over 21 percent were not able to read any words. Of note, overage students accounted for the majority of zero scores in both grades (Cloutier 2010). *Zero score results on this exam and the NEA indicate that large numbers of children have passed through three or six grades of school having learned little to no English.*

The missing-middle is associated with broad based inequities in basic education and poor system performance. Specifically, children from Ghana's northern regions and deprived districts, poor and rural households and ethnic and linguistic minorities—students who require the most support to meet learning outcomes—receive, on average, disproportionately fewer resources from the government than their peers. Low scores from these populations create a *missing middle* and drag down system performance.

Ghana's 2007 TIMSS scores in mathematics and science were much higher than 2003 scores; however, 2007 scores remain lower than almost all other countries participating in the assessment. The Trends in International Mathematics and Science Study (TIMSS) is an international assessment in math and science in which a random selection of Ghanaian JHS2 students participated in 2003 and 2007. Table 5.1 shows selected mathematics and science TIMSS scores. In 2003, Ghana's score for mathematics of 276 was higher only compared to that of South Africa and much lower than the international average score for mathematics of 467. In 2007, Ghana demonstrated substantial improvement in the mathematics score, which increased to 309. Even so, this score is still one of the lowest among the participating countries, ranking 47th among the 48 participants. The science score realized a big increase from 255 in 2003 to 303 in 2007.[3]

TIMSS categorizes students into four benchmarks: advanced, high, intermediate and low. In 2003, 3 percent of Ghanaian students met the intermediate benchmark; 13 percent of Ghanaian students met the low benchmark and the rest of the students (87 percent) fell below this benchmark. Anamuah-Mensah summarizes, "The performance of Ghanaian JSS students was abysmally low compared to students from other countries. …It is hoped that measures will be taken…to bring about improvement in mathematics and science education in basic schools" (2004, 133).

Compared to their ability to recall factual information and use concepts, Ghanaian JHS2 students' demonstration of higher-order cognitive skills (for example, problem solving, analysis) on TIMSS was low. Table 5.2 shows content

Table 5.1 Selected Mathematics and Science TIMSS Scores

Country	Mathematics		Science	
	2003	2007	2003	3007
Singapore	605	593	578	567
Tunisia	410	420	404	445
Botswana	366	364	365	355
Ghana	276	309	255	303
International average	467	500	474	500

Source: Anamuah-Mensah et al. 2009.

Table 5.2 TIMSS Content and Cognitive Domains, 2004

Math content domains	Science content domains	Cognitive domains
Numbers	Life science**	Factual/procedural knowledge
Data	Physics**	Conceptual understanding
Algebra**	Chemistry	Reasoning and analysis**
Geometry**	Earth science	Solving routine problems (maths)
Measurement**	Environmental science	

Source: World Bank data.
**Represents low-score areas.

domains in each subject area and the cognitive domains covered in both subject areas. Ghanaian JHS2 students showed strongest results in the mathematics domains of numbers and data and in the science domains of chemistry and environmental science. In mathematics, students posted the lowest scores with algebra, geometry, and measurement. In science, low scores were posted in physics and life science. With respect to cognitive skills, Anamuah-Mensah et al. write: "Students' problem solving, reasoning and analytic abilities in science and mathematics were therefore low compared to their abilities to recall factual information or use concepts" (Anamuah-Mensah 2004, 123).[4]

Student performance on international assessments appears to have some relationship with country income status. TIMSS comparison countries, such as Tunisia, the Arab Republic of Egypt, Botswana, and South Africa have a GDP per capita that is two to four times larger than that of Ghana. Figure 5.6 illustrates the relation between country income status and performance on international assessments (using PISA 2009 data). The graph shows the percentages of 15-year-old students scoring at "high," "average," and "below basic" levels. While it is likely that a large number of factors contribute to differences in TIMSS scores, it is also worth remembering that Ghana has fewer resources than comparison countries that could be utilized to improve learning outcomes.

The Basic Education Certificate Examination (BECE) is primarily a screening mechanism as opposed to a tool designed to measure learning outcomes. The NEA and the TIMSS are competency-based assessments, meaning that results are designed to show the extent to which students have mastered particular competencies. The purpose of the BECE is to determine whether or not a pupil is able

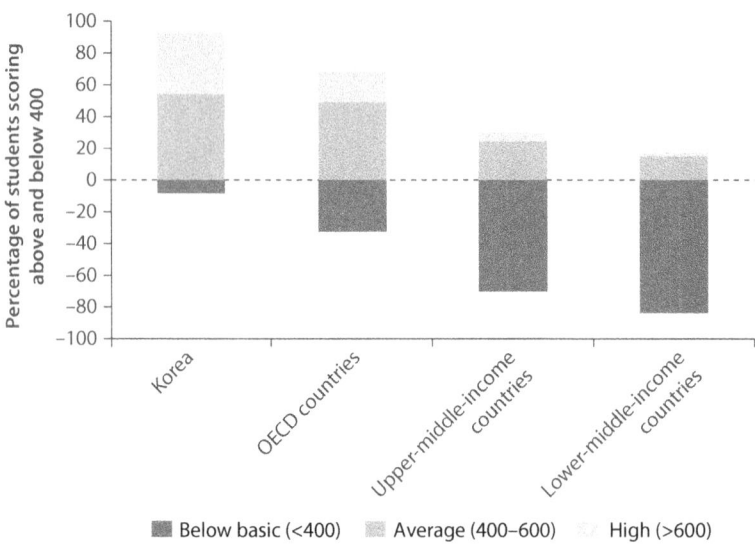

Figure 5.6 Comparative PISA Math Proficiency, by Country Income Status

Source: Bruns, Filmer, and Patrinos 2011.

to progress to second cycle education. As such, the BECE is structured so that approximately 60 percent of students each year obtain an aggregate 6–30 (Ampiah 2010). One criticism of such end-of-cycle exams is that they distort educational priorities and objectives toward the factual knowledge covered on the exam and away from higher-level cognitive skills. It is important to note that while aggregate BECE pass rates provide an indication of quality differences between regions or schools, comparison of national BECE pass rates over time or equating national BECE pass rates with "quality" misunderstands the structure and scoring of the BECE. Additional information in the BECE is in the Equity chapter.

Box 5.1 The Teacher Community Assistant Initiative (TCAI)

Demonstrating Possibilities for Improving Equity and Quality

Many primary schools across the developing world fail to equip pupils with basic literacy and numeracy skills, often because schools are not able to target teaching to the actual learning levels of pupils. Facing heterogeneous classrooms, teachers need either support in the form of assistants focused on basic skills or the opportunity and skills to target instruction at the child's level.

The TCAI Pilot in Ghana tests four programs that aim to target instruction to children's actual learning levels in basic numeracy and literacy. The program is based on research on the highly successful Pratham Balsakhi program in India, where a community volunteer teacher provides targeted instruction on basic skills to the lowest-performing primary students. In Ghana, TCAI program implementation began in May 2011, as a collaboration between Innovations for Poverty Action (IPA), National Youth Employment Programme (NYEP), the Ghana National Association of Teachers (GNAT), and Ghana Education Services (GES). Each program includes 100 government schools and using a randomized control trial (RCT), compares these schools against a control group of 100 schools which receive no treatment. Programs in the TCAI pilot are as follows:

1. A teacher community assistant (TCA), paid a small salary through the NYEP and trained in a simple teaching methodology, focused on targeting basic literacy and numeracy instruction, provides remedial education to a group of lowest-level learners pulled out during the school day.
2. TCAs provide the same remedial education support to lowest-level learners, but classes are held after school.
3. Teachers are trained to group their classes by learning levels and tailor their instruction accordingly.
4. To test the effect of reducing classroom size by adding an assistant, TCAs provide homework help to a randomly selected pull-out group during the school day.

---

box continues next page

Box 5.1 The Teacher Community Assistant Initiative (TCAI) *(continued)*

Program evaluation tests the relative impact and cost-effectiveness of each of the following factors:

- Does providing schools with teacher assistants (TCAs) focused on remedial instruction for the lowest half of the class improve learning levels?
- If so, is it due to the mere addition of an assistant (smaller class size), or to the focus on targeted instruction?
- Is it more effective during or after school hours?
- Can teachers trained in differentiated instruction produce the same results?

Initial results are promising, demonstrating impact on basic literacy and numeracy skills after only 10 weeks of exposure to the program. These results indicate that TCAs providing targeted instruction focused on the lowest-level learners have a positive impact on literacy and numeracy skills after only 10 weeks. This effect is strongest for the after-school intervention in deprived schools, while the program works better during school hours in nondeprived Districts. Teacher-led classes with targeted teaching methods seem to affect literacy skills, but only for pupils who are already above the median. However, simply reducing class size by adding another TCA without training on remedial instruction shows little impact.

TCAI and Innovations for Poverty Action are currently working with GES to look at the impact of these programs as they mature, further refine these programs and determine how best to integrate successful mechanisms into already-operational programs, such as those run by the National Youth Employment Programme.

The TCAI experience suggests:

- Spending focused time on basic skills with the lowest-level learners can improve literacy and numeracy
- Community members with limited training can be effectively used to improve children's literacy and numeracy, when they are given the right tools to target their lessons to the lowest-achieving pupils.
- GES engagement with innovative partners and leveraging of existing resources can support cost-effective interventions which improve equity, quality and efficiency.

Source: IPA 2012.

Factors Affecting Learning

Why is broad-based improvement in numeracy and literacy so challenging? In writing this chapter, the authors want to acknowledge the puzzlement that we have heard from many educators and policymakers as to why more rapid improvement in system quality appear so difficult to realize. This chapter outlines some possibilities for improving learning outcomes. However, it is also important to recognize that, in general, systemwide improvement in learning outcomes occur at a slow pace and year-on-year changes are often difficult to detect. Even the

McKinsey (2010) study, which includes Ghana, compares learning outcomes at 4- to 6-year intervals. However, the same study shows that significant improvements in learning are achievable during this span of time.

School-level factors associated with a positive effect on NEA scores include the proportion of trained teachers, availability of textbooks and the proportion of female teachers.[5] Separate, independent analyses of NEA results in 2011 (MoE 2012), NEA results in 2009 (Joseph and Wodon 2012) and NEA results in 2007 and 2005 (USAID 2009) found an association between a high proportion of trained teachers and female teachers with higher NEA scores. Joseph and Wodon (2012) and MoE (2012) found a positive association of textbook availability with NEA scores.[6] Recent studies also found positive effects of infrastructure quality (Joseph and Wodon 2012; USAID 2009), number of circuit supervisor visits (MoE 2012) and presence of updated administrative registers (MoE 2012) on NEA scores. Findings from these studies are consistent with other international findings on the effect of trained teachers and textbooks.

Factors negatively associated with NEA achievement included presence of high repetition and dropout, multigrade classrooms and a high percentage of orphans (MoE 2012).[7] *Language spoken at home (if it is not English) may also explain low exam scores.* At the district level, high poverty rates, incidence of adult illiteracy and malnutrition are associated with lower NEA scores (Joseph and Wodon 2012). Findings on negative associations should not be surprising as the identified factors are associated with poverty, rural conditions or poor family or guardian support structures. Mitigating effects of these factors is taken up in the Equity chapter, as well as in the final chapter on policy options. Analysis of TIMSS scores found that the majority of the Ghanaian 8th grade students rarely speak English at home and found home language to be associated with lower achievement in both mathematics and science. *Factors such as low "time on task" and high rates of teacher absenteeism, are also associated with low learning outcomes and are discussed in the Efficiency chapter.*

As noted in the Equity chapter, inequality in NEA learning outcomes is largely explained by differences between (i) major population center districts—Accra, Tema, Kumasi, and Shama-Ahanta East (Takoradi)—and the rest of the country, (ii) urban-rural status and (iii) regional status. These three factors are also associated with inequitable distribution of inputs, including trained teachers.

Analysis of Ghana TIMSS data found that student characteristics including coming from household where English is not spoken as the main language, influenced test scores. Anamuah-Mensah (2009, 124) found that the majority of the Ghanaian 8th grade students (66 percent) rarely spoke English at home and found frequent use of English as the home language to be associated with higher achievement in both mathematics and science. This finding is consistent with both 2003 and 2007 analyses of Ghana TIMSS scores and aligns with findings in Kenya and South Africa on the effect of home language on test performance. Both Kenya and South Africa are multilingual countries where

English is usually a second or third language. Two separate analyses of SACMEQ exams (a multicountry test written in English covering multiple subject areas for upper primary pupils) indicated that a student whose home language was not English was more likely to have a lower score on the exam (Shimada 2010; Spaull 2011).

Teacher characteristics (that is lack of professional training, limited teaching experience) and curriculum/classroom activities influenced Ghanaian pupils TIMSS scores. Anamuah-Mensah (2004) found that Ghanaian teachers were among the least-experienced teachers (with an average of 6 years of teaching experience and below 30 years of age) compared to countries with high achievement. Less than

---

Box 5.2 Multigrade Multilevel Schools

Several recent studies argue that additional support should be given to improving learning in multigrade multilevel (MGML) classrooms. There are more than 5,000 schools with MGML classrooms in Ghana. The number of these schools is increasing. More than 20 percent of MGML schools have only one or two teachers and the majority of teachers in these schools (64 percent) do not have relevant training. The below figure shows that pupils in multigrade classrooms perform significantly worse in language learning than counterparts in nonmultigrade classrooms. According to the MoE (2012, 38), "Teaching in multi-grade classrooms presents particular challenges as the teachers must prepare multiple lessons to be able to teach students learning at different grade level." A study by Open Learning Exchange and Ghana Education Service, Teacher Education Division recommends that meeting basic education learning objectives will requires giving more attention to MGML classrooms and providing additional support MGML classroom teachers through initial preparation and continuous professional development.

Figure B5.1 Percentage of Students Reaching Minimum Competency and Proficiency, by Classroom Type, P3 English, 2011

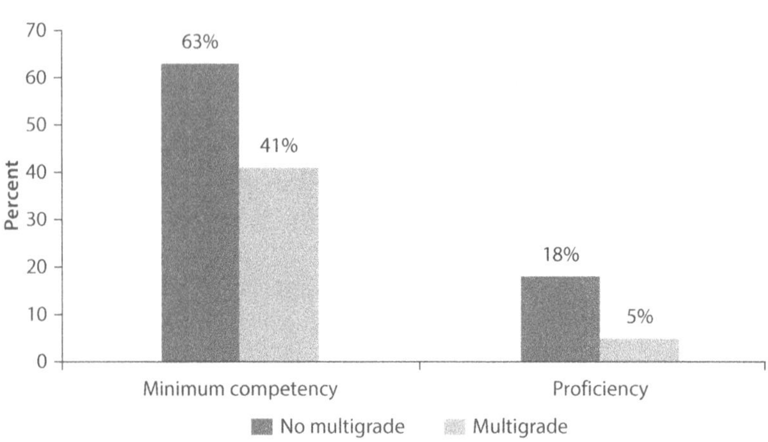

Category	No multigrade	Multigrade
Minimum competency	63%	41%
Proficiency	18%	5%

Source: OLE 2011.

10 percent of JHS teachers have a university degree compared to nearly all teachers from high-achieving countries. Notably, only half of JHS students in Ghana are taught by a teacher with a major in the respective field (for example, science or mathematics). Study findings suggest that the low percentage of female teachers (and thus lack of female science and math role models) may be associated with girls' lower performance on TIMSS. More time spent on homework was positively associated with higher scores; lack of textbooks and learning materials and teacher emphasis on factual knowledge (as opposed to "reasoning" and other mathematics and scientific processes) were associated with poor performance.

Qualified Teachers

Ampiah (2010, 3) notes, "The issue of providing quality education to pupils is directly related to the quality of teachers in the system." This statement is confirmed by research in Ghana and internationally that recognizes qualified teachers as one of the most important in-school inputs to support pupil learning. **Meeting the MoE target of 95 percent qualified teachers requires the addition of more than 50,000 qualified teachers in basic education schools.** Figure 5.7 shows the percentage of trained public primary and JHS teachers from 1987 to 2010 (MoE EMIS). In the past 5 years, the percentage of trained primary teachers has been nearly flat (between 58 percent and 62 percent). Figure 5.7 trends are explained in Thompson and Casely-Hayford (2008):

> A major impetus for the launching of the educational reforms in 1987 was the shortage of trained teachers as a result of years of outward migration. At the time of the reforms, an estimated 50.0 percent of such teachers had left the teaching field. Against this background, teacher training formed a major part of the reforms. However, 20 years after the initiation of the reforms, the proportion of trained

Figure 5.7 Percentage of Trained Teachers in Primary School and JHS, 1987/88–2009/10

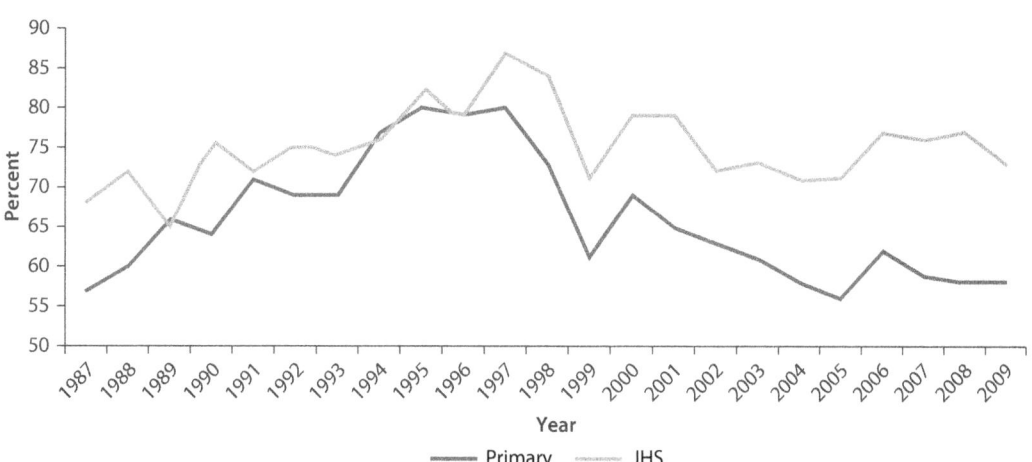

Sources: Thompson and Casely-Hayford 2008; ESPR 2011 (2006/07–2010/11); ESPR 2008 (2003/04–2005/06). Public school only.

teachers in primary schools, at 56.3 percent [in 2005], is lower than the 57.4 percent at the time the reforms were launched.

…The decline in the percentage of teachers was due in part to a combination of inadequate funding, attrition and/or measurement problems. Anecdotal evidence also suggests that large numbers of teachers are leaving the country for South Africa, Gambia and England. (Thompson and Casely-Hayford 2008, 32)

In the past 5 years, between 30 percent and 40 percent of the KG teaching force has been comprised of trained teachers whereas 70–80 percent of JHS teachers hold a Diploma in Basic Education. Like the primary subsector, in both KG and JHS subsectors, deprived districts are substantially worse off than non-deprived districts with respect to the percentage of "trained teachers" (ESPR 2011). From an equity standpoint, the high percentage of untrained teachers working in KG and lower primary is highly disadvantageous to poorer students—who require strong instruction in basic subjects in early years.

Deployment of individuals from the National Youth Employment Program (NYEP) and the National Service Scheme (NSS) into primary teaching positions has increased the number of untrained primary teachers in recent years. However, it does not appear that the addition of more untrained teachers has improved quality. Several studies have NOT found a link between PTR (which has ranged from 31 to 35 in the past 8 years) or the increased presence of untrained teachers in primary schools to improved learning outcomes. In 2007, approximately 70,000 unqualified teachers were employed in Ghanaian basic schools.[8] Two separate studies found that students who were taught by trained teachers scored significantly better than did those who were taught by untrained teachers (MoE 2012; USAID 2009). USAID notes:

> The proportion of teachers in a school who are untrained had a strong association with P6 students' English achievement, holding other variables in the model constant. A student in a school where half of the teachers were untrained would have a predicted English score 3.5 points lower than a student in a school with no untrained teachers…While this may not initially appear to be a practically significant difference, it is nearly the same difference in expected scores between a student in a rural school and an urban school, and in education research, this is a moderately strong effect. (USAID 2009, 15)

The same report (using a small case study sample) found that unqualified teachers often had limited formal training in pedagogy, low educational attainment and demonstrated low commitment to teaching. PPVA (2011) echoes this concern, noting,

> In several communities, serious questions were raised about the competence (and commitment) of NYEP teachers—referred to as "Zoom Teachers" …Ghana Education Service (GES) presumably has little control over them because they are answerable principally to the Ministry of Employment and Social Welfare (MESW)… Some who were interviewed at Gbare admitted that they had received no proper training before being posted to the classrooms. (PDA-PPVA 2011 88)

Recent experience suggests that future support of NYEP teachers should be considered critically; these individuals are not the equivalent of a teacher holding a DBE.[9] As noted in the previous section, having a higher proportion of female teachers at a school has been associated with higher learning outcomes. However, over the past decade the proportion of female teachers in primary schools has been flat, accounting for 32–35 percent of the primary teaching force.

Improving supply and retention of qualified teachers for basic schools may be the most critical priority facing basic education quality over the medium term. As background, the Diploma in Basic Education (DBE) is considered the minimum standard for considering a teacher qualified to teach at a basic school. The DBE is offered through 38 Colleges of Education (CoE), which are the institutions charged with training teachers for basic schools.[10] Table 5.3 summarizes the three paths a trainee can follow to earn a DBE. All CoEs offer a three-year residential program for trainees with a secondary education but no previous teaching experience. Trainees spend the first 2 years in class and in their final year, they work in schools as teachers under a mentor. The Untrained Teachers Diploma in Basic Education (UTDBE) is a four-year nonresidential program for individuals currently teaching as untrained teachers. Trainees follow a distance learning course using prepared modules and have face-to-face contact with their tutors at cluster and college levels. A recent study supported by TED/DfID-Ghana (2012) argues that UTDBE offers a cost-effective route to professional development compared to site-based training (cost of US$2,000 compared to US$20,000, respectively.[11] A third program is a two-year sandwich program designed to upgrade practicing Certificate-A teachers to a DBE (Adu-Yeboah 2011; World Bank 2010).

A recent report by GNAT and TEWU identifies teacher attrition as a critical problems facing education in Ghana. GES estimates that about 10,000 teachers leave the classroom on an annual basis.[12] Low pay (this study was completed prior to implementation of the Single-Spine Salary Structure) and poor working conditions are identified as the two main factors influencing teacher attrition. The GNAT survey found that more than 72 percent of teachers are either "dissatisfied" or "very dissatisfied" with their job as a teacher and that 50 percent of respondents plan to leave before they retire (for higher pay, 24.8 percent of respondents; and for improved conditions of service, 59.8 percent of respondents). The survey also

Table 5.3 DBE Programs and Output of New Teachers

DBE program	Description	Results
Residential DBE	Three year residential program for secondary graduates at Colleges of Education	Intake of 8,000–9,000 annually. Annual DBE graduates number 5,000–7,000
UTDBE	Four-year nonresidential program for untrained teachers	UTDBE program has graduated 30,000 new DBE-holders since 2005
Sandwich DBE	Two-year sandwich program for upgrading Certificate "A" teachers	From 2007–2010, more than 11,000 Certificate A teachers upgraded to DBE status

Source: Adu-Yeboah 2011; World Bank 2010; ESPR 2008; Interview, S. Baiden, GES/TED.

found that more than one-third of teachers have plans to leave the classroom after study leave (GNAT 2010).

The current shortage of teachers, high rates of teacher attrition and continued growth of the pupil population suggest that the demand for qualified teachers will be very strong over the medium term. *If one considers enrolling the over 1 million KG and primary -aged children who are still out of school, the demand for additional qualified teachers becomes much greater.* In later chapters, the book will discuss the interrelated nature of teacher policy issues—including policies related to teacher supply, training and quality, deployment and remuneration.[13]

Literacy Instruction

Given the importance of literacy and learning materials to quality, this section briefly discusses the National Accelerated Literacy Program. Textbooks are discussed in the efficiency chapter.

Improving broad-based acquisition of literacy in basic education requires policymakers and other education stakeholders to critically review policy and implementation issues related to the National Literacy Accelerated Programme (NALAP). As background, NALAP is a transitional bilingual literacy program in 11 Ghanaian languages for implementation in grades KG-P3. NALAP curriculum and materials focus on improving literacy learning through mother tongue instruction in Kindergarten through third grade with an early transition to English. NALAP represents a break from the past in that the mother tongue is used as the foundation for a child to become literate. In earlier grades, NALAP uses local language materials and exercises to help children become literate in their mother tongue. In later grades, less time is spent in the mother tongue instruction and more time is spent on English language instruction. The transition to NALAP and the priority given to mother tongue instruction has been a contentious issue between policymakers, education experts, and the MoE.

Box 5.3 National Standards of Performance

Several recent reformers have argued for creating national Minimum Standards of Performance (MSP), which define competencies to be mastered in each subject at all levels (for example, Anamuah Mensah Committee Report, 200).

The current curriculum for primary schools identifies learning objectives, content to be covered, a general evaluation method and a grading scale for each subject in each grade. However, it does not identify minimum performance standards or specific guidance for teachers in each subject and grade.

This lack of guidance in the curriculum may contribute to low learning outcomes, discourage accountability and frustrate attempts to link inequity to low quality. Creating Minimum Standards of Performance would provide clearer guidance to teachers and support efforts to improve accountability and link inequities to quality deficiencies.

NALAP pilot schools outperformed public schools in English on the NEA in 2009 and 2011. On the 2011 exam, P6 students at NALAP pilot schools were 55 percent more likely than their peers in public schools to achieve proficiency in English. A recent formative evaluation found that understanding of the local language is quite high—which supports the rational for NALAP (using local language literacy acquisition as a bridge to English). However, NALAP emphasis on local language instruction means that teachers must be proficient in both the local language and English which is challenging for teachers who are not proficient in the community mother tongue or in English.[14] NALAP implementation is affected by teacher posting and deployment policy, which at present does not take into account teacher proficiency in the community mother tongue.

Closing Notes

The link between equity and quality can be made by observing that areas with comparatively low levels of education inputs also demonstrate comparatively lower learning outcomes. While progress remains to be made in addressing equity issues, MoE and GES have taken on many initiatives to support quality improvement. Such initiatives include support to expanding and improving the quality of KG and the provision of after-school remedial learning support to struggling students through the Teacher Community Assistant Initiative (TCAI).

Akyeampong (2010, 13) writes, "What reforms in education has taught Ghana is that it is much easier to fix the 'hardware' problems of education than the 'software' ones." This suggests that in addition to addressing some fundamental equity and inputs issues, there also needs to be space for flexibility and creativity. Given the great differences between Ghana's geographic regions and student populations, educators may recognize that some equity and quality improvement strategies which work in Greater Accra may not work in Wa, Hohoe, or Sunyani.

Box 5.4 Private Schools

The issue of private schools, school choice and sending public resources to private schools is, globally, and in Ghana, a contentious one. The Education Act (2008) formally recognizes the status of private schools. In Ghana, enrollment in private schools at the basic level has been growing rapidly in the past decade. Private school enrollment accounts for over 20 percent of total primary school enrollment—though such enrollment varies greatly by region and urban-rural status. Learning assessments generally show private schools (which are registered) outperforming public schools (Djangmah 2011). On the 2011 NEA, private schools outperformed public schools and NALAP schools (MoE 2012). Trends in access and learning outcomes as well as concerns about the contribution of private basic schools to the "reproduction of inequality" suggest a need for more policy-oriented research.

box continues next page

Box 5.4 Private Schools *(continued)*

There is a wide range of private schools. The best private schools (as measured by BECE results) are most likely registered with GES and cater to pupils from wealthier, urban, and better-educated families. As such, pupil recruitment to private schools results is what is called cream skimming (that is selecting the best students out of public schools and into private schools). This leaves public basic schools with students from poorer, more rural and less-well educated families. Djangmah (2011) discusses this phenomenon and notes that the vast majority of pupils in the best secondary schools come from private basic schools. However, there are also many unregistered private schools which cater to pupils coming from less wealthy households. There is some anecdotal and research evidence indicating that some of the characteristics of private schools (for example, lower rates of teacher absenteeism, greater availability of learning materials) draw students (who are able to afford the fees) away from public schools.

This dialogue continues to be played out in the press with hard news stories and opinion columnists asking: What type of basic education do Ghanaian's want? How (and to what extent) should the private sector be involved in delivering this public good, guaranteed by the Constitution to be available to all?

Notes

1. The following article provides more detailed discussion on basic education quality, teacher quality and teacher education: Akyeampong A. K., J. Pryor, and J. G. Ampiah. 2006. "A Vision of Successful Schooling: Ghanaian Teachers' Understandings of Learning, Teaching and Assessment." *Comparative Education* 42: 155–76.
2. The MoE 2011 report indicates "For comparability reasons, this report presents NEA's traditional classifications of proficiency (≥55 percent), but readers should be aware that this definition does not effectively identify students who truly are proficient in the subject area."
3. TIMSS (2007) is constructed to have a mean of 500 and a standard deviation of 100. This means that the average math and science scores in Ghana were nearly two standard deviations below the mean.
4. NEA assessments test two levels of cognitive abilities (knowing and understanding, applying) and do not measure higher-order skills (analysis, synthesis, and evaluation/creation). Results are in MoE (2012).
5. USAID 2009 analyzed 2005 and 2007 NEA scores against EMIS. Of note, an earlier evaluation found that widening access to textbooks contributed to improvement in English and Maths scores between 1998–2003 (World Bank 2004).
6. USAID statistical analyses did not find the same result, but interviews with teaching staff suggested that shortages of textbooks and learning materials negatively affected NEA scores.
7. Multigrade classrooms should not be seen as a "cause" of low quality. The social/rural conditions which may lead to the use of a multigrade classroom may offer more power in explaining low NEA scores.

8. In extreme cases, PTR likely makes a difference (for example, once a classroom has a PTR of greater than 60). Studies on effect of untrained teachers include USAID (2009), MoE (2012), Joseph and Wodon (2012). About 22,000 were NSS, 12,000 NYEP, 9,000 teacher trainees in the final year of their program and the remaining number were teachers classified as underqualified, such as those with a Certificate A.

9. In other settings, underqualified and contract teachers have been shown to be effective teachers. The example of complementary basic education in Ghana, discussed in the Equity chapter suggests that such teachers, properly trained and supported, can make a difference in hard to reach areas. At present, however, few studies exist on the impact of NYEP teachers; those that do suggest that they do not have a positive effect on learning. In recent years, some districts have taken advantage of available NYEP teachers and have taken the lead in training and supporting them.

10. The DBE started in the 2004/05 academic year to fulfill a teacher education policy directive that requires basic school teachers to possess a minimum professional qualification of Diploma in Basic Education.

11. The quality and effectiveness of UTDBE graduates requires further evaluation. If weakness in the program or graduates exist, then steps should be taken to strengthen the UTDBE program to ensure graduates meet required standards.

12. Reasons for leaving include the following: study leave, secondment, retirement, and resignation to take up a nonteaching job.

13. The draft "Pre-tertiary Teacher Professional Development and Management" policy touches on many important teacher policy issues, including professional development, standards, induction, mentoring licensing, and career path.

14. MoE (2012) notes that "there are significant percentages of teachers assigned in schools and grades that do not have sufficient facility with the mother tongue to teach reading in that language. [and] …The findings show that a full 60% of the teachers were not completely comfortable teaching in English." This concern is echoed by members the academic community in Ghana (Ampiah 2010).

CHAPTER 6

Efficiency

Improving efficient utilization of core basic education inputs, including instructional time, money, qualified teachers, infrastructure, and textbooks, is one of the three themes comprising the strategic framework of the Education Strategic Plan 2010–20. Information included in this chapter suggests that changes in policy guidance, management practices and institutional arrangements have not kept pace with the needs of a much larger basic education system. This chapter provides information on the extent to which selected core inputs are efficiently used and identifies factors which contribute to existing inefficiencies.

Overview

Efficiency in education is making the best possible use of available resources to meet education goals. In education, efficiency is measured by comparing education inputs with education outputs and outcomes. Efficiency analyses such as cost-benefit and cost-effectiveness analysis provide information that can help policymakers improve utilization of available resources such as money, human and physical resources and time. Table 6.1 presents an overview of internal and external efficiency.

Table 6.1 External and Internal Efficiency

Type of efficiency	Sample query	Data
Internal efficiency (cost-effectiveness)	Are teachers efficiently distributed and utilized?	PTTR by district
		Extent of teacher absenteeism
	Is the completion rate high?	Unit cost per completer
	What percentage of P6 students are proficient in English?	Unit cost per learning outcome
External efficiency (cost-benefit)	What are the social returns of ensuring girls complete primary school?	Lower maternal mortality, increased child spacing
	What is the private return on investment in primary education?	A rate of return to primary investment

Source: Patrinos 2007; Tsang 2002.

Internal efficiency relates the production of educational outputs to educational inputs (usually at the subsector level) and asks the question: Are available resources used as efficiently as possible? Internal efficiency is improved when more education outputs are produced at a given level of education resources or fewer education resources are used in producing the same amount of education outputs (Tsang 2002). Internal efficiency questions include the following: (i) are inputs (teachers, textbooks, classrooms) efficiently distributed, (ii) are inputs maximally utilized (for example, issues of teacher absenteeism and instructional time), (iii) does the system show high dropout and repetition or low-learning outcomes, and (iv) is fund leakage a problem? Cost-effectiveness analysis is often used to measure internal efficiency and can provide information on unit costs such as "cost per completer" or "cost per learning outcome."

Internal efficiency may also take into account opportunity costs and direct costs of education financed by poor and rural households which negatively affect pupil dropout, completion and learning (Tsang 1995). Gains in internal efficiency may include making better use of existing resources or cutting one program area (such as a subsidy deemed "inefficient") and providing resources to fund something presumed to have a greater educational benefit (Tsang 1997, 2002). Djangmah (2011, 15) writes, "unless the poorest are identified for enhanced special assistance … the additional costs which must go into quality improvement will be wasted on many parents who hardly need assistance." Providing disadvantaged populations with additional support (for example, remedial instruction and afterschool programs) to help them attain basic education learning and completion goals, even if it costs a little bit more, may result in an overall efficiency improvement.

External efficiency is concerned with the economic and social returns to investment in education. External efficiency is improved when more education outcomes are produced at given education resources or fewer education resources are used in producing the same amount of education outcomes. External efficiency is related to improvements in economic growth, social returns and social equity, or poverty reduction (Tsang 2002). External efficiency analysis is usually called "cost-benefit" analysis, where return is usually measured in financial terms. Given the widespread recognition of the economic and social returns to basic education and since most countries recognize the "right to basic education," measuring the "rate of return" of basic education in relation to other education subsectors as a means of determining state investment is becoming a less common practice (Colclough, Kingdon, and Patrinos 2009). External efficiency is discussed in more detail at the end of this chapter.

Applying internal efficiency analysis to education policy can be problematic. This is because education has multiple goals, policy options have a range of pros and cons and because no two interventions are exactly alike.[1] For example, NYEP teachers lower PTR and help reach disadvantaged areas at a fraction of the cost of qualified teachers, but it is not clear if the NYEP initiative improves student learning.

Efficiency gains related to core basic education inputs (for example, qualified teachers, infrastructure and textbooks) and instructional time could help the education sector make great progress toward equity and quality goals. The Strategic Framework of the ESP 2010–20 recognizes *efficiency gains* and *cost-savings* as important to meeting ESP objectives. Efficiency gains proposed include improving the distribution of teachers, reducing teacher absenteeism, improving "time on task" and making improvements in GES administrative and management systems. Cost-cutting strategies (ESP Section 3.4) include eliminating certain regressive subsidies including SHS, BECE/WACE and study leave subsidies.

Internal Efficiency: Teachers and Instructional Time

Sources of inefficiency in basic schools include inefficient teacher allocation, teacher absenteeism and teacher delay, loss of instructional time during the school day, fund leakage and inefficient allocation of other inputs (for example, textbooks, classrooms).

Inefficient allocation of qualified teachers, teacher absenteeism and loss of instructional time during the school day are three of the greatest inefficiencies in the current system. As noted earlier, student achievement is higher in schools with more qualified teachers. A more equitable distribution of these teachers would likely support improved overall learning. Regarding teacher absenteeism, a 20 percent reduction in teacher absenteeism would be the equivalent of hiring 5,200 additional new teachers. *Improving efficient use of qualified teachers should be a priority.*

Teachers are inefficiently allocated by region, district and deprived district status. Figure 6.1 shows great variation in PTR by primary school. For example, if a school has ten teachers ("10" on the x-axis), it may have as few as 100 pupils or as many as 600 pupils (on the y-axis): a range in PTR from 10 to 60. Analysis of

Figure 6.1 Student-Teacher Scatter Plot for Primary, 2008/09

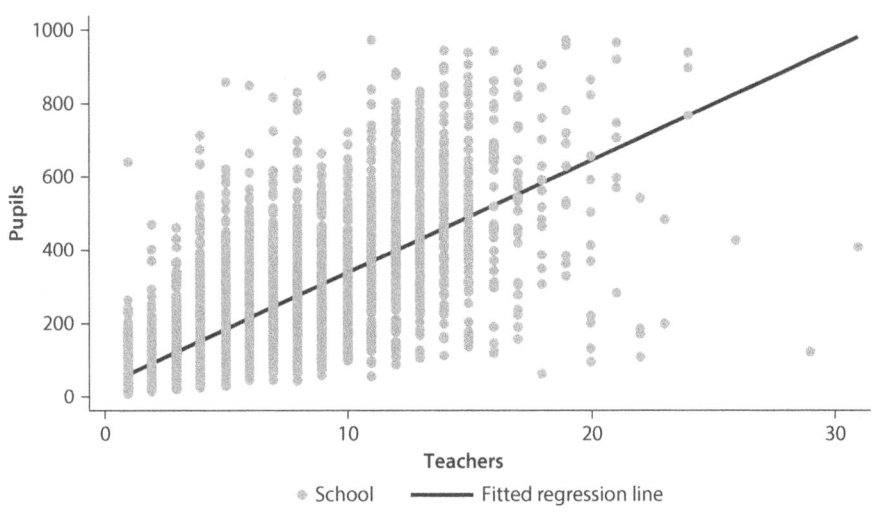

Source: World Bank, 2010, using EMIS 2008/09.

school-level PTR data from 2008/09 found that only 29 percent, 46 percent and 55 percent of teacher presence could be explained by *enrollment* in Kindergarten, primary and junior high school, respectively. Put another way, while the policy for declaring teacher vacancies is based on enrollment, statistical analysis shows that factors other than enrollment explain the distribution of more than half of primary school teachers. Teachers are less efficiently distributed in primary schools in deprived districts than in nondeprived districts.

Figure 6.2 shows the efficiency of teacher allocation for the Northern and Upper East regions using 2010/11 EMIS data. These two regions offer extreme examples of inefficiency in teacher allocation, where enrollment in primary schools explains only 35 and 34 percent of teacher placement, respectively. Each circle represents a basic school. The x-axis is number of students and the y-axis is number of teachers. The chapter on Equity provides additional data on inequitable (and therefore inefficient) distribution of teachers and qualified teachers.

Teachers are often unequally distributed at the school level, with less qualified teachers working in early grades which have large numbers of students. Improving literacy acquisition in early grades (one of the ESP targets) is undermined by sending less qualified teachers to lower grades classrooms with more students. More research is needed to understand the extent to which this phenomenon is a problem in Ghana.

Inefficiencies at the school level, led by teacher absenteeism and teacher delay, may account for the loss of more than 50 percent of available instructional time at primary school. Several studies point to a teacher absenteeism rate of between 20 percent and 30 percent in Ghana. This is the equivalent of more than one day per week. Once teacher and student presence are accounted for, Abadzi (2007) found that 70 percent of available instructional time is used for engaging students in learning

Figure 6.2 Student-Teacher Scatter Plot for Northern and Upper East Regions, 2010/11

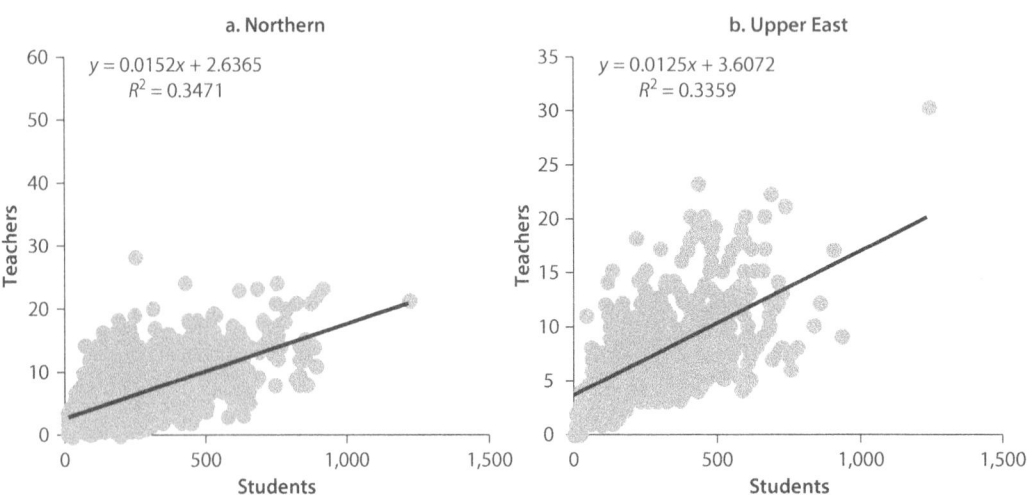

Source: World Bank 2011.

activities. Figure 6.3 shows information from studies on "instructional time use" in four countries. In Ghana, out of 197 school days, teachers were, on average, absent for 43 days and delayed for 40 days. Other factors, including student absence (11 days) and student delay (9 days) and poor use of instructional time led to the finding that, out of the 197 day school year in Ghana, students were engaged in learning activities for only 76 days. In comparison countries of Brazil, Morocco and Tunisia, students were engaged in learning activities for 126, 145, 148 day.

Abadzi (2007, vi) notes "Within each country, time use among schools showed substantial variability. Most of them used the time rather well, but a minority had substantial losses and skewed the averages." While evidence is not conclusive, Abadzi's study points to poorer use of instructional time in the

Figure 6.3 Instructional Time in Basic Schools in Four Countries

Source: Abadzi 2007.

Figure 6.4 Effective Instructional Time Basic Schools in Four Countries (EQUIP2)

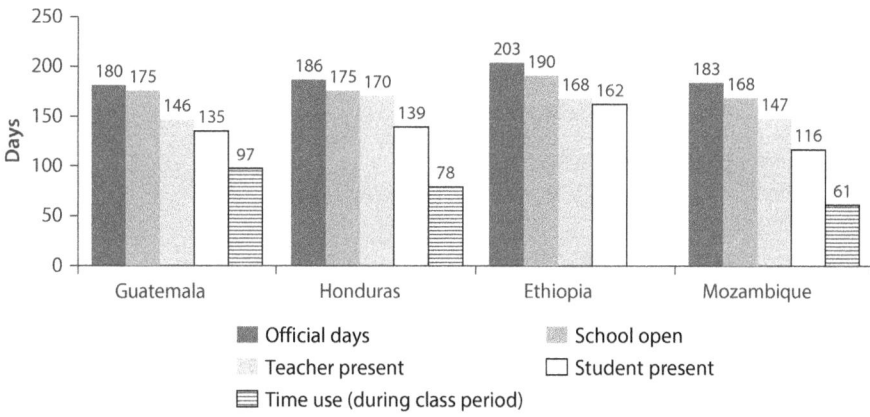

Source: EQUIP2 2011.

northern regions and in rural schools. A study by EQUIP2 (2011) provides data showing a similar trend. EQUIP2 findings suggest similar efficiency challenges in countries striving toward EFA access and quality goals (see Figure 6.4). Teacher absenteeism appears to be a bigger problem in Ghana than in many other countries; however, Mozambique and Honduras are more inefficient in their use of the class period.

"Loss of Instructional time" studies highlight the insufficiency of an inputs-only focus. Improving the amount of time students are engaged in learning activities is a critical challenging facing many countries which have recently realized large enrollment increases. Mereku (2005) in *Opportunity to Learn in Ghana* provides evidence similar to Abadzi (2007).

Explanations for teacher (and head-teacher) absenteeism include illness, participation in official teaching related duties, administrative matters (for example, salary collection, HR issue), funeral attendance, religious practices, farming activities (rural teachers) and participation in continuing education courses. Table 6.2 provides a list of the most frequent explanations for teacher absenteeism. CDD (2008) suggests that reasons underlying the high rate of absenteeism include lack of supervision, distance (from teachers' homes to schools and from schools to health care and banking facilities) and, in many cases, poor working conditions at the school (for example, poor infrastructure, lack of toilets and potable water). Teacher absenteeism and delay is a bigger challenge in rural areas than in urban areas. This is because teachers working rural areas often live in town and thus require transport on a daily basis. PPVA (2011) findings on teacher absenteeism are worth quoting at length.

> In schools of the rural savannah, trained teachers generally live in their district capitals and commute relatively long distances daily, making them late to school. … Teachers at Gupanarigu travel from Tamale, some 33km away, and are late when they do come. On market days (every third day or so) and Fridays, those in Islamic communities often do not show up at all. The Gupanarigu community had made attempts to provide their teachers with accommodation but this had been politely turned down. …At Wungu and Bansi, community members observed that lateness and absenteeism usually intensify from around the middle of the month when teachers' salaries ran low and it becomes difficult to pay for public transport.

Table 6.2 Factors Explaining Teacher Absenteeism

- Teacher illness/health clinic visits***
- Official teaching duties (for example, in-service training/workshop)**
- Funeral attendance**
- Religious practices (for example, Friday prayers for Muslim teachers)**
- Farming activities
- Continuing education (study leave, sandwich course)
- Official nonteaching duty

Sources: Abadzi 2007; CDD 2008; EARC 2003; Transparency International 2009b
** Indicates a frequently cited reason.
***Maternity leave is included in "health."

> ... In a few schools, teachers demonstrated impressive commitment to duty (Bongo Soe, Nyogbare, South Natinga), giving of their best against huge odds to ensure high levels of achievement. However, this was the exception. (PDA-PPVA 2011, 84)

PPVA (2011, 84) further notes that in some areas, teacher absenteeism is such a challenge, that "where parents can, they simply opt for private schools in an attempt to protect their children's futures. This is, however, a *luxury* few poor parents can afford."

It is important to note that absenteeism is not necessarily a reflection on teachers' commitment to their work. Rather, high rates of absenteeism reflect the realities of a challenged policy and management environment (for example, salary delays or other HR issues; schedules for training and upgrading) and social and economic forces (for example, the draw of urban centers) in which teaching professionals work. Some factors that appear to reduce absenteeism include improving teacher work conditions (for example, infrastructure, management support, lower PTRs and providing near site salary collection, especially in rural areas), the presence of "dedicated and disciplined" school leadership, increasing circuit supervisor visits, preparedness to sanction recalcitrant staff (from the head-teacher, circuit supervisor, or DEM), altering the academic schedule of DBE and sandwich courses and supporting increased parental involvement (World Bank 2010; PDA-PPVA 2011). Providing teacher accommodation is worth consideration; however, such initiatives should be considered carefully as many teachers working in rural school prefer to live in urban areas and mass provision of teacher housing may not be cost-effective when compared to other options (for example, providing a rental allowance).

Policy and institutional arrangements guiding deployment (allocation) of new DBE teachers are not structured to reduce current inefficiencies and inequities. Decisions for deployment of new DBE teachers follows the below process.

> First, every year, districts identify the number of teacher vacancies they have. Vacancies are declared against the number of positions established. Identified vacancies usually far outnumber the number of new DBE teachers available. For example, in 2010, the number of teacher vacancies was over 60,000. Available new teachers numbered less than 10,000.
>
> Second, the majority of DBE teacher trainees, usually in the first or second year at the College of Education, will write to the district to request "sponsorship." If the district agrees to the request, then the district will "sponsor the teacher." This means the district will sign a contract guaranteeing that the teacher has a job in the district following CoE graduation. Teachers may have many reasons for requesting sponsorship from a district: often positions in urban and wealthy districts are highly sought; sometimes districts offer financial and other incentives.
>
> Teachers who are not sponsored are allocated according to the formula at regional, and then the district level.

The challenge with this process is that the majority of teacher trainees (80–90 percent in recent years) are not affected by the third criteria as they have already made agreements with districts. The poorest districts appear least able to sponsor teachers meaning that they receive disproportionately low numbers of new DBE teachers.[2]

Internal Efficiency: Output Production, Other Inputs

Key basic education outputs include primary completion and pupil acquisition of literacy and numeracy skills. High dropout and repetition and low primary completion and learning reduce internal efficiency. In Ghana, the primary completion rate has improved from 85 percent to 90 percent in the past 5 years while repetition has decreased from 7 percent to 3 percent. Dropout appears to be a bigger problem in JHS than in primary school. JHS completion rates are 71 percent for boys and 63 percent for girls.

Unit cost for achieving desired learning outcomes (at 3,670 GHc) is more than twice as expensive as unit cost for meeting primary completion goals (at 1,427 GHc). Table 6.3 uses unit costs from the 2011 ESPR to calculate cost per completer and cost per learning outcome. To support primary completion, the government must pay for 6 years of education for all children, of whom 90 percent complete the full cycle. To support P6 pupil development of English proficiency, the government must pay for 6 years of education for all children. Of this group, 35 percent score at the proficiency level on the P6 English NEA exam.[3] This information could be interpreted in several ways. One interpretation is that learning is expensive. Inputs are lacking nationwide (especially so in deprived districts), and more resources are needed. Another interpretation is to ask what MoE/GES can do to get more primary completers to attain desired learning outcomes: where are the opportunities for efficiency gains? How can improved learning be attained within the same resource environment?

To keep up with expanding enrollment, the number of primary schools has increased by over 20 percent in the past decade. However, pupil enrollment explains less than 50 percent of the distribution of classrooms. This distribution may in part be explained by differences in school catchment areas and in part by the complexity of funding school construction. In 2008/09, average enrollment in KG, primary and JHS schools was 90, 225 and 138, respectively. However, as shown in figure 6.5,

Table 6.3 Cost Per Primary Completer and Cost to Produce a P6 Student Proficient in English

Output	Rate (2011)	Unit cost (2010)	Cost per output (Calculated)
Primary completion	90%	214 GHc	1,427GHc
P6 English proficiency	35%	214 GHc	3,670GHc

Source: ESPR 2011; World Bank data.

Figure 6.5 Distribution of KG, Primary, and JHS Schools, by Enrollment

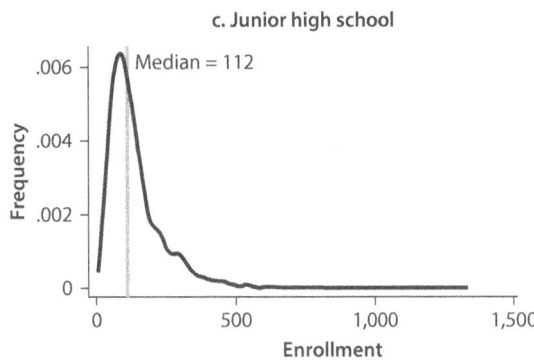

Source: World Bank 2010, using EMIS 2008/09.

primary education is largely delivered in small and medium schools. The median primary school enrolls 193 pupils. JHS follows a similar pattern, with a median enrollment of 112 pupils. Given the significant variation of catchment area populations around the country, it is unreasonable to expect the distribution of classrooms to be fully explained by enrollment. However, that only 40 percent and 46 percent of the variation in number of classrooms between schools can be explained by pupil enrollment (in primary and JHS, respectively), suggests large inefficiencies in infrastructure provision. From 2005 to 2009, efficiency of classroom distribution improved in primary schools, but declined in KG and JHS (World Bank 2010).

The number of institutions involved in infrastructure and textbook provision, complex policy guidance and the recent pattern of large one-off procurements and campaigns are likely to contribute to the inefficient distribution of these inputs. Officially, establishment and maintenance of pretertiary infrastructure is the responsibility of the districts (Education Act 2008). However, districts' limited resources mean that often it is the central government (using GETFund resources) which provides the financing to build or refurbish schools. Thus, while the official policy is clear, it does not appear to be the main avenue through which pretertiary infrastructure development is financed and procured.

Table 6.4 Efficiency in Core Textbooks Distribution in Primary and JH, 2004/05–2008/09

	2005	2006	2007	2008
Primary school				
Average number of core textbooks per child	1.54	1.64	1.44	1.45
Efficiency in distribution	0.69	0.68	0.72	0.63
N	6,193	6,250	6,446	6,598
Junior high school				
Average number of core textbooks per child	2.06	2.16	1.96	1.93
Efficiency in distribution	0.60	0.62	0.56	0.47
N	6,193	6,250	6,446	6,598

Source: World Bank 2010, Calculation based on EMIS 2004/05-2008/09. Unadjusted N indicates the number of observations used to compute the coefficients.
Note: Data are not adjusted for nonresponses.

In recent years, around 70 percent of textbook distribution in primary schools and a range of 50–60 percent of textbook distribution in JHS schools have been explained by pupil enrollment. Between 2005/06 and 2008/09, the average number of textbooks per pupil in primary schools declined more in deprived districts than in nondeprived districts. Table 6.4 shows efficiency in core textbooks distribution in primary and JHS, 2004/05–2008/09.

As referenced in "Quality" core textbooks, especially for English and mathematics at primary level, are recognized as essential components of the Government's strategic agenda. A comprehensive evaluation of basic education in Ghana found that widening access to textbooks contributed to improvements in English and Math scores between 1988 and 2003 (World Bank 2004). Unfortunately, in the past 5 years, the pupil-core textbook ratio has realized a greater than 50 percent decline, to one (of three required) core textbook per primary and JHS pupil.

The textbook policy has decentralized textbook procurement to the district level. As such, detailed guidance on textbook procurement is not included in annual budgets or operational plans. To a greater degree than infrastructure, textbook provision has taken on a campaign-like (and haphazard) nature with large numbers of textbooks procured by the center and distributed unevenly across the country.

Basic education enrollment is expected to continue to expand over the next decade. ESPR 2011 notes:

> Increased enrolments have placed pressure on pupil classroom ratios, which have increased at all levels, suggesting that infrastructure investments have not managed to keep pace with the increase in enrollment. The strong enrolment growth witnessed in Kindergarten has led to the sharpest rise in PCR in basic education, increasing by 11% in 2010/11 to reach 64. (p. 42)

With expansion, more classrooms, toilets, water points (for potable water) and classroom repairs will be needed. Efficiency gains would ensure that available resources reach a greater number of students and could also improve equity. *Leakage of capitation grant and DACF funds also reduce internal efficiency. These issues are discussed in the Management chapter.*

External Efficiency

External efficiency is related to improvements in economic growth, social returns and poverty reduction. Low private returns to basic education in Ghana have been evidenced by several recent studies. GLSS5 (2005/06) estimates that one additional year of basic schooling adds about 4 percent to individuals' annual earnings, against 8 to 12 percent on average in developing countries (Lejarraga 2010, as quoted in World Bank 2011, 32; qtd. World Bank 2011a). Colclough et al. (2009) offer similar findings on private rates of return (RoR) but also recognizes the limitations of RoR analysis to sufficiently capture external efficiency of basic education. This is because we have still not been able to capture fully the externalities in estimating the social rates of return related to basic education (for example, improvements in maternal health in women with higher levels of educational attainment) nor can we accurately predict the impact of basic education in labor markets where the majority of workers are in the semi-formal or informal sectors.

Two common external efficiency questions are whether government is spending the appropriate amount on each level or type of education (for example, basic v. secondary) and whether government is making the appropriate investment choices and trade-offs on basic education access and quality. However, in absence of solid data on externalities, answering these questions remains difficult. As indicated in the Equity chapter, basic education is necessary, but not enough for individuals seeking employment in the formal sector in Ghana. That said, effective investments into interventions improving basic education quality (for example, functional literacy) would be recognized as contributing to external efficiency. The next chapter looks at education expenditures and makes an assessment of whether these expenditures provide adequate support to improvements in equity and quality.

Notes

1. GES budget staff recognize that diversity in geographic circumstances means that implementing an initiative (or building a school, or deploying a teacher) in one district may cost more than implementing it in another district.
2. Information for this section comes from author interviews with GES heads of department in TED, HRMD and IPPD (October, 2010).
3. Calculation of internal efficiency by wealth quintile or deprived district status is not possible in this analysis. However, information presented in earlier chapters clearly show that deprived districts show lower primary completion and learning, higher levels of teacher absenteeism and disproportionately lower levels of public investment.

CHAPTER 7

Education Expenditure

This chapter provides information on education expenditure in Ghana. Information in this chapter includes historical and cross-country data on funding sources and expenditure trends over time, by budget category (PE, admin, service, and investment) and by subsector (KG, primary, JHS, etc.).

Education Expenditure

Between 1976 and 1984, government spending on education plummeted from 6.4 percent of GDP to 1.5 percent, considerably constraining physical and human resources and creating challenges in maintaining quality. From 1990, this share has fluctuated between 5 percent and 6 percent of GDP. In the past decade, public finance of education in Ghana has demonstrated four characteristics.

1. A lot of money is spent on education in Ghana: education accounts for 18–27 percent of public expenditure, equal to 5–6 percent of Ghana's GDP.
2. Personal emoluments have accounted for over 97 percent of government expenditure in basic education over the past 5 years. PE expenditure does not appear constrained by Ministry of Finance budget ceilings and annually crowds out expenditures in other budget categories (for example, service and investment).
3. Education financing is fragmented among a number of sources and among an even larger number of flows of funds. Basic schools in Ghana have very little financial autonomy—teachers and resources for goods and services generally flow from centralized structures.
4. The complexity of education finance sources and delivery systems complicate efforts to improve accountability.

This chapter provides information on the first two issues. The next chapter provides more detail on education finance.

In 2011, public expenditure on education in Ghana as a percentage of GDP stood at 6.3 percent—above the African Union average and suggested target of 6 percent for a middle-income country. Figure 7.1 shows education expenditure increased from 5.3 percent in 2008 to 6.3 percent of Ghana's GDP in 2011.

Table 7.1 compares public expenditure on education as a percentage of GDP and total public expenditure with other countries. Expenditure on education in other African countries equals 11–28 percent of total public expenditure (compared to 18–27 percent in Ghana) and ranges from 2 percent to 8 percent of GDP. Public expenditure on education as a percentage of GDP in OECD countries stands at 5.6 percent and ranges from 4.5 percent to 7 percent of GDP (UIS

Figure 7.1 Public Education Expenditure as a Percentage of GDP

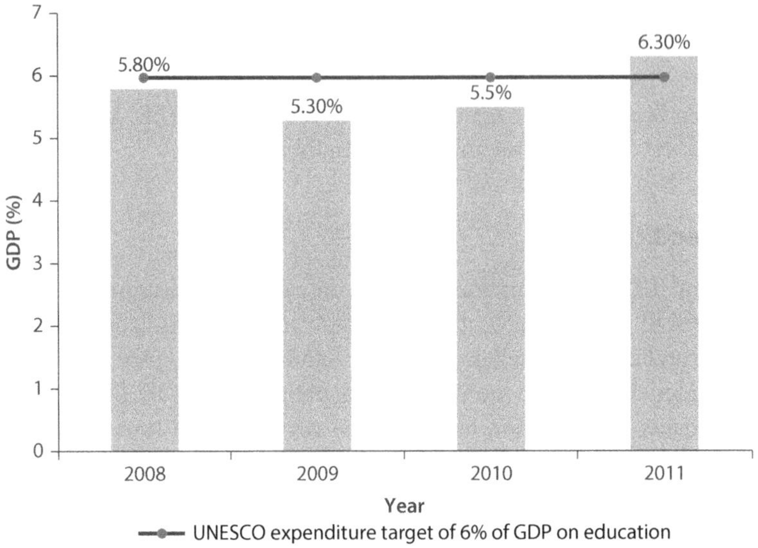

[Bar chart showing GDP (%) by Year: 2008 = 5.80%, 2009 = 5.30%, 2010 = 5.5%, 2011 = 6.30%. Line shows UNESCO expenditure target of 6% of GDP on education.]

Source: ESPR 2012.

Table 7.1 International Comparative Analysis of Public Spending on Education

	Public spending on education as a percentage of GDP	Public spending on education as a percentage of total public spending
Ghana, 2008	5.8	18
Low-income countries (i)		
Sub-Saharan Africa	4.3	17
Other regions	4.3	14
Middle-income countries (ii)		
Sub-Saharan Africa	5.7	16
Other regions	4.2	17
High-income OECD	5.6	12

Source: Preliminary Education Sector Performance Report, MOE (2012, 2009) based on data from UIS.
Note: (i) Countries eligible for lending from IDA. (ii) Countries eligible for lending from the IBRD. Table does not include (i) countries in the World Bank's Europe & Central Asia region, and (ii) countries, mostly island states, with population less than approximately 300,000.

2011). National income and country demographic features influence these indicators: high-income countries with lower dependency ratios usually spend less on education as a percentage of GDP and public expenditure.

Figures used for Ghana were calculated using the rebased GDP. In November, 2010, the Ghana Statistical Service "rebased" Ghana's GDP. This revision changed Ghana's 2010 GDP from 24 billion Ghana Cedi to 45 billion Ghana Cedi—an increase of 60 percent (GSS 2010). The rebasing exercise included changing the base year from 1993 to 2006 and updating data sources and classification systems which allowed for more accurate representation of fast-growing service sectors (for example, telecommunications and banking) in the revised GDP (GSS 2010, Moss 2012). Prior to rebasing the GDP, it was estimated that Ghana was spending the equivalent of 8–10 percent of its GDP on education on an annual basis. The ESP 2010–20 was developed before the GDP was re-based and there was a perception that Ghana was spending a large amount on education with lower-than-expected outcomes.

In the 9 years from 2003 to 2011, public expenditure on education in Ghana has tripled. Table 7.2 shows trends in education expenditure in (GH¢) by source for 2003–11. Ghana has seen a massive increase in GDP over the past decade. Section 7.2 will identify the wage bill as the primary driver of GoG public expenditure increases. Main sources of education finance have all realized steady increases. Measured using 2005 prices in Ghana Cedi, total expenditure on education has increased from 534m GH¢ in 2003 to 1,736 m GH¢ in 2011. GoG expenditures have followed a similar trend, nearly tripling during this period. GETFund and IGF contributions to education have also steadily increased, though GETFund expenditures appear slightly more erratic than GoG and IGF contributions. Financing from specific donors and through HIPC, MDRI and the

Table 7.2 Education Expenditure, 2003–11
in millions of GhC, in 2005 prices

Source	2003	2005	2007	2009	2010	2011
GoG	438	486	706	857	966	1,248
Donor	24	62	63	56	34	62
IGF	—	69	90	123	160	173
GETFund	52	72	134	88	166	252
HIPC/MDRI	15	31	36	19	31	1
DCAF	6	9	—	—	—	—
EFA-Catalytic	—	3	8	—	—	—
SIF	—	3	—	—	—	—
Total expenditure	534	736	1,037	1,142	1,357	1,736
Education expenditure as a percentage of GDP	5.6	5.6	—	5.3	5.5	6.3
Education expenditure as a percentage of Government of Ghana expenditure	26.7	23.1	25.8	22.3	22.2	25.8

Source: Ministry of Finance and Economic Planning and MoE; Source: ESPR, 2008; ESPR, 2012. CPI used to calculate expenditure drawn from Ghana Statistical Service and the IMF Statistical Database.
Note: — = not available.

EFA Catalytic fund have made significant contributions. Donor contributions have ranged from 4 percent and 18 percent over the past decade. Given Ghana's recent growth, in the past 4 years, external financing to education accounted for a smaller portion of total expenditures—from 4 percent to 8 percent.

GoG share of total education expenditures have been in the range of 70–75 percent from 2008 to 2011. After GoG, the GETFund is the second biggest contributor to the education resource envelope followed by IGF, Donor and HIPC sources, respectively. Figure 7.2 shows table 7.3 data as a pie chart with each source's contribution to total education expenditure. GoG finances the bulk of education expenditure (71.9 percent) followed by the GETFund (14.5 percent). More than 95 percent of GoG expenditure is on the personal emoluments (PE). Internally Generated Funds account for 9.9 percent of expenditure and donors and HIPC account for 3.6 percent and 0.1 percent of expenditures, respectively. Funds from other sources, including DCAF, MP Fund and other private (often household) funds also contribute to financing of basic education in Ghana. Other sources (PPVA 2011; World Bank 2011b) note that parents finance a range of schooling expenditures including lunch, uniforms, examination fees and transportation, which sum to a much larger amount than the capitation grant. Notably, figure 7.2 captures only expenditure data collected at the national level.

Table 7.3 shows expenditure by subsector in 2011 as a percentage of total resources used by source (for example, GETFund). In 2011, GETFund allocation to SHS surpassed allocation to tertiary for the first time in the history of the GETFund. SHS accounted for the greatest share of GETFund execution (30.4 percent) followed by tertiary with 20.4 percent. The allocation increase to SHS is explained by the extensive increase in SHS construction across the country (ESPR 2012). IGF is concentrated at the second cycle level and tertiary where a

Figure 7.2 Total Education Expenditure, by Source, 2011

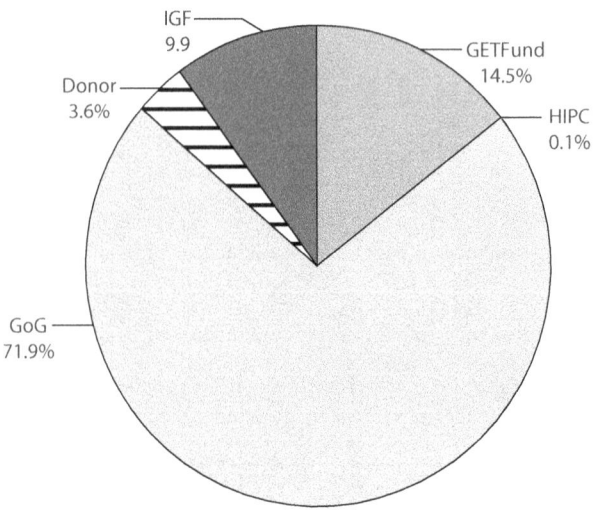

Source: ESPR 2012.

Table 7.3 Expenditure, by Level of Education as a Percentage of Total Expenditure, by Source, 2011

	GoG	GETFund	IGF	Donor	HIPC	Total
Preschool	3.5	1.0	0.3	5.9	5.0	**2.9**
Primary	43.1	12.3	5.3	35.9	60.0	**34.6**
JHS	13.2	7.4	2.4	20.2	30.0	**11.5**
SHS	8.0	30.4	40.0	15.9	—	**14.8**
Tertiary	14.3	20.4	45.0	6.2	—	**17.9**
Management	15.5	13.5	1.4	12.6	—	**13.7**
Other[a]	2.5	15.1	4.9	3.3	5.0	**4.5**
Total (%)	100	100	100	100	100	**100**
Source total (millions of GH Cedi)	2,663	518	354	127	2	**3,566**

Source: ESPR, 2012.
Note: — = not available. For this table, 2011 prices are used.
a. "Other" includes TVET, SPED, NFED, and HIV/AIDS.

Table 7.4 Subsector Expenditure as a Percentage of Total Education Expenditure, 2008–11

	2008	2009	2010	2011
Preschool	3.8	3.1	2.8	2.9
Primary	35	30.5	27.9	34.6
JHS	16.8	15.3	14.4	11.5
SHS	9.8	17.3	15.6	14.8
Tertiary	21.7	20.6	20	17.9
Teacher education	3.2	2.6	2.4	—
Management	7.5	8.2	14.1	13.7
Other[a]	2.2	2.4	2.8	4.5
Total (%)	100	100	100	100

Source: ESPR 2012.
a. "Other" includes TVET, SPED, NFED, and HIV/AIDS.

cost sharing policy is in place. Donor and HIPC spending continues to emphasize basic education.

Over the past 7 years, basic education (KG, primary, JHS) has accounted for between 45 percent and 55 percent of total education expenditures. However, there is large variation in year-on-year expenditure in each subsector. Table 7.4 presents expenditure trends by level of education from 2008 to 2011. Over the last four years, while gross preschool expenditures have increased, the preschool share of total education expenditure has decreased. From 2003 to 2007, primary accounted for 28–40 percent of education expenditures. In the past 4 years, it has ranged from 28 percent to 35 percent. From 2003 to 2007, JHS accounted for 16–22 percent of education expenditures. In the past 4 years, the share of expenditure has steadily declined from 16.8 percent to 11.5 percent. As a whole, basic education still captures the largest share of expenditures followed by tertiary and SHS.

These trends suggest some interpretations. First, if preschool continues to expand and increase the number of qualified preschool teachers employed, it may expand its budget share to equal one third of primary share (about 10 percent). Second, while some of the erratic trends over time are not easily explained, some variation in SHS and tertiary may be explained in year on year differences in GETFund expenditures (ESPR 2012, 2008). The level of inconsistency in expenditure share by subsector suggests that budget execution does not follow guidance offered in Strategic Plan or Medium-Term Expenditure Framework documents. Third, declining share of tertiary expenditure is consistent with ESP guidance and efforts to increase cost-sharing at the tertiary level.

Personal emoluments account for the majority of total education expenditures and the vast majority (95 percent) of GoG education expenditures. Figures 7.3 and 7.4 show budget execution by budget category for the 2011 budget year. The first figure shows total education expenditure (expenditure from all sources) by budget category. PE constitutes 68.7 percent of the total expenditure followed by investment (14.7 percent); service (14.1 percent) and admin (2.4 percent). The second figure, figure 7.4, shows GoG-only education expenditure by budget category for 2011. PE constitutes 95.6 percent of the total expenditure followed by investment (2.1 percent); admin (1.6 percent) and service (0.7 percent). Over the past decade, PE (salaries) expenditures account for over 90 percent of GoG basic education expenditures. Note that these data show recurrent and capital costs and that GoG expenditure does not include GETFund, IGF, or external financing expenditure. Three observations related to the below charts and earlier tables: PE consumes the majority of the GoG budget, investment expenditures come primarily from the GETFund, external sources and IGF and, in basic education, the GoG budget provides very few resources to Services. Service resources appear to come mainly from external funders. In the 2011 budget year, SHS

Figure 7.3 Total Education Expenditure, by Budget Category, 2011

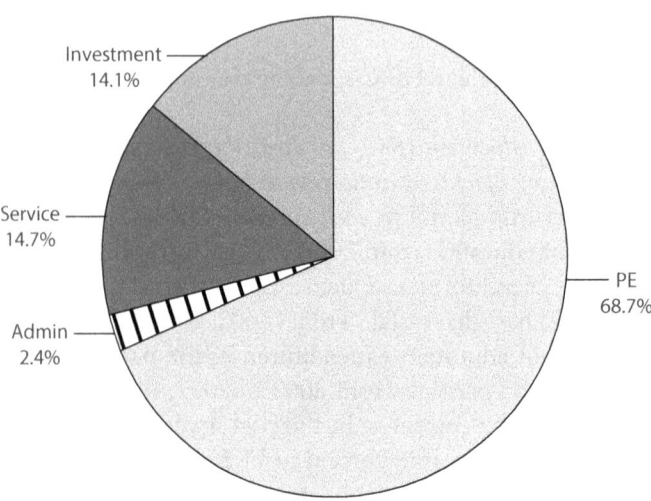

Source: ESPR 2012.

Figure 7.4 GoG Education Expenditure, by Budget Category, 2011

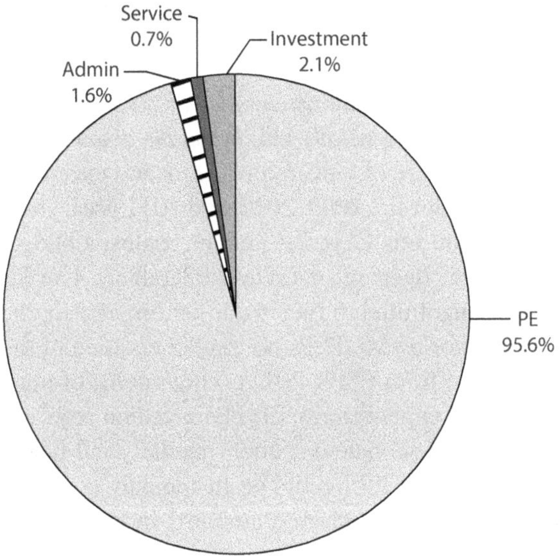

- Service 0.7%
- Admin 1.6%
- Investment 2.1%
- PE 95.6%

Source: ESPR 2012.

Table 7.5 PE as a Percentage of Total and GoG-Only Education Expenditures, 2011

	Total	GoG
Preschool	86.4	99.2
Primary	89.0	99.4
JHS	81.3	99.0
SHS	32.7	83.9
Tertiary	53.1	92.6

Source: ESPR 2012.

spent nearly equal amounts in PE, service, and investment (the latter two budget categories funded by IGF and GETFund, respectively). Table 7.5 shows expenditure on PE by subsector as a percentage of total education expenditure and GoG-only education expenditure.

In the 2013 budget, wages, salaries and allowances accounted for 99 percent of the GoG basic education budget.[1] *Expenditure on salaries and allowances in 2013 is expected to be 3,700 million Ghana cedis, or 179%, of the budgeted amount.* The trend in the wage bill poses two critical challenges:

1. *The wage bill crowds out expenditures in other critical areas.* In 2012, GES received just over a third of their goods and services budget allocation. Consequently, districts were heavily dependent on non-GoG funds to manage their day-to-day expenses.
2. *Increasing the percentage of trained teachers will require the wage bill grow faster than GDP in the medium term.* Increasing the number of trained teachers is

important for improving equity and quality; however, given the size of the 2013 wage bill and the higher cost of trained teachers, it is unclear if there is room for such growth absent salary reform.

In the past 5 years, PE budget execution has regularly exceeded the budget. Budget execution in service and investment categories generally falls below the amount budgeted. Table 7.6 shows budget category share of GoG expenditure and execution as a percentage of the amount budgeted for the 2009, 2010, and 2011 fiscal years. In 2011, the MoE's total PE expenditure was GH₵ 2.45 billion against a budget of GH₵ 1.42 billion creating a budget overrun of GH₵ 1.03 billion. The PE execution rate of 172 percent can be attributed to two major factors, namely the low level of PE ceiling given to the sector by MOFEP and implementation of the Single-Spine Salary Scheme (some text from ESPR 2012). Three items of note: (i) PE accounts for the majority of GoG expenditures; (ii) PE execution regularly exceeds the budget, (iii) investment and service execution regularly fall below budgeted amounts. Investment execution in 2011 could be an anomaly, given the significant cost overrun (593 percent of the budgeted amount) in the tertiary subsector. The ESPR (2012) notes:

> The investment budget allocation of GH₵53.9 million includes a supplementary budget of GH₵49 million for the construction of the schools under trees program, classrooms and dormitories for Senior high schools and the revamping of Science Resource Centers. The budget execution rate indicates a budget overrun of 5%.

GETFund provides the majority of financing used for capital expenditures. Table 7.7 shows GETFund expenditure as a percentage of total education expenditure (selected years). The Ghana Education Trust Fund (the GETFund), a statutory fund partially funded by collecting 2.5 percent of total VAT receipts in Ghana, was established in 2000. GETFund resources tend to be allocated on an ad hoc basis. Approximately 70 percent of GETFund releases are in capital

Table 7.6 GoG Budget Share, by Budget Category and Execution in Relation to Budget Amount

	2009		2010		2011	
Budget category	Share (%)	Execution (%)	Share (%)	Execution (%)	Share (%)	Execution (%)
PE	97	136	97	147	97	172
Admin	2.1	130	1.9	101	1.6	137
Service	0.7	31	0.7	52	0.7	83
Investment	0.1	56	0.1	58	2.1	105

Source: ESPR 2010, 2011.

Table 7.7 GETFund Expenditure as a Percentage of Total Education Expenditure

2003	2005	2007	2009	2010	2011
10.0	9.8	12.9	7.7	12.2	14.5

Source: ESPR, selected years.

investment. The largest receiver of GETFund investment is the tertiary subsector, followed by senior high school and primary. There remains debate on the extent to which VAT operates as a regressive or progressive tax. Recent analysis of the National Health Insurance Scheme suggests that as many small businesses and basic consumables in Ghana are excluded from the VAT, the VAT is progressive in nature. However, as the majority of GETFund resources finance SHS and tertiary capital projects, which preponderantly benefit individuals from wealthier households, utilization of GETFund may demonstrate less progressive tendencies.

Per pupil recurrent expenditure in primary education in Ghana is above the Sub-Saharan average. Per pupil recurrent expenditure in Ghana progressively increases from primary to tertiary subsectors. Figure 7.5 shows relative and absolute unit costs of primary education in several Sub-Saharan African countries using 2007 and 2008 data. Ghana spent more in terms of absolute unit costs of education ($413 in PPP) in comparison to most other African countries. Spending the equivalent of 16.5 percent of per capita GDP per primary student, Ghana was slightly above average in terms of relative unit costs (Motivans 2010).[2] Table 7.8 shows subsector unit costs from 2008 to 2011. Trends show rising primary, JHS SHS and TVET costs while unit costs at the tertiary level have remained flat. Figure 7.6 shows public current expenditure per tertiary student as a ratio of current expenditure per primary student for selected countries. Ghana has recently reduced this ratio both by implementing increased cost-sharing in tertiary and by increasing level of expenditure in primary education.

Figure 7.5 Relative and Absolute Measures of Per Primary Pupil Public Expenditure in Several Countries in Sub-Saharan Africa, 2010

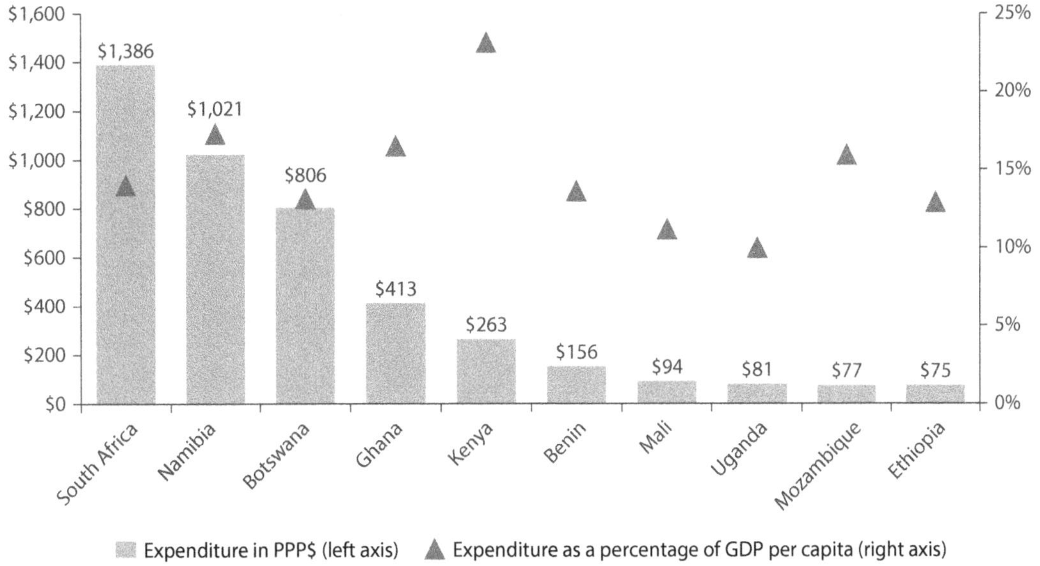

Source: Motivans 2010.

Table 7.8 Education Unit Costs across Different Subsectors
Unit cost GH¢

Level	2008	2009	2010	2011
Primary	189.02	180.55	213.75	372.02
JHS	256.73	259.74	319.60	340.28
SHS	281.12	636.35	397.33	471.26
TVET	304.81	649.94	775.35	1,143.12
Tertiary	2,012.37	2,034.48	1,932.05	—

Source: ESPR 2012.
Note: Student unit cost is the recurrent expenditure per student, by level of education.

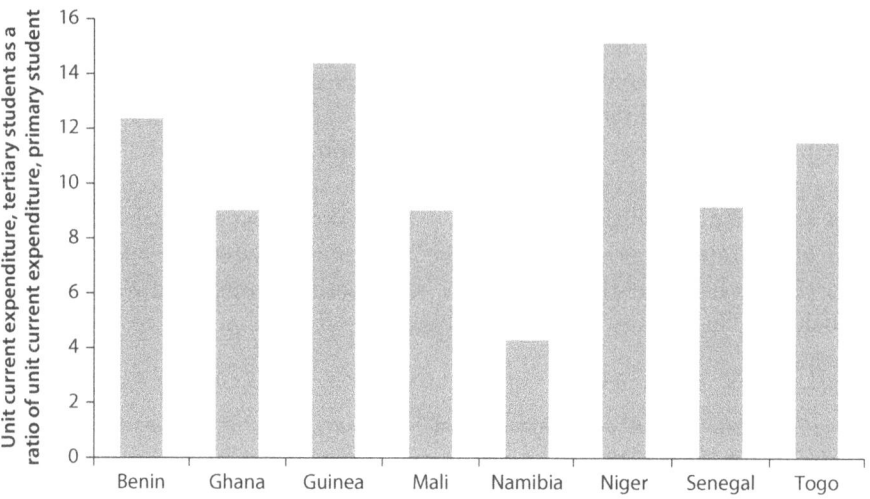

Figure 7.6 Public Current Expenditure Per Tertiary Student as a Ratio of Current Expenditure Per Primary Student (Selected Countries)

Source: UNESCO/UIS 2011.

Figure 7.7 shows composition (by budget category) of per student recurrent expenditure by subsector. This analysis did not identify how IGF funds were used.

The significant disparity in the public expenditure on education by district is one of the most important concerns in education finance. As noted in "Equity," since teacher salaries account for the majority of education expenditures, unequal distribution of qualified teachers largely explains the inequity in expenditure.

The Wage Bill

The wage bill accounts for the bulk of public expenditure (nearly 90 percent in 2010) in basic education. The government wage bill went from the equivalent of 3.9 percent of GDP in 2000 to 4.7 percent in 2004 and 7.6 percent in 2008. Over the same period, the number of public sector employees increased from 371,000 to 478,000—a pace consistent with Ghana's population growth. Education was

Figure 7.7 Composition of Per-Student Recurrent Expenditure, by Subsector, 2011

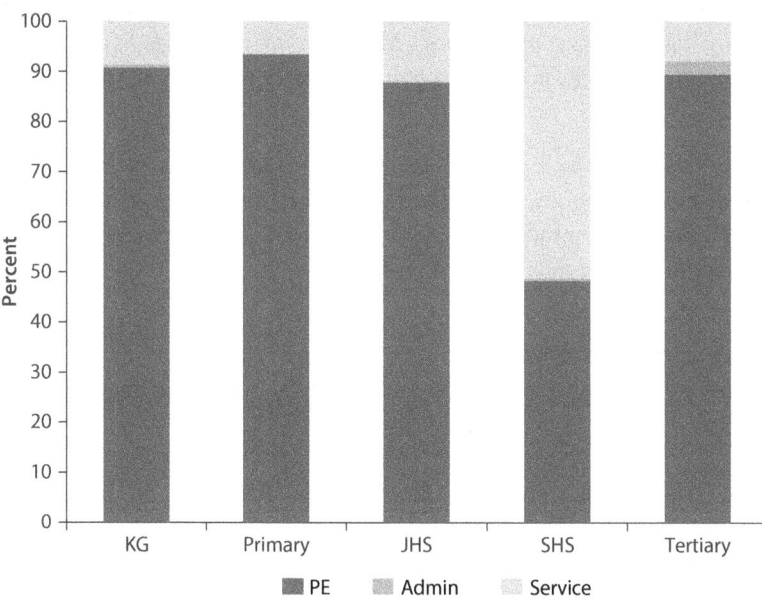

Source: ESPR 2012.

the main contributor to the growth in public sector labor force adding more than 65,000 employees over this same period of time. Accounting for consumer price inflation, individual remunerations were multiplied by 3.6 between 2000 and 2008, corresponding to an average 17 percent annual growth rate in real terms (World Bank Public Expenditure Review, 2011). As noted in earlier sections, NYEP and NSS teachers account for an increasing percentage of the basic education teaching force.[3]

World Bank PER (2011) notes that the rapid increase in the wage bill since 2000 was driven to a large extent by the health and education sectors with population growth and social demand for these services driving Government employment and remuneration in these sectors. The two services together accounted in 2008 for 71 percent of public sector employment and 4.8 percent of GDP, up from 67 percent and 2.6 percent in 2000. Notably, increases in the public sector wage bill have captured a substantial part of GDP growth.

With respect to comparison countries in the region, Ghana stands as an outlier on several grounds. The size of the public sector labor force is twice as high as (2.1 against 1.0 percent) as the average in comparison countries. However, individual remunerations in the public sector with respect to GDP per capita are much lower in Ghana (3.6) than in the rest of Sub-Saharan Africa (7.1). This may be because of the large number of untrained and NYEP/NSS teachers on GES payroll. One the one hand, the large number of civil servants means that PTR in basic schools in Ghana compares favorably with neighboring countries. On the other hand, the effectiveness of underqualified teachers is questionable.

The government wage bill regularly exceeds annual budget appropriations. In the past 5 years, expenditures in PE have come in at 15–78 percent above the budget ceiling given by the Ministry of Finance. Migration to the Single-Spine Salary Structure has resulted in a significant short-term increase in the government wage bill. IMF (2011) notes:

> In the medium term, the single-spine structure should bring considerable benefits. These include more pay equity, easier salary negotiations, better oversight of outlays, and the potential for productivity gains. However, in the short term, it has raised the wage bill significantly. (IMF 2011, 10)

An In-Depth Analysis of the Wage Bill

A 2008 analysis of the GES payroll and salary distribution offers the following insights:

- Teachers in basic school account for the majority (more than 60 percent) of teachers and the wage bill
- Distribution of teachers by qualification is as follows: teachers with low qualification (35 percent), a Cert-A (42 percent), and a diploma or above (21 percent)
- Teachers in Greater Accra have 4 more years of experience than does the average teacher; teachers in deprived districts have 2 fewer years of experience on average than do teachers in nondeprived districts
- Teachers on study leave account for 5 percent of the teaching force and a similar percentage of the wage bill.

This section presents a description of the structure of the Ghana Education Service (GES) payroll from 2008 to 2009 and analyzes variations in teacher remuneration across subsectors. The GES payroll in 2008 counted approximately 250,000 individuals, classified as teaching and nonteaching (see figure 7.9, from World Bank, 2010). Teaching staff constitute 85 percent of the total and absorb 91 percent of the total expenditure. Staff numbering 146,000, mainly teachers and head-teachers, are paid for by GES in Kindergarten, primary and junior high schools and account for about 63 percent of all GES salary costs. In addition, at least 30,000 staff are paid by the National Service Fund and 25,000 staff are paid by the National Youth Employment Agency (NYEP figure is from 2011). At senior high school level, GES pays for 33,500 staff, of whom about 19,250 are teachers. In 2008, 12,650 teachers were on study leave. The cost of salaries spent on study leave teachers (over GHc51 million) is equal to more than the than the total cost of all 138 district education offices. Payroll figures for 2011 are also shown for comparison.

Two thirds of the total teaching and nonteaching staff are employed in the basic cycle, receiving approximately two thirds of the total expenditure. Within the basic cycle, 95 percent of staff is classified as teaching staff. Primary education employs 60 percent of the total staff, Kindergarten 10 percent and junior high

Table 7.9 Payroll Numbers, GES Payroll Figures, 2008

Cost center	Number of staff	Total wage bill '000 Gh cedis	Share of wage bill (%)
Headquarters	676	3,301	0.4
District education offices	10,309	51,262	5.6
Regional education offices	780	3,967	0.4
Educational units	1,428	510	0.1
Study leave	12,650	52,376	5.6
Trainees	22,689	24,492	2.7
Training college staff	3,371	14,721	1.6
Senior high schools	33,512	148,038	16.1
Technical schools	2,161	9,328	1.0
Special schools	1,162	4,696	0.5
Newly trained	11,806	24,499	2.7
Basic schools	146,710	578,912	63.0
Total	**247,254**	**921,103**	**100**

Source: Financial Controller, GES, from World Bank 2010.

Payroll Numbers, GES Payroll Figures, 2011

Cost center	Number of staff	Total wage bill '000 Gh cedis	Share of wage bill (%)
Headquarters	626	3,560	0.3
District education offices	11,413	73,570	5.3
Regional education offices	738	4,571	0.3
Educational units	1,642	8,964	0.6
Study leave	8,335	44,859	3.2
Trainees	23,102	54,454	3.9
Training college staff	3,312	18,719	1.4
Senior high schools	42,820	252,903	18.3
Technical schools	2,443	14,576	1.1
Special schools	1,199	6,086	0.4
Basic schools	163,737	898,931	65.1
Total	**259,367**	**1,381,197**	**100**

Source: Financial Controller, GES, 2013.

30 percent. Per unit expenditure on teaching staff is highest in JHS, followed by primary and KG (table 7.10). Teachers in the upper secondary cycle are better paid than those in the basic cycle.

Before the SSSS, the GES payroll was made up of a 22-grade scale with a number of steps in each for a total of 211 different salary points, known as the Ghana Universal Salary Scheme (GUSS). This was based on the principle of equal pay for work of equal value. There are four entry points to the payroll. Unqualified teachers with GCE O levels begin at Level 5 (GHc 1,279 p.a.). Unqualified teachers with A levels enter at Level 7 (GHc 1,719 p.a.). Qualified teachers with a Certificate A begin at Level 10 (GHc 2,678 p.a.). Over their career, such teachers can move up to Level 16 (GHc 8,237 p.a.). Graduate

Table 7.10 Staff in the Basic Cycle, 2008

	Number	Expenditure	Per-unit expenditure
KG			
Teaching	13,711	39.37	2,871.09
Nonteaching	756	1.64	2,172.68
Primary			
Teaching	86,923	299.57	3,446.42
Nonteaching	4,191	9.72	2,319.46
JHS			
Teaching	41,907	164.88	3,934.35
Nonteaching	2,991	7.32	2,446.94
Basic			
Teaching	1,42,541	503.82	3,534.53
Nonteaching	7,938	18.68	2,353.51

Source: World Bank 2010, 2008 payroll.
Note: Expenditure in million GHc, All figures in 2008 GHc.

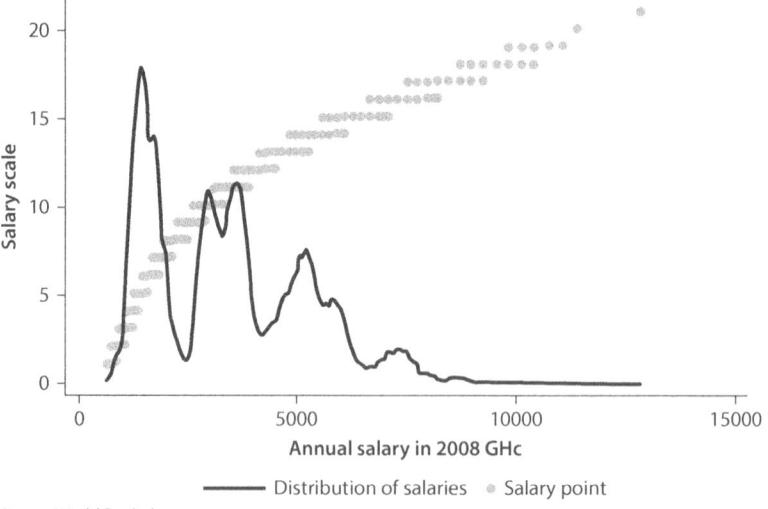

Figure 7.8 Distribution over the GES Salary Scale, 2009

Source: World Bank data.

teachers commence further up the scale at level 14 (GHc 4,837 p.a.). The salary scale, with the correspondent salaries is plotted in figure 7.8.

Figure 7.8 overlays the active GES payroll in 2009 (red dots) to the relative frequency with which each salary point is found in the 2009 payroll (black line). The peaks in the black curve indicate the point on the salary scale with a higher concentration of individuals. There are three major salary classes: unqualified, qualified, and graduate.

Figure 7.9 shows the relative frequency of salary points against the entry points. The first salary class, covering approximately 35 percent of the total number of staff, is made of staff entering the payroll with low qualifications. The second

Education Expenditure

Figure 7.9 Distribution of Salaries and Entry Levels, 2009

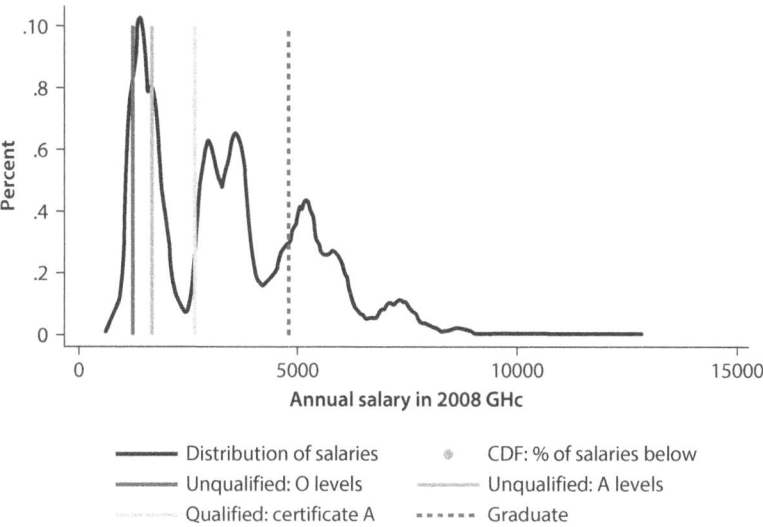

Source: 2009 Payroll.

Figure 7.10 Average Teacher Years of Service, by Region, 2009

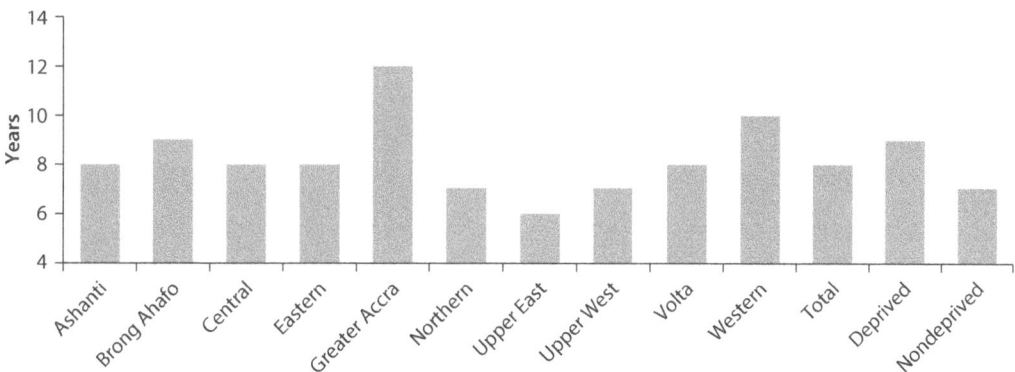

Source: World Bank 2010, from GES Payroll.

salary class, covering approximately 42 percent of the total staff, is made of staff entering the payroll with Certificate A, and the last salary class, approximately 21 percent, is made of graduate teachers.

Teachers in Greater Accra have on average 4 more years of service than in the rest of the country. Teachers in deprived districts are, on average, 2 years less experienced than teachers serving in nondeprived districts and receive lower pay. Figure 7.10 (World Bank, 2010) offers data for each region. An analysis of nonteaching staff is beyond the scope of this section, but the large number of nonteaching and auxiliary staff cannot be overlooked.

Notes

1. Total 2013 GoG basic education budget: 2,070 million cedi; Budget for wages, salaries and allowances: 2,051 million cedi. In the 2012 budget, wage bill expenditure was 3,471 million against 1,279 million allocation: a difference of 2.192 million. Budgets for 2014 and 2015 are expected to follow a similar trajectory (GES, 2013).
2. Ghana calculations based on World Bank and IMF data. In Ghana, primary unit costs were US$172 in 2008 where GDP per capita (Atlas method) was US$1040. Using purchasing power parity, unit costs were US$413 in 2008 and GDP per capita was measured at US$2500. (World Bank 2012; IMF World Economic Outlook 2011). Primary unit costs equal 16.5 percent of Ghana's per capita GDP. Exchange rate used. 1.1 Ghana Cedi per USD (average for 2008).
3. This section is adapted from World Bank, 2010 and uses a data set on wage bill–related expenditures for the years 2000, 2004, and 2008, as well as data gathered from the OHCS on age and information from the Controller Accountant General (CAG) through the automated Integrated Payroll and Personnel Database (IPPD).

CHAPTER 8

Management, Finance, and Accountability

Basic education equity, quality, and efficiency can be improved with improvements in management and accountability. This chapter provides an overview of education management and discusses how management characteristics can strengthen or weaken service delivery. The chapter outlines the responsibilities of the Ministry of Education and the Ghana Education Service, describes influences on education strategy and finance, provides an outline of the planning, implementation and evaluation and provides discussion on accountability. The chapter concludes with sections on decentralization and teacher management.

Overview

In this chapter, we consider how the Government of Ghana, through the MoE and GES, uses human and financial resources to achieve education objectives. Before discussing specific goals and objectives however, it is useful to situate education management in the Ghanaian political, economic and social context. To do this requires revisiting some material discussed in earlier chapters.

Factors Influencing Education Management

Some of the following factors influence the education management environment:

Significant growth: Ghana has realized significant growth in the past 15 years. All of the following have grown: the population, the economy, migration to urban areas, use of electricity and access to media and the number of basic school pupils, teachers and classrooms. This growth has placed significant demands on all government service delivery agencies, including the Ghana Education Service.

Increased expectations: Extraordinary growth has created new tensions and expectations. With economic growth, nearly 50 percent of the current population can be defined as middle class or near-middle-class status. Improved education attainment means that increasing numbers of JHS and second cycle leavers are competing for a limited number of formal sector jobs. The existence of a larger, and politically active, middle class and the increasing importance of education to securing a good job have resulted in increased pressure on service delivery agencies to improve education. Development of a more highly educated population, with higher expectations, absent corresponding increases in employment growth or reductions in inequality threaten growth, stability and social cohesion.

Increased expectations are also influenced by greater popular access to the media (for example, internet, radio, television, newspapers). The growth of the media, which offers daily coverage on education issues, has greatly increased information available to the public and increased pressure on government and GES staff at all levels to address specific and general issues. Such issues include addressing problems related to procurement, financial management, staff or negotiations with teachers' unions.

Increased complexity: Compared with 15 years ago, the policy and management environment has become more complex. Education and education management in 2012 simply requires more inputs, processes and access to information than a generation ago. Increased complexity also reflects an increase in the number of management layers between central management and the classroom and the larger number of stakeholders and other influences affecting education policy, financing, and service delivery. In terms of management, for MoE and GES to deliver education, they must work with, through or in collaboration with the following: more than 15 "sub-vented" agencies (which operate in full or partial autonomy of MoE), at least three other Ministries, Universities and Colleges of Education, Regional Ministers, MMDA governments, Teacher's Unions, Civil Society Groups and Development Partners. Ongoing decentralization of roles and responsibilities has resulted in new complexities.

Competing interests and unequal power: Snyder (1999, 1) notes that different interest groups in education, "promote different educational priorities, and [that] greater consultation does not result in clarity of intents but rather in compromises and complexities." The structure of the current education system (for example, the existence of the NIB, DEOCs or GETFund) is not the result of careful implementation of a strategic plan, but rather evidence of a history of contested reforms and initiatives. As with most nations in the world, in Ghana, the education sector provides more resources to those who need it least and thereby helps to reproduce social and economic inequality. Kenny (2011) argues that increasing levels of domestic resources mean that reduction in poverty and inequality will become increasingly determined by domestic politics and the increasingly influential middle class. In the context of these competing interests, it is important to consider the role of the state and service delivery agencies in protecting the rights of poor and marginalized populations, who have less voice in the political process.

Characteristics of education reform: Sustained education system reform is complex and ridden with dilemmas. Most reform measures have powerful "anti-reform" constituencies and attainment of expected reform results is far from guaranteed. MoE and GES goals to improve access, equity, quality, and efficiency require a variety of measures and interventions—many of which may not be highly visible, would require several years to show substantive results, and may require implementation flexibility, given the diversity of the country and student population. While efficiency gains are possible, moving resources from popular, if inefficient subsidies (for example, SHS, BECE or Study Leave subsidies), toward expenditures which may have a more focused impact on improving quality or equity risk upsetting influential constituencies. Equity improving programs designed to provide direct support to vulnerable groups show great promise, but require improvements in targeting and reductions in implementation costs.

Impact of Above Factors on Education Management and Accountability
The following are some of the impacts of the aforementioned factors:

Multiple influences on education affect reform priorities and service delivery. "Performance improvement" activities included in strategic plans are often displaced by wage bill expenditures and/or ad hoc and high-visibility projects advocated from outside of the MoE. The multiple and, often competing, influences on education strategy and planning, is a significant challenge to MoE and GES implementation of annual AESOP priorities—many of with focus on critical equity, quality and efficiency issues. Since this happens every year, it is difficult for initiatives with strong potential, but few influential advocates to gain traction.

Management and finance fragmentation and complexity negatively influences accountability. That MoE and GES are highly dependent on other Ministries and agencies for key inputs and management and financing of education is fragmented across a large number of institutions from the central to the school level. Holding particular management units accountable for specific service delivery issues is challenging. Clarifying accountability structures could be an important step in efforts to strengthen education management.

Teacher utilization, management, and conditions of service remain critical management issues. As mentioned in the Quality chapter, qualified teachers are the most important and most expensive input to the education system. The diffusion of management responsibility for teachers across school, circuit, district and central levels greatly challenges the effective management of teachers. While the political, social and economic context of Ghana will continue to change, better utilizing, managing and supporting teachers, so they can focus on their work in the classroom, would go a long way toward resolving many of the issues identified in previous chapters.

Even taking into account the above contextual factors, this chapter argues that there is a lot of room for the public sector to be held more accountable for delivery of basic education. This chapter provides some discussion on strategies at the national, district and school level to improve accountability. Some prominent educators in Ghana contend that nothing less than a change in the organizational culture of the education bureaucracy and school leadership is required. Elaborating and providing recommendations on this critique is beyond the scope of this report, but should be a consideration in further public debate.[1]

The next four sections discuss strategy and influence at the national level, financing of basic education and planning, program implementation and evaluation and accountability.

Strategy and Influence

Influences on education strategy and planning have multiplied and thus increased the complexity of leading change in education. This section discusses factors influencing education strategy and planning in Ghana. **Four key factors influence education priorities and expenditures: (i) MoE/education planners, (ii) political institutions and processes, (iii) teachers and civil society, and (iv) recurrent commitments (see Figure 8.1).** *The Ministry of Education and the Ghana Education Service are the main institutions responsible for education in Ghana.* The MoE is responsible for education policy and planning and representing the sector in strategic dialogues. The MoE leads regular strategic planning exercises (for example, ESP 2003–15, ESP 2010–20) and is responsible for submitting Annual Education Sector Operational Plans and budgets to Parliament. GES is responsible for service delivery, including provision of inputs and oversight and management of teachers and District Education Directorates. In most other countries in Africa, these responsibilities are housed under one Ministry. The split in education policy, management and service delivery responsibilities between MoE and GES is unlike the arrangement in most other African countries.

Political institutions and processes are the second main influence on strategy. Government influencers include the Cabinet, the NDPC and political parties. Through the political process (for example, during the presidential election cycle), these groups identify and promote priorities which reflect popular interests and interests of specific constituencies. These priorities and interests are reflected in debates and commitments made by campaigning political parties. Once elected, the winning party seeks to fulfill election promises by implementing identified education priorities.

Teachers, unions and civil society organizations are third main influence on strategy. Teachers exert significant influence on the budget and other policy priorities. Given the critical importance of teachers to education, the significant political influence of teachers and the dissatisfaction of the majority of teachers with conditions of service, the government is in regular dialogue with teachers' unions.

Figure 8.1 Influences on Education Priorities and Expenditure

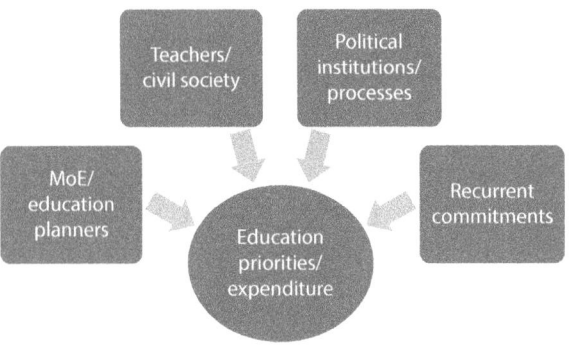

Recurrent commitments are a final influence on strategy. Recurrent commitments (for example, salary, admin and maintenance costs) account for the vast majority of annual expenditures and projected future expenditure. Often these commitments are seen as "running costs" and simply increased year-on-year. However, close interrogation of recurrent commitments could identify potential efficiency gains.

"Performance improvement" activities (for example, regular supply of textbooks; remedial language/mathematics instruction) identified through MoE-led strategic and annual planning exercises are often displaced by the wage bill and priorities identified through the political process. This statement does not seek to suggest that activities or priorities influenced by teachers or the political process do not support "performance improvement." However, as these priorities often displace those articulated through MoE planning processes, it is important to look at evidence and ask, how much have priorities articulated through teacher interests or the political process supported improvements in access, quality and equity? Of course, an alternative perspective would question the extent to which MoE-led strategic planning exercises are open to and consider the varied interests of teachers.

The two main "system reform" types seen in the past two decades are those articulated through the political process and those developed through MoE-led strategic planning processes. The first type of system reform may involve a White Paper or political party commitments to Ghanaian citizens made during the election cycle. These reform initiatives include the White Paper (2004), NERIC (2007), The Education Act (2008) and commitments to deliver school uniforms and eliminate schools under trees. A second type of system reform is development of strategic plans (for example, Education Strategic Plan 2003–15 and ESP 2010–20) designed to inform annual MoE planning processes (for example, the rolling three-year Annual Education Sector Operational Plan). Development of the ESP 2010–20 was led by the MoE and provides a broad and detailed outline of education priorities in Ghana. Development of both the ESP 2003–15 and ESP 2010–20 were aligned with efforts to secure funding from the EFA-Fast Track Initiative (now called Global Partnership for Education) and provide a framework for organizing how other external financing agencies could support the education sector. It must be noted that development of the Education Strategic Plan is also a political process, with all influencers including political parties involved, especially during the NESAR. However, the process may be less explicitly aligned with a political party compared to agendas developed during national political campaigns. Table 8.1 shows policy commitments outlined by the 2008 incoming government.[2]

Reforms articulated through the political process are usually small in number, fairly specific and have a good record of being implemented. Of note, commitment to teacher salaries (outlined in Table 8.1) has been supplanted with GoG implementation of the Single-Spine Salary Scheme, while decentralization objectives outlined in the Education Act (2008) are expected to be phased in over time.

Annual planning documents (based on the ESP 2010–20) may be best viewed as providing a "menu" or "catalogue" of programming options rather than a prioritized list. Table 8.2 shows an excerpt from ESP 2010–20 Volume II. The table shows two

Table 8.1 Incoming Government Policy Commitments, 2008

(a) Motivation of parents and learners through fee abolition, feeding programs, school uniform provision, reducing distance between home and school

(b) Provision of incentives through salary increments for licensed teachers (+15%), mathematics and science teachers (+≈9%), technical and vocational teachers (+10%), and teachers in deprived areas (+20%)

(c) Abolition of shift systems at JHS and the retention of 3 years of SHS

(d) Provision of at least one SHS and two technical schools per district

(e) The establishment of two new public universities at Ho and Sunyani

(f) Allocation of 2 percent of the GETFund for bursaries/scholarships for needy tertiary students in pure and applied mathematics, science and technology; also the construction of a modern office complex for NUGS and affiliated student bodies

Source: World Bank data.

basic education "outline strategies" and "indicative activities" associated with each strategy. There are a total of twenty-one outline strategies for basic education. Over 48 pages, the ESP 2010–20 Volume II, provides extensive detail on outline strategies and indicative activities for each subsector. ESP 2010–20 informs the Annual Education Sector Operational Plan (AESOP), a 3-year costed plan, and district budgeting exercises. While several activities included in respective strategic plans and AESOPs are successfully implemented, a review of the ESPR in 2008 and 2012 indicate that a large number of priority activities were not completed.

Strategic plans developed by the MoE are regularly disrupted by emergent priorities articulated by other influences. The ESP 2010–20 included an education finance scenario whereby teacher salaries would raise at the pace of inflation. Implementation of the Single-Spine Salary Scheme completely revised the picture for education expenditures over the medium and long term. Another important difference between ESP 2010–20 and priorities articulated through the political process (for example, the White Paper (2004), NERIC (2007), and recent dialogue) is the high priority placed on expansion of secondary school. This dialogue influenced the revision of the ESP 2010–20 to include a target of 75 percent Secondary GER by 2020 and the 2011 use of GETFund resources to finance extensive expansion of secondary school infrastructure.

Implementation of the Medium-Term Expenditure Framework highlights the challenge of matching planning with budget execution. A review of the MTEF as implemented under the Ghana Poverty Reduction Strategy II notes:

> At present, the MTEF appears to be neither strategic nor medium term. In practice, budget formulation takes the form of annual incremental line item budgeting. The MDAs' MTEF volumes are focused on presenting detailed items with little or no link to the overall strategic policy context.
>
> During budget implementation, poor predictability of resource flows may lead to *ad hoc* prioritisation of resources. Higher-than-expected payroll requirements may require adjustments in other spending items, particularly service and investment, which are likely to have a significant impact on the efficiency of resources used to deliver basic services. (World Bank Ghana MTEF Review 2009, 26)

Table 8.2 Excerpt from ESP 2010–20, Vol. II, Basic Education Section

Policy objectives	Indicative targets (outcomes and outputs)	Outline strategy	Indicative activities	Time frame	Unit-agency responsible
3 Improve quality of teaching and learning	• Minimum National Standards applied in literacy and numeracy in English and Ghanaian languages at primary and JHS • Literacy and numeracy in a Ghanaian language by 60% of primary 6 pupils by 2012 • Literacy and numeracy in English by 60% of primary 6 pupils by 2012	12. Ensure that all P6 graduates are literate and numerate in English and a Ghanaian language	1. Strengthen internal monitoring and supervision of literacy and numeracy teaching in schools through head-teachers and SMCs 2. Provide at least one specialist teacher in literacy and one in numeracy to serve a cluster of primary schools 3. Support the development of textbooks and other teaching/learning materials in English and Ghanaian languages in line with language policy 4. Distribute the recommended textbooks and teaching guides for the Ghanaian Languages 5. Revise Ghanaian languages syllabus at CoEs to focus on the teaching of literacy and numeracy 6. Develop and implement effective methodologies for teaching in local languages ("Language 1") particularly in P1 to P3 7. Develop and implement an effective methodology for the use of English ("Language 2") as a medium for teaching and learning, particularly in P4 to P6 …	Ongoing from 2010 2010–2012	1. TED, NTC 2. TED, NTC 3. CRDD 4. SL 5. CRDD 6. HRMD 7. BED

table continues next page

Table 8.2 Excerpt from ESP 2010–20, Vol. II, Basic Education Section *(continued)*

Policy objectives	Indicative targets (outcomes and outputs)	Outline strategy	Indicative activities	Time frame	Unit-agency responsible
6. Improve management of education service delivery	• Reduce percentage of untrained teachers from 21.2 percent at the primary level and 21.8 percent at JSS to not more than 5 percent by 2020 (% defined by payroll criteria) • Ongoing IEC for teacher recruitment, especially females in hard-to-reach areas • Motivational packages for teachers to go to hardship areas • 9,000 "pupil teachers" (at least 2/3 of whom are female) identified in rural hard-to-reach areas • All head-teachers trained by 2020	14. Improve the preparation, upgrading and deployment of teachers and head-teachers especially in disadvantaged areas with emphasis on female and pupil teachers.	1. Develop district-level Establishment Control instruments for the effective mobilization and deployment of trained teachers 2. Provide "deprived area incentive package" 3. Implement district sponsorship program for teacher trainees in all districts 4. Support teacher recruitment in deprived areas, through scholarships to "pupil teachers" (mostly young girls) who will be identified by local chiefs/heads/SMCs, trained through the UTTDBE and receive 35% salary payments) 5. Provide IEC to chiefs to provide local support to teachers in remote areas 6. Review policy on paid study leave (to reduce the number of teachers taking annual study leave, reducing the financial burden of the study leave system, and placing a greater emphasis on distance education as a means of professional development). See BE18 7. Strengthen supervision and inspection systems. 8. Introduce a teacher rotation/redeployment system to supply remote rural areas with qualified teachers on an equitable basis 9. Develop and implement phased head-teacher training for those in service and those about to be promoted)	From 2010	BED with REO, DEO

Source: MoE, ESP 2010-20

Management, Finance, and Accountability

A review of the past two decades of reform shows that the MoE is not sole influencer of system reform. In fact, this review suggests both the possibilities and limitations of MoE-led strategic reform initiatives. Education reform and change is not necessarily a linear process—but rather reflects the multiple, and often competing, interests, affecting the development of new priorities, institutions and reform initiatives.

A more detailed analysis would identify that the path taken on each reform issue is affected by a number of interests. Increasing time on task is highlighted in the ESP 2010–20—but may not reflect teacher or political priorities; free SHS is prioritized in the political process, but may face severe financial and human resource limitations; implementation of the Single-Spine Salary Scheme, which reflects MoE, teacher, civil society and political interests, may not significantly improve quality and may in fact capture resources which could have been used for targeted access, equity or quality interventions. These interests show powerful and divergent perspectives on education reform priorities, which in turn are reflected in the education expenditures, achievements and challenges reflected in prior chapters.

Fragmentation of Financing

Education financing is fragmented among a number of sources and among an even larger number of flows of funds. Given expansionary pressures and efforts to meet EFA goals, the government of Ghana has more than doubled its financing of basic education in the past 15 years. In this same time, the financing of basic education has become more complex. Figure 8.2 shows sources and flows of funding and resources for a government primary school in Ghana. It is worth noting that basic schools in Ghana have very little financial autonomy. Teachers and resources for goods and services generally flow from centralized structures.

Figure 8.2 Sources and Flows of Funding and Resources for a Primary School in Ghana

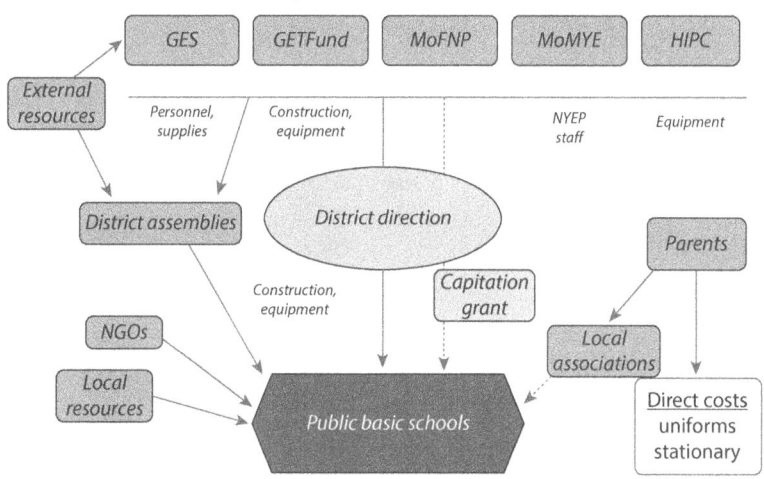

Source: Adapted from UIS 2011.

The authority to allocate the key resources is divided among four agencies: The Ministry of Finance is responsible for setting the overall budget and determining Civil Service Agency (CSA) remunerations; the Ghana Education Trust Fund (GETFund) is responsible for investments; Ghana Education Service (GES) is responsible for allocating recurrent expenditure and to set teacher numbers; the Ministry of Education (MOE) is responsible for allocating donor funds and proposing the annual budget to the government. This fragmentation of budgetary responsibilities is, perhaps, the main reason why planned and executed budgets differ. As noted earlier, districts have some responsibility for infrastructure and textbook provision but often have insufficient resources.

Funding flows for each of the four budget lines follow different paths. Figure 8.3 shows funding flows for PE, administration, service, and investment budget

Figure 8.3 Funding Flows for MoE Budget Category

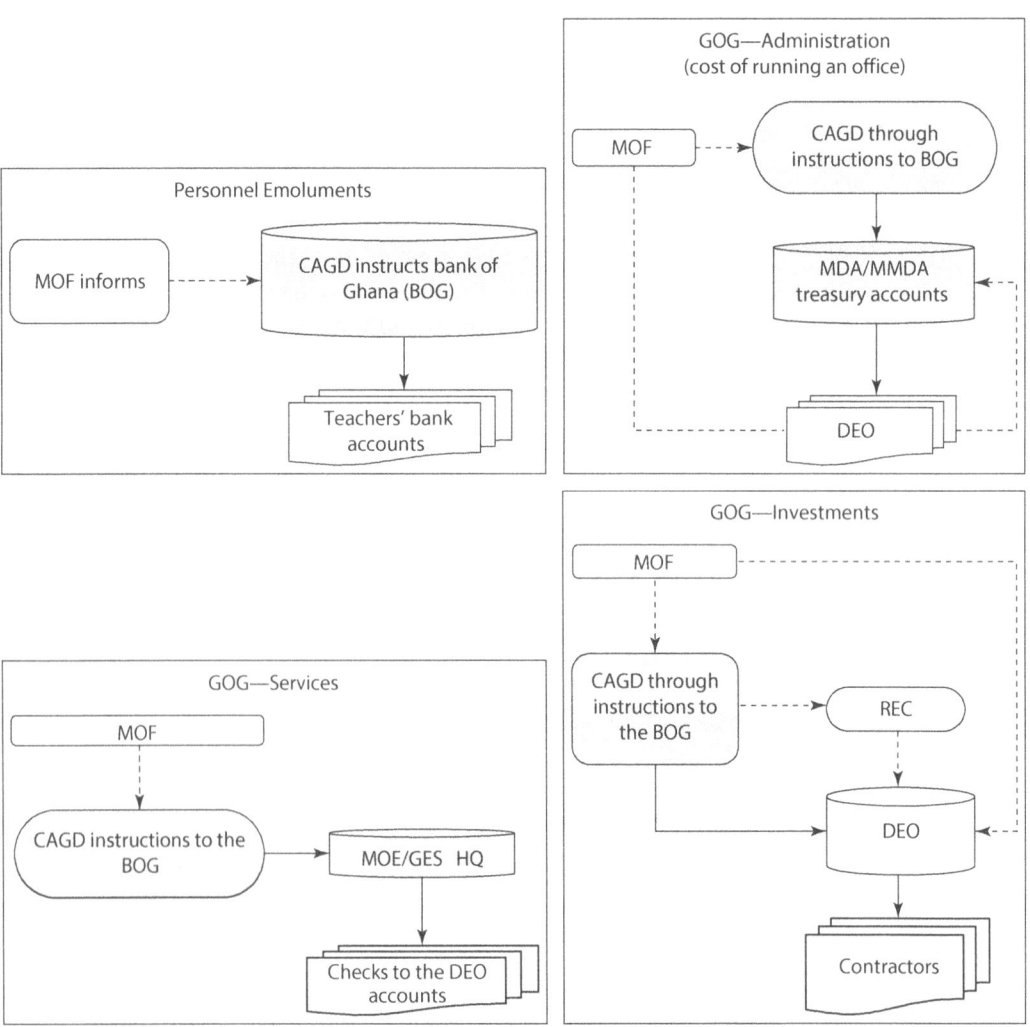

Source: Steffensen 2006.

categories. The IPPD department in GES is responsible for managing payroll information. Based on this information, the CAGD disburses teacher payroll to teacher bank accounts. Administrative funds are directed to MMDA treasury accounts by the CAGD and are then forwarded to the DEO. Service funds flow from CAGD to GES and then on to DEO accounts. Investment funds overseen by MoE (which are far smaller than those managed by GETFund) flow directly from CAGD to the DEO, which is then responsible for overseeing contractor activity (Steffensen, 2006).

However, even the above illustrations provide an incomplete picture. Classroom construction provides a good example of the complexity of financing. Infrastructure is financed through a great number of sources including: GOG investment budget, Donor support (on-budget), GETFund, HIPC-MoE budget funds, HIPC-MMDA funds, DACF nonsectoral funds, various targeted education programs such as the Pilot Programmatic Scheme being implemented with World Bank funding support, and nonsectoral district support programs (for example, the CIDA-supported DWAP). Differences in funding source and flow are accompanied by differences in management of specific projects—with MoE, FPMU, and various DAs overseeing infrastructure projects depending on the funding source. Although most textbooks are purchased directly by MoE, textbooks are also procured through numerous funding sources including GOG, GETFunds, HIPC and donor funds.

Education finance issues have important implications on education management. Implications include the following: the effectiveness of linking planning to budget execution, safeguarding service and investment priorities in the face of annual PE overruns and the need for MoE to negotiate with multiple stakeholders to secure resources for core education expenditures.

Planning, Implementation, Evaluation

The MoE follows an annual planning, implementation and monitoring cycle framed by the Annual Education Sector Operational Plan. Figure 8.4 provides an overview of the annual planning, budgeting, and monitoring cycle. The ESP 2010–20 informs the development of the AESOP. The AESOP informs the budget (which is sent to Parliament for approval) and the Medium-Term Expenditure Framework (used by districts for budgeting). At the end of the cycle, EMIS and educational expenditure data and other monitoring and evaluation reports inform the completion of the Education Sector Performance Report (ESPR) by the MoE Planning, Budgeting, Monitoring and Evaluation Unit. The ESPR informs the National Education Sector Annual Review (NESAR), which is a forum for debate and discussion about education priorities in Ghana. An Aide Memoire, outlining priorities for the next AESOP is drawn up following the NESAR. The new AESOP is developed and used to inform development of the annual budget, which must be submitted to Parliament for review and approval.

To adequately plan for and finance annual education costs, MoE must negotiate with several other institutions. Importantly, many key decisions affecting education

Figure 8.4 Annual Planning, Budgeting, and Monitoring Cycle

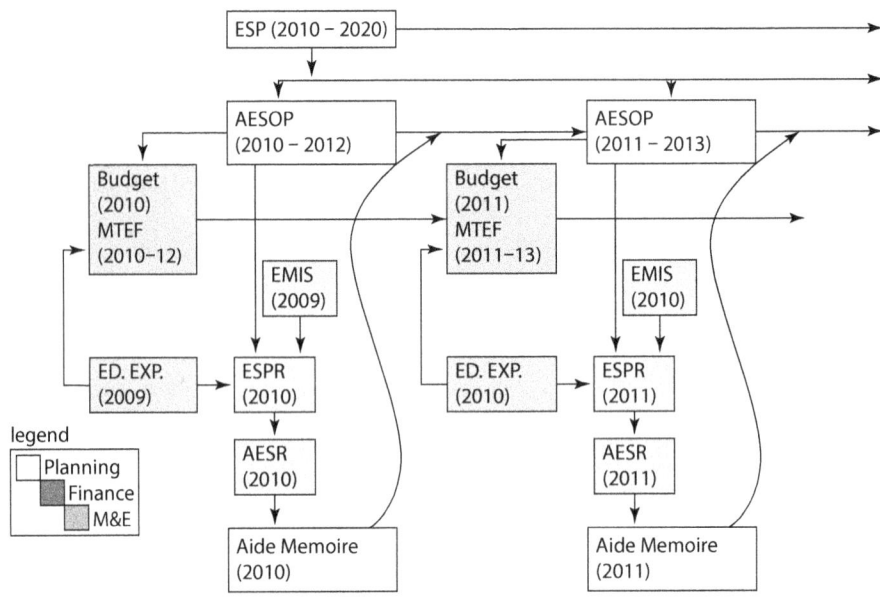

Source: MoE ESP 2010–20, vol II, 2010.

Figure 8.5 Partners with Whom MoE Negotiates to Secure Resources

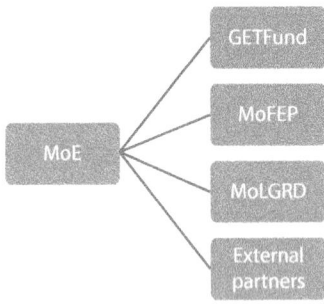

(for example, teacher salary negotiations, recruitment and posting of NYEP teachers) are made outside of the MoE/GES. Figure 8.5 shows some of the partners with whom the MoE must negotiate to fund "core" educational costs—such a teachers, infrastructure and textbooks. In 2011, GETFund resources were used to fund infrastructure, textbooks, the capitation grant and NYEP teachers. MoFEP plays a critical role in deciding annual changes in the salary bill. MoLGRD arranges implementation of the Ghana School Feeding Program through district assemblies. MoE also works with development partners to provide resources for items such as grants to deprived districts, sector budget support and project support to purchase textbooks and infrastructure and train head-teachers.

As education finance is fragmented among several MDAs, the MoE spends a lot of time negotiating with other MDAs and DPs to secure the resources required to cover core education costs (for example, teachers, capitation grant, textbooks) on an annual basis. The case of the capitation grant in 2011 highlights the interconnectedness of these responsibilities. The capitation grant, a relatively new scheme, is critical to service delivery and equity targets affecting the school level. However, in 2011, MoE did not have sufficient resources to fund the capitation grant in its internal budget. To address the shortfall, MoE worked to fund the capitation grant using GETFund resources.

In terms of budget execution, the biggest issue appears to be the wage bill, which crowds out other expenditures; however, the decentralized budgeting process, the implementation of ad hoc initiatives and fund leakage also weakens the ability of the MoE to enforce strategic priorities or targets. For the last decade, basic education wage expenditures have always exceeded budget ceiling approved by the Parliament. These cost overruns crowd out budgeted spending on "service" items such as textbook procurement, district support activities and teacher professional development. *The lack of alignment between annual salary negotiations and hiring practices suggest that the wage bill does not face a hard budget constraint*

Adding to this challenge is the introduction of new initiatives not linked to MoE planning processes (such as the provision of school uniforms and exercise books or the schools under trees program). While these new initiatives may be valuable, paying for them usually requires resources drawn from other budgeted activities. The decentralized budgeting process, in which planning templates distributed by GES recommend annual priorities, further weakens the influence of the AESOP and the ability of the MoE to enforce AESOP priorities or targets. That said, decentralized budgeting may end up having more pros than cons as GES becomes more decentralized.

Accountability

Education accounts for 20 percent of government expenditures and touches the lives of more than 7 million children in basic schools. Yet the use and distribution of resources is often unclear to the general public and many communities are uninvolved in the life of the school. In addition to serving as stewards of public expenditures and resources, MoE and GES staff annually commit to completing a large number of activities and meeting several ambitious targets. This section discusses factors affecting accountability to meeting sector goals at the national level, factors affecting accountability at the district and subdistrict levels (including social accountability at the school level) and financial management.

Accountability exists when the performance of tasks or functions by an individual or institution are subject to the oversight of another individual or institution. Simply put, accountability requires that one institution "answer to" another and, should a task or function not be met, that the second institution must be able to enforce a penalty or remediating action on the first. *For example, if a school or district is accountable to a community, then if the school fails to provide adequate textbooks, ensure that teachers present during the school day, or support pupil progress toward numeracy and literacy attainment then the community should have the power to force the school to address these deficiencies. As noted in this chapter, GES, districts and schools should be held accountable for effective management and use of public resources (for example, capitation grants, textbooks, use of the DCAF).*

While the MoE and GES hold regular monitoring exercises (for example, audits, collection of EMIS data and evaluation activities) to provide data and analysis on education sector performance, the fragmented and decentralized nature of education management arrangements may compromise efforts to hold particular levels of management accountable for meeting particular expectations.

National level dialogue and "accountability" exercises have a mixed record of strengthening accountability. The National Education Sector Annual Review (NESAR) provides a forum to discuss successes and failings of annual program priorities. ESPR's from 2008 and 2012 each highlight a long list of planned activities and targets either not initiated or only partially completed during each program year. While the NESAR provides a space to air these challenges, there does not appear to be a system of accountability for addressing performance challenges against key priorities. Two issues may contribute to this. First, given the size of the wage bill and the regular inclusion of new, unbudgeted activities, stakeholders may recognize, realistically, that it is not possible for MoE and GES to complete all planned activities and meet all targets. Second, given the reality of decentralized budgeting and the large number of activities and targets included in each AESOP, MoE and GES may either (i) find it difficult to influence the completion of priority activities or (ii) not offer a realistic, or short enough, list of prioritized activities.

Another explanation is that media outlets and the political process often give greater prominence to "visible" education issues (for example, schools under trees, SHS construction, free school uniforms) compared to less visible activities such as teacher professional development or providing remedial learning support to children. The "high-visibility" of some initiatives creates a strong incentive for MoE and GES managers to focus on these issues in relation to plans and targets presented in the AESOP. A second example of an accountability challenge was the loss of $15 million in multidonor budget support (MDBS) in 2010. MDBS works with MoE and GES to create a set of annual targets, which, if met provide MoE with access to MDBS funding. In 2010, one of the targets was the completion of the annual school census (EMIS) survey. In failing to complete the census, the education sector did not secure the $15 million available through the MDBS.

Circuit supervisors and head-teachers play critical management and accountability roles at the school level; however, several factors, including lack of resources to fulfill their responsibilities and insufficient professional development, hinder their successful fulfillment of job responsibilities.

Many circuit supervisors don't observe and assess teachers during instruction time, but rather visit schools to simply verify student and teacher attendance figures (World Bank 2004). According to the CDD (2008) study, less than 6 out of 10 teachers (57 percent) said circuit supervisors visit their schools at least once a month. Over time, visits from circuit supervisors have become slightly more frequent: the number of visits averaged about six per year in 1988 and increased to about nine per year in primary and slightly lower in junior secondary by 2003 (World Bank 2004). An analysis of EMIS data indicates that in 2008 circuit supervisor visited schools more than once a year in only 77 percent of schools. Table 8.3 provides data on the frequency of head-teacher and circuit supervisor activities. Studies have shown that rigorous and frequent school visits by circuit supervisors, though uncommon, play an essential management role. Improving the teacher supervision structures and offering teachers incentives tend to directly decrease teacher absenteeism and lateness (Akyeampong et al. 2007).

Head teachers are often promoted without training on their roles and are not always seen as figures of authority at the school level. In a school survey conducted by Akyeampong and Asante, head-teachers were asked about the general behavior of their staff. Whilst rural school heads seem generally happy with the behavior of their teachers, urban heads complained that teachers were increasingly becoming rude and difficult to manage. The school survey also showed that dismissals rarely occur. Most primary head-teachers, as one union official pointed out, "lack the authority that goes with being a head," and therefore are unable to initiate disciplinary measures against teachers. GES has produced a training program for school head-teachers; however, at the time of this publication, it is unclear how many school head-teachers have been trained, and the extent to which the training has been recognized by participants as useful.

Strengthening local participation (through SMCs and PTAs), information transparency and social accountability through the School Report Card, the School Performance Improvement Plan and the School Performance Appraisal Meeting show some promise. The role of PTAs and SMCs in improving "social accountability" at the school level is promising and some evidence supports the importance of an active PTA and SMC on selected management issues. When parents are actively involved in their children's schools through productive and effective PTAs, parental oversight can have a direct impact on teacher attendance patterns (CDD 2008; Brookings Institution 2007). Survey results have shown that the degree of community support for PTAs is strongly linked to its level of income such that financial support for PTAs in schools located within wealthier areas is on average tenfold that of schools in the poorest areas (World Bank 2004). The CDD study (2008) shows that enhancing effective supervision as well as strengthening evaluation have proven effective measures to increase teacher attendance in public schools.

As part of the 1993 decentralization, School Management Committees (SMCs) were introduced. As with PTAs, the presence of SMCs will not necessarily have a positive impact on schools unless they are run effectively. School Management Committees practice some level of community oversight, but their focus is limited to overseeing the use of the capitation grant and does not extend to educational issues, including whether teachers are present and whether students spend their school time on task. Recent efforts to implement School

Table 8.3 Frequency of Head-Teacher and Circuit Supervisor Activities, 2003
percent

	Sits in on class		Looks at a sample of students' work		Looks at lesson plans		Discusses lesson plans		Discusses career development	
	Head-teacher	Circuit supervisor	Head-teacher	Circuit supervisor	Head-teacher	Circuit supervisor	Head-teacher	Circuit supervisor	Head-teacher	Circuit supervisor
Never	10.6	58.6	8.2	56.4	2.3	48.7	10.9	58.3	42.8	72.6
Less than weekly	28.1	38.4	39.4	41.6	2.4	49.2	43.4	40.3	48.7a	22.0a
At least weekly	49.4	2.5	46.4	1.7	95.4	2.2	45.7	1.5	8.5a	5.5a
Daily	11.9	0.4	6.0	0.2	—	—	—	—	—	—
Total	100	100	100	100	100	100	100	100	100	100
Schools sampled	3,013	3,120	3,009	3,119	3,011	3,121	3,007	3,097	3,005	3,114

Source: World Bank 2004.

Note: Schools sampled also include a small share of schools that are part of USAID and DFID programs (i.e. Quality Improvement in Schools [QUIPS] and Whole School Development [WSD]), which had virtually no impact on variations of the frequency of visits. — = not available.

a. Indicates per month and not weekly.

Report Cards, School Performance Improvement Plans (SPIPs) and School Performance Appraisal Meetings (SPAMs) also show promise, but evaluation of the effectiveness of these interventions has not yet been completed. Importantly, these tools can strengthen community participation and access to important *comparative* data on school quality and public resources (for example, trained teachers, textbooks, capitation grant). Providing democratic space and information at the school level can allow community members to ask important questions which can improve accountability. Such questions may include the following: *Why does school X have more qualified teachers? Why does school Y have higher BECE scores? Are we being short-changed by the school, district, or national government?*

There is extensive evidence of fund leakage in the Capitation Grant scheme and school books expenditures. A public expenditure tracking survey (PETS) implemented in 2007 found that the CG amounts distributed by MoFEP to the GES and then to DEOs revealed no "leakage" or delay from the center to the district. However, delays from the DEO to the school occurred and this, along with the inexistence of records of these transfers, suggests that the capacity at the district level to manage funds needs to be improved. The study found a one- to two-month delay in the transfer of funds from the DEO to schools, with the third tranche payment arriving very late in the school year, with negative implications for nonsalary school expenditures. Moreover, the DEOs failed to keep records on the distribution of funds in 50 percent of the schools surveyed. Lack of data about the distribution of funds to schools raises questions about accountability at the DEO level, with funds actually received by schools falling both short and in excess of DEO allocations, depending on the district. Reviews by CDD (2010) and PBME (2011) evidence similar issues.

The PETS also shows that there were large inconsistencies in DACF's records of allocations and that large amounts of funds were retained at the center. Large anomalies in both allocations and executed expenditures argue for in-depth examination of DACF procedures and their implementation.

Many effective "accountability" exercises have originated from outside of the education sector: led by civil society organizations or development partner efforts to track public funding of education communicate critical challenges through public forums and the media. Civil society actors such as the Center for Democracy and Development and the Ghana National Education Campaign Coalitions have played an important role in the national education debate. Reports, studies and position papers produced by these groups have provoked important discussion on inequities and leakages in public expenditures and capitation grant expenditure and inequities between urban and rural areas and the allocation of trained teachers. Absent efforts from these organizations, evidence of fund leakage in the Capitation Grant scheme and school books expenditures and anomalies in District Assembly Common Fund (DCAF) fund use may not have come to light.

In an effort to strengthen accountability at all levels, the Education Act (2008) provided the legal framework for the establishment of a National Inspectorate Board

(NIB). ESP 2010–20 recognizes the NIB as playing a central M & E role through the following activities:

- School inspection through sample surveys of 1st and 2nd cycle institutions
- Oversight of district inspection and supervision systems
- Setting and overseeing norms and standards in educational attainment and performance
- Monitoring the CSSPS (computerized school selection and placement system)
- Establishing inspection panels to provide independent evaluation of quality and standards in educational institutions (including management, teaching and learning, school facilities, testing and examinations, community values, and student achievement).

Ensuring full funding of the NIB and the independent exercise of its authority is expected to improve accountability.

Decentralization and Teacher Policy and Management

At present, most MMDAs are not fully autonomous in most expenditure decisions, especially in the areas of teacher management, remuneration (salaries and allowances), investment budget (classroom, school buildings, teachers' houses etc.) and textbooks provision (Steffensen 2006).

Ongoing decentralization poses both a great opportunity and significant challenge. From a district perspective, problem solving in this complex and fragmented system is very challenging. The decentralization process promises to provide local authorities with more authority and capacity to supervise and manage service delivery and resource allocation activities. Part of this support includes strengthening the professionalization of management staff at the district, circuit and school level.

The GES Act (1995) and the Education Act (2008) provide the legal framework for GoG efforts to deconcentrate line management functions to the District Education Department and devolve decision-making and financing authority to the MMDAs. Ongoing work on decentralization offers a framework whereby MoE and MoLGRD support decentralization at the district level through the Education, Youth and Sports Department (DoEYS) of the DA to perform functions as stipulated in section 3.3 of the Legal Instrument1961 (USAID 2012).

Effective management of teachers is hampered by several factors. While GES has the mandate to assure that schools have the appropriate number of teachers, it does not have effective tools to assure that teachers who are assigned to one school or even to one district take the assignments or remain in the district. Factors contributing to excused and unexcused teacher absenteeism can greatly frustrate efforts by head-teachers, circuit supervisors, and DEOs to effectively manage teachers. Many head-teachers, and circuit supervisors have limited job-specific training and in most cases they may have limited authority to address teacher work performance and disciplinary issues. As noted throughout this volume, NYEP staff accounts for a large portion of basic school teachers and GES has little control over the training, deployment or management of these staff.

Planners face several genuine policy dilemmas when it comes to teacher policy and management.

1. *GES requires more than 50,000 qualified basic education teachers, but does not have sufficient resources to finance salaries of this many more qualified teachers. Using less qualified teachers will likely reduce school quality.*
2. *The majority of teachers are not satisfied with the conditions of service—however, most changes to conditions of service require more resources. Taking away costly benefits (for example, Study Leave) may have highly negative results.* A recent survey by GNAT (2010) found that respondents would quit teaching before they retired, for higher pay (24.8 percent), improved conditions of service (59.8 percent) or to change their profession (6.5 percent). At the time of the survey (which was before the implementation of the SSSS), 98 percent of respondents said they were not satisfied with their current pay (GNAT 2010). Notably, in a growing economy and amid increasing urbanization, both of which are happening in Ghana, there are an increasing number of employment opportunities offering better conditions of service (including higher salary or potential for career advancement) than teaching.
3. *Posting teachers to rural and deprived areas continues to be especially challenging. Unfortunately, the posting process for new teachers appears to reproduce the unequal distribution of qualified teachers instead of serving as a mechanism to address this issue.* It is often argued that, beyond incentives in the form of higher remuneration and career promotion, the absence of amenities in deprived districts (for example, good schools and hospitals for staff children, incentives for spouses) are major brakes to effective deployment of human resources throughout the country (PER, 2011). One of the government policy commitments is the provision of incentives through a salary increment of 20 percent for teachers working in deprived areas. On this issue, ESPR (2012, 12) notes:

> Supply of trained teachers has not managed to keep up with the expanded enrolment witnessed in recent years, reflected in the high PTTR …Provision of trained teachers [in deprived districts] is however a greater problem, with a PTTR of 52 at the national level and of 87 for deprived districts…This has led to calls for incentives to be provided for teachers taking up postings in rural and remote areas. There was extensive discussion around the 20% top up for teachers in deprived districts during 2011 but this policy was not deemed to be feasible at present in light of the move to Single-Spine Salary Scheme.

Teacher policy and management issues are nearly always interconnected and complex. Figure 8.6 outlines the interrelated nature of teacher policy issues. Mulkeen (2010, 8) notes:

> Measures to improve teacher supply or improve deployment may require recruitment of teachers with lower entry standards, with implications for quality.

Figure 8.6 Interrelated Dimensions of Teacher Policy

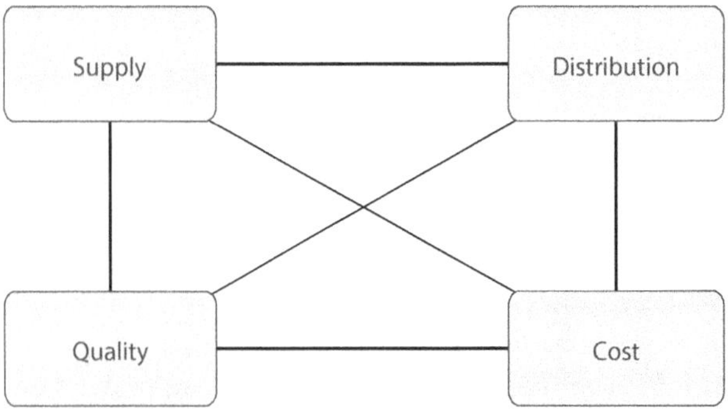

```
   Supply ────────── Distribution
        \          /
         \        /
          \      /
           \    /
            \  /
             \/
             /\
            /  \
           /    \
          /      \
         /        \
        /          \
   Quality ─────────── Cost
```

Source: Mulkeen 2010.

Conversely, measures to improve quality by raising the certification requirements, such as requiring a degree for secondary teaching, may reduce supply and exacerbate deployment problems by drawing in more teachers from urban backgrounds. Any measure involving financial incentives, accelerated promotion, or increased training or supervision has cost implications. ...Developing the right teacher policies is likely to require careful examination of the range of challenges, and making difficult trade-offs between these four dimensions.

Box 8.1 Expanding Senior High School

The ESP 2010–20 identifies expanding access to SHS as a critical priority. In the political arena, there is also expensive discussion on the option of providing "free" SHS. As the debate continues, further research and analysis should be completed on the actual cost of SHS expansion and the potential effects of increased SHS access on employment, inequality and poverty reduction.

At the moment, there are nearly 600,000 students enrolled in SHS making for a gross enrollment ratio of 37 percent and a net enrollment rate ratio of 24 percent. Ghana has about 550 senior high schools. Schools tend to be large: half of SHS institutions had more than 850 students in 2008/09. Significant expansion would require significant investment in infrastructure expansion, some of which is already happening. The elimination of fees would most likely subsidize students from wealthier households at the expense of students from poor households and students in the northern regions who do not yet have access to high-quality basic education. Given low NEA proficiency scores, it is worth asking whether all JHS leavers will have the background needed to take advantage of SHS education.

Expanding access to secondary education or other postbasic skills development programs will not in and of itself lead to more and better paying jobs. This is true in Ghana, and many other countries in Sub-Saharan Africa, where the informal sector accounts for the majority of jobs and job growth in the formal sector has been anemic. King (2011) notes:

box continues next page

Box 8.1 Expanding Senior High School *(continued)*

...there is nothing automatic about the utilization of skills, whether basic literacy or more specialized vocational; they both require supportive local economic environments. And these are in turn affected by the wider international, national economic, political, socio-cultural environments, and especially the labour market environment. The latter might include: the growth in the economy and availability of more and better employment opportunities; the advancement, accessibility and adoption of technological capabilities; the development of an equitable infrastructure for formal and informal enterprises; the presence of meritocratic access to both the formal and informal labour markets; and the availability of financial capital. (King 2011, 3)

At present, most children are not able to continue their education following JHS completion. The government characterizes unemployed youth who complete 6 years of primary and 3 years of JHS as "NEET" people, that is, no education, employment, or training. The "NEET" characterization raises questions about the relevance of basic and postbasic education and also the condition of the labor market that provides limited options for this youth. Many of these low-skill JHS leavers are not likely to benefit from free SHS in the short or medium term. As such, the effect of SHS expansion and "free" SHS on poverty reduction is unclear.

Notes

1. Publications from Prof. Jophus Anamuah-Mensah, ex-Vice Chancellor, University of Education, Winneba and Chairman of National Council for Curriculum and Assessment and Prof. J.S. Djangmah, ex-Director of Ghana Education Service, ex-Chairman of the West African Examination Council.
2. There are other types of "reform," such as NALAP. However, the two reform types mentioned are initiatives seeking to direct change in the entire sector, as opposed to change in a specialized area.

CHAPTER 9

Options for Policymakers

Implicit in the basic education strategic goal is government commitment to full implementation of FCUBE and that, at a minimum, all pupils should leave primary schools with proficiency in numeracy and literacy.[1] This report argues that pupils should leave primary schools with proficiency in numeracy and literacy, teachers should have the knowledge, skills and institutional support to effectively instruct students, schools should be equitably resourced and supported and children who require additional support to access school and to learn should have access to it.

Ensuring continuous improvement in equity and quality in a rapidly changing environment is an ambitious task. In the medium term, basic education access and finance requirements will continue to increase, management of a growing and decentralizing education system will become more complex, and economic growth and increasing urbanization will affect the core aspects of service delivery, including the location of pupils in need of education services and the availability and employment expectations of qualified teachers. However, amid these challenges are also important opportunities and significant resources to effect equity-improving reforms.

Recommendations included in this section seek to support national progress toward the basic education strategic goal, prioritizing improvements in quality and equity. Recommendations below offer a prioritized list of strategic areas for reform, priority interventions and provocative ideas which we hope stimulate a lively and productive debate on basic education reform in Ghana. Many of these recommendations are drawn from ESP 2010–20, Volume 2 and the experience of GES pilot programs and interventions.

Recommendations

1. *Improve the equitable allocation and increase the number of qualified teachers.* Accelerating progress toward learning goals requires addressing the national shortage and inequitable distribution of qualified teachers. *Some strategies to consider:*
   - *Reform the teacher deployment system.* Centralized recruitment and deployment of teachers has not managed to address persistent inequities in

teacher allocation. As long as this system remains in place, poorer and more rural schools and districts will not have equitable access to qualified teachers.

- *Introduce location-specific recruitment of teachers and ensure teachers' language skills match school needs.* In location-specific recruitment, newly qualified teachers would compete for positions posted by schools or districts. Providing schools more choice in hiring decisions and teachers' more choice in deployment can help fill unpopular posts and improve retention and gender balance.[2] Furthermore, Ghana has more than 5,000 multigrade, multilevel basic schools. Recruitment and deployment should ensure teachers' language skills match school needs.

- *Upgrade qualifications and strengthen professional support for underqualified teachers.* Ghana's basic schools are likely to rely on a large number of unqualified teachers over the next two decades. The Untrained Teachers Diploma in Basic Education (UTDBE) offers a cost-effective way to upgrade the skills/qualifications of underqualified teachers. Attention should be paid to ensuring the quality of the UTDBE program to ensure it produces effective teachers.

- *Provide incentives for teachers and head-teachers in deprived areas.* Newly qualified teachers are attracted to the amenities and incentives in urban districts. To help schools in deprived areas compete, positions at these schools could be linked to benefits, such as accelerated promotion, salary top-up, study leave with pay, transport or accommodation allowances or loan forgiveness. Pilot studies should be used to determine how to best target benefits and which benefits offer the best value for money.

- *Improve transition rate of CoE and university graduates into the teaching profession; improve retention; reduce attrition. Agressively recruit SHS graduates for CoE studies.* Every year, a large number of CoE, UEW and UCC graduates do not enter the teaching profession and 10,000 teachers leave basic education. *On these issues, this report has more questions than answers especially since the causes and remedies likely point beyond education policy and education reform.*

- *Deploy more qualified teachers to KG1-P3 classes.* Anecdotal evidence suggests that qualified teachers are more likely to teach upper primary and JHS classes and that KG and lower primary classes are likely to have high pupil-teacher ratios. Learning in early grades provides the foundation for future learning. School leaders should be encouraged to direct appropriately qualified teachers to teach KG1-P3 classes and lower PTRs in early grades.

- *Eliminate study leave.* If wage bill reductions are not considered politically feasible, GES could access the equivalent of 3.4 percent and 3.8 percent of the total annual education budget by eliminating paid study leave and eliminating allowances to trainee teachers. Over 3,000 teachers take paid study leave on an annual basis and do not return to the classroom.

2. *Strengthen instructional support for children in early grades and for children who need it most.* The Government of Ghana made a positive step toward improving equity and quality by adding Kindergarten to basic education. More can be done to improve early grades learning. *The following are some strategies to consider:*
   - *Provide additional instruction to children with low learning outcomes.* There is an increasing body of evidence about which schools fall behind in performance, what the reasons are and what can be done to improve learning outcomes of students who falling behind. One example: A study implemented by the Teacher Community Assistant Initiative shows that providing after-school numeracy and literacy instruction using a trained teacher-community assistant has a positive impact on literacy and numeracy skills of lowest level learners in deprived schools (TCAI 2012).[3] Performance data and information on promising practices should be brought into the annual performance reporting system to support discussion on mainstreaming and scale-up.
   - *Further strengthen national literacy efforts.* The National Accelerated Literacy Program (NALAP) shows promise, however to sustain progress, KG1-P3 teachers needs more guidance, skills and resources to effectively teach literacy in multilingual environments.
   - *Ensure the provision of sufficient teaching and learning materials.* In the past 5 years, the pupil-textbook ratio has declined to one (of three required) core textbooks per primary and JHS pupil. ESPR (2012) identifies lack of textbook provision to basic schools over the past 4 years as a critical failure in GES service delivery. This situation leaves children from low literacy environments and poor households at a disadvantage to their peers.
3. *Improve equitable access, demand for schooling and funding for basic education through existing programs.* In the past decade, GES has piloted several innovative programs which have helped children from vulnerable households attend school. The second generation of programs should seek to address critical targeting, implementation and cost-effectiveness challenges. *Some strategies to consider include the following:*
   - *Strengthen equity of the capitation grant scheme and the resource allocation model.* GES introduction of the Resource Allocation Model, which provides additional funding to schools in deprived districts, shows great promise. Reforming the capitation grant scheme along the same lines (e.g. providing a base grant for all schools or providing additional money to schools in deprived areas or with insufficient teachers) could support equitable progress toward learning goals in small schools and schools in deprived districts.
   - *Strengthen demand-side interventions, especially LEAP.* Livelihood Empowerment Against Poverty (LEAP), a conditional cash transfer program, supported increased access to basic schools. However, the program has high implementation costs and does not reach children from the most vulnerable households. The Ghana School Feeding Program and the Take

Home Rations program face similar issues. Ghana could provide a continent-leading example of improving social protection and interministerial collaboration by significantly strengthening design, targeting and cost-effectiveness of these programs.

- *Continue efforts to support out-of school children, children from marginalized and disadvantaged groups and children with disabilities.* GES partnerships with School for Life, IBIS and others have made a large impact in improving school access to children from disadvantaged and marginalized populations, especially in the three northern regions. Growing informal settlements in urban areas point to new challenges and the need to continue creative access-promoting interventions.[4] GES can build on partnerships with CAMFED, USAID-TAP, UNICEF and PAGE to continue to address challenges facing girls and children with disabilities.

4. *Strengthen management accountability for results, transparency and democratic participation at all levels.* Education accounts for 20 percent of government expenditures and reaches over 7 million children in basic schools. Yet, the use and distribution of resources is often unclear to the public. Action on several fronts—in civil society, within MoE and GES, in communities, and with the newly established National Inspectorate Board—can improve transparency and accountability. *Some strategies to consider include the following:*

- *Give local authorities power and develop local capacity to supervise and manage service delivery.* District authorities should be given authority to hire, dismiss and deploy teachers and more resources to support professional development and supervise teacher performance. The current, fractured, system for teacher management allows for high absenteeism and leaves districts with no power to enforce professional standards of conduct.

- *Professionalize school management and strengthen instructional leadership.* Head-teachers and circuit supervisors should have the educative, management and leadership capacities, the authority and sufficient resources to execute the managerial and instructional leadership responsibilities of their position.[5] GES-led training of head-teachers and circuit supervisors should be complemented with increased responsibilities and resources for school and circuit leaders.[6]

- *Reduce teacher absenteeism and teacher delay.* A 20 percent reduction in teacher absenteeism would have the equivalent effect of hiring an additional 5,200 teachers. Policymakers in Ghana are discussing options for reducing high absenteeism, including reducing the number of days allowed for "unexcused absence" or due to participation in teacher education courses and allowing district officers to freeze teacher pay. In rural areas, targeted provision of a transportation allowance may reduce absenteeism and delay of teachers living off-site.

- *Increase time on task.* Increasing the amount of time in the school day spent on learning activities will likely improve learning outcomes with minimal cost to government. Supporting this effort may require guidance and supervision from the National Inspectorate Board and buy-in and capacity development of circuit supervisors, head-teachers and classroom teachers.

- *Increase support to civil society stakeholders and the media.* Civil society actors such as the Center for Democracy and Development and the Ghana National Education Campaign Coalition have provoked important debate on critical issues, including inequities and leakages in public expenditures and inequities between urban and rural areas and in teacher allocation.
- *Implement the School Report Card, the School Performance Improvement Plan and the School Performance Appraisal Meeting.* Implementation of the SRC, SPIP, and the SPAM can strengthen accountability for results, transparency and community participation. These tools provide access to *comparative* data on school quality and public resources (for example, trained teachers, textbooks, capitation grant) and create a space for community dialogue on education.[7]
- *Fully back the National Inspectorate Board (NIB).* The NIB requires full funding and independent exercise of its authority in setting and overseeing educational attainment and performance standards and oversight of district inspection and supervision.

5. *Improve efficiency of PE and infrastructure expenditure.* PE and infrastructure costs account for the vast majority of public expenditures on basic education. Improving value for money would release resources which could be directed toward equity and quality goals. *Some strategies to consider include the following:*

- *Enforce a hard budget constraint on the GES wage bill. The wage bill presents a true dilemma: balancing the priority for more trained teachers (who have higher recurrent costs) with efforts to manage public expenditure.* In 2013, the wage bill accounted for 99 percent of the GoG basic education budget; wage bill expenditures regularly crowd out expenditure on other education priorities. Setting targets for the overall composition of spending (that is the ratio of PE to other recurrent funding in the final approved budget), ring-fencing critical admin and service items, or rationing the number of centrally-paid teachers per school are possibilities worth exploring.
- *Strengthen district procurement and infrastructure project management.* Infrastructure costs in Ghana are high in comparison to other countries in West Africa. Basic education infrastructure responsibilities (for example, classrooms, water points, toilets) has been decentralized to the districts, however, capacity to plan for, procure (for example, transparent and competitive bidding) and oversee infrastructure projects varies greatly by district.

6. *Foster a culture of innovation and collaborative learning, everywhere.* In education, "learning is the work" (Fullan 2011). Just as people, cities and nations grow and change, so to must education. For Ghana to meet the possibilities and challenges of the twenty-first century, a *learning culture* should be fostered. Characteristics of such a culture could include the following: collaboration

and shared learning; seeking out and funding promising ideas for pilot programs; developing habits of collecting and using relevant data and evaluation at the school level (for example, so teachers are continuously learning about themselves and their pupils) and system level (for example, to consider policy relevance and scale-up potential of promising programs) and encouraging local innovation (since different contexts may require different education interventions). If change is the only constant, change-orientation and learning must be built into the DNA of the education sector.

7. *Other recommendations*
   - *Professionalize the teaching profession.* The draft policy on teacher professional development and management of the NTC needs to be finalized, approved, and implemented.
   - *Aggressively recruit College of Education candidates from deprived areas.* A "grow your own teachers" approach would recruit high potential SHS graduates into local CoEs, cover their fees and incentivize them to work in local basic schools for a bonded term. This approach has the advantage of providing a career path for local talent with a strong knowledge of local context and language.
   - *Reform the salary structure. Consider introducing a hedonic wage model.* A hedonic model is a model where teacher wages would vary across Ghana according to teacher demand for particular positions and employer demand for teachers. Absent a significant increase in revenue, it is unlikely that GES can afford the wage bill associated with a significant increase in the number of qualified teachers. Introducing a hedonic wage model could more efficiently allocate PE resources.
   - *Strengthen school-based and cluster-based continuing professional development.* Continuing in-service training workshops in individual schools or clusters can contribute to improved performance of teachers. At the same time, it promotes sharing of information and experiences among teachers, which can support the development of a professional community.

Notes

1. The basic education strategic goal is to "provide equitable access to good-quality child-friendly universal basic education, by improving opportunities for all children in the first cycle of education at Kindergarten, primary and junior high school levels" (MoE, ESP 2010–20, 2010).
2. Evidence is based on (Mulkeen 2010, on location specific recruitment in Lesotho, Uganda and Zambia). Implementation of location-specific recruitment may not work by itself. This policy option may also need to include introduction of local incentives and equity-protecting safeguards overseen by NIB.
3. In TCAI, a trained Teacher-Community Assistant from the NYEP supported the program. Untrained NYEP teachers should not take the place of a qualified teacher, however with sufficient training, NYEP staff can provide effective tutoring support.
4. Notably, girls' access, especially in the three northern regions, and girls' dropout in upper primary and JHS, remain critical challenges.

5. Prominent educators in Ghana contend that nothing less than a change in the organizational culture and attitudes of the education bureaucracy and school leadership is required. Elaborating and providing recommendations on this critique is beyond the scope of this report, but an important consideration in further public debate. [This footnote references the important work of Prof. Jophus Anamuah-Mensah, ex-Vice Chancellor, University of Education, Winneba and Chairman of National Council for Curriculum and Assessment and Prof. J.S. Djangmah, ex-Director of Ghana Education Service, ex-Chairman of West African Examination Council.]
6. Responsibilities include circuit supervisor visits, in-service professional development, supervisory and disciplinary actions. The teacher education universities (UCC & UEW) could be approached to support such training.
7. Providing democratic space and information will allow community members to ask important questions: Why does school X have more qualified teachers? Why does school Y have higher BECE scores? Are we being short-changed by the school, district or national government? However, we should also add a note of caution against an overreliance on community participation as a "solution" to low quality in poor or marginalized areas. Participation efforts, in the absence of increased professional development and resources and professional support for teachers and deprived schools, is not sufficient.

Bibliography

Abadzi, Helen. 2007. *Absenteeism and Beyond: Instructional Time Loss and Consequences.* Washington, DC: World Bank.

Addae-Mensah, I. 2000. "Education in Ghana: A Tool for Social Mobility or Social Stratification?" Delivered at the J.B. Danquah Memorial Lectures. Accra: Ghana Academy of Arts and Sciences.

Adu, J. K. 2006. "Report on 2005 Administration of National Education Assessment Primary 3 and Primary 6 English and Mathematics." Ministry of Education, Accra.

Adu-Yeboah, Christine. 2011. "Teacher Preparation and Continuing Professional Development in Africa." University of Sussex.

African Development Bank. 2010. "The Middle of the Pyramid: Dynamics of the Middle Class in Africa." Market Brief.

———. 2011. *The Middle of the Pyramid: Dynamics of the Middle Class in Africa.* Abidjan, Ivory Coast: Africa Development Bank.

Akyeampong, Kwame. 2008. "Public Private Partnership in the Provision of Basic Education for Poor and Disadvantaged Groups in Ghana and Rwanda: Possibilities and Constraints." Brighton, UK, University of Sussex, Sussex School of Education, Centre for International Education, unpublished paper.

———. 2009a. "Access and Educational Equity in Ghana." Centre for International Education, University of Sussex, Brighton, commissioned by the World Bank for this Country Status Report, unpublished.

———. 2009b. "Revisiting Free Compulsory Universal Basic Education (FCUBE) in Ghana." *Comparative Education* 45 (2): 175–95.

———. 2010. "50 Years of Educational Progress and Challenge in Ghana." CREATE Pathways to Access Series, Research Monograph Number 33.

———. 2011. (Re)Assessing the Impact of School Capitation Grants on Educational Access in Ghana. CREATE.

Akyeampong, Kwame, J. Djangmah, A. Seidu, A. Oduro, and F. Hunt. 2007. "Access to Basic Education in Ghana: The Evidence and the Issues." Country Analytic Report. CREATE.

Akyeampong, Kwame, John Pryor, and Joseph Ghartey Ampiah. 2006. "A Vision of Successful Schooling: Ghanaian Teachers' Understandings of Learning, Teaching and Assessment." *Comparative Education* 42 (2): 155–76.

Ampiah, Joseph. 2010. "Quality Basic Education in Ghana: Prescription, Praxis and Problems." Paper delivered at Experience Sharing Seminar. University of Cape Coast, Accra.

Ampiah, Joseph Ghartey, and Christine Adu-Yeboah. 2009. "Mapping the Incidence of School Dropouts: A Case Study of Communities in Northern Ghana." *Comparative Education* 45 (2): 219–32.

Anamuah-Mensah Committee Report. 2002. "Meeting the Challenges of Education in the Twenty First Century- Executive Summary." Report of the President's Committee on Review of Education Reforms in Ghana. Adwinsa Publications (Gh) Ltd., Ghana.

Anamuah-Mensah, Jophus, Akwasi Asabere-Ameyaw, and Kofi Damian Mereku. 2004. "Ghanaian Junior Secondary School students' Achievement in Mathematics and Science." Results from Ghana's participation in the 2003 Trends in International Mathematics and Sceince Study (TIMSS), Ministry of Education, Accra.

Anamuah-Mensah, J., D. K. Mereku, and J. G. Ampiah. 2009. *TIMSS 2007 Ghana Report: Findings from IEA's Trends in International Mathematics and Science Study at the Eighth Grade.* Accra: Adwinsa Publications (Gh) Ltd.

Bennell, P., and K. Akyeampong. 2006. *Is There a Teacher Motivation Crisis in Sub-Saharan Africa and South Asia? Key Findings and Recommendations of an International Research Project, Knowledge and Skills for Development.* Brighton, UK: Knowledge and Skills for Development.

Berg, Andrew G., and Jonathan D. Ostry. 2011. "Inequality and Unsustainable Growth: Two Sides of the Same Coin?" International Monetary Fund, Washington, DC.

Brookings Institution. 2007. "Review of Trends in Public Spending for Education and Health in Ghana (2002–2006)." Transparency and Accountability Project.

Bruneforth, M. 2006. "Interpreting the Distribution of Out-of-School Children by Past and Expected Future School Enrollment." Background paper for *EFA Global Monitoring Report* 2007.

Bruns, Barbara, Deon Filmer, and Harry Anthony Patrinos. 2011. *Making Schools Work.* Washington, DC: World Bank.

Casely-Hayford, Leslie. 2011. "Political Economic Analysis of Education in Ghana." STAR-Ghana/DfID.

Casely-Hayford, Leslie, and A. Ghartey. 2007. "An Impact Assessment of School for Life." Accra, Ghana.

CDD (Center for Democratic Development). 2008. "Tracking Leakage of Public Resource in the Education Sector: A Pilot Investigation of Teacher Absence in Public Primary Schools in Ghana." In collaboration with: the Transparency and Accountability Project/ Brookings Institution. Ghana.

———. 2010. "Public Expenditure Tracking Survey." Tracking capitation grant in primary schools in Ghana.

Chijioke, Chinezi. 2012. "The Journey from Poor-to-Good: How School Systems Start the March to Excellence." Presentation. Ghana School Systems Improvement. McKinsey and Company.

Cloutier, Marie-Helene. 2010. "Making the Grade." Ghana Case Study. Development Impact Evaluation Initiative. World Bank.

Colclough, Christopher, Geeta Kingdon, and Harry Patrinos. 2009. "The Patterns of Returns to Education and Its Implications." RECOUP Policy Brief No. 4.

CREATE. 2010. "Fosterage and Educational Access among the Dagomba of Savelugu-Nanton, Ghana." Create Ghana Policy Brief 4.

Djangmah, Jerome. 2011. "Inequitable Access to Basic Education in Ghana: The Way Forward for Free Compulsory Universal Basic Education (FCUBE)." CREATE Occasional Paper 2, University of Sussex, Brighton.

Dunne, Máiréad, F. Leach, B. Chilisa, T. Maundeni, R. Tabulawa, N. Kutor, L. Forde, and A. Asamoah. 2005. *Gendered School Experiences: The Impact on Retention and Achievement in Botswana and Ghana*. Education Series Research Report No. 56, DfID, London.

EARC. 2003. "Teacher Time on Task." United States Agency for International Development, Grant No. 641 G-00-03-0055 unpublished report. Educational Assessment and Research Center, 35 Dabebu Rd. Osu, Ghana.

Education Management Information System (EMIS). EMIS School Census Database and Administrative WAEC Data. Ministry of Education, Accra.

Education Development Center. 2007. "Islamic Education Sector Study." Ghana.

EQUIP2. 2011. "The Cost-Effectiveness of Education Reform: Improving the Use of Existing Resources for Learning Gains." CIES Conference. Montreal, Quebec, Canada.

Fobih, D., K. A. Akyeampong, and A. Koomson. 1999. "Ghana Primary School Development Project: Final Evaluation of Project Performance." Ministry of Education, Accra.

Fobih, D. K., and A. K. Koomson. 1998. *Ghana's Educational Reform: Historical Perspective in Education and Development in Africa—A Contemporary Survey*. Jonathan Nwomonoh (ed.). San Francisco-London-Bethesda: International Scholars Publications.

Foster, Philip J. 1965. *Education and Social Change in Ghana*. Chicago: University of Chicago Press.

Fullan, Michael. 2011. "Learning Is the Work." Unpublished Paper.

Gershberg, A. I., and A. Maikish. 2008. "Targeting Education Funding to the Poor: Universal Primary Education, Education Decentralization and Local Level Outcomes in Ghana." Background paper for EFA Global Monitoring Report 2009.

Ghana Demographic and Health Survey. 2009. *Ghana Demographic and Health Survey 2008*. Accra, Ghana: Ghana Statistical Service, Ghana Health Service, and ICF Macro.

Ghana Education Service and Ghana National Association of Teachers. 2000. *Conditions and Scheme of Service and the Professional Code of Conduct for Teachers*. Accra, Ghana: GESC and GNAT.

Ghana Education Service and University of Cape Coast (Institute of Education). 2007. *Two Year Diploma in Basic Education Brochure*. Teacher Education Department, GES, Accra, Ghana.

Ghana National Association of Teachers (GNAT) & Teachers & Educational Workers (TEWU) of Ghanatrades Union Congress. 2010. Teacher Attrition in Ghana: Results of a Questionnaire Survey.

Ghana National Education Campaign Coalition (GNECC). 2010. *Tracking Survey for Textbooks, Exercise Books, School Uniforms, Capitation Grant, School Infrastructure and Teachers*. Accra: GNECC

Ghana Statistical Service (GSS). 2003. *Core Welfare Indicators Questionnaire*. Accra: Ghana Statistical Service.

———. 2008. "Ghana Living Standards Survey Report of the Fifth Round (GLSS 5)." Ghana Statistical Service, Accra.

———. 2010. "Rebasing of Ghana's National Accounts to Reference Year 2006." Ghana Statistical Service, Accra.

———. 2011. "Ghana Multiple Indicator Cluster Survey." Final Report. Ghana Statistical Service, Accra, Ghana.

———. 2012. "2010 Population and Housing Census." Summary Report of Final Results. Ghana Statistical Service, Accra, Ghana.

Government of Ghana (GoG). 2004. "White Paper on the Report of the Education Review Committee." Government of Ghana, Accra.

———. 2008. *Education Act*. Accra: Government of Ghana.

———. 2009. *Underserved Areas in Ghana, A study on Teacher Placement*. Accra: Government of Ghana.

Hanushek, E., and L. Woessmann. 2008. "The Role of Cognitive Skills in Economic Development." *Journal of Economic Literature* 46 (3): 607–68.

———. 2009. "Do Better Schools Lead To More Growth? Cognitive Skills, Economic Outcomes, and Causation." NBER Working Paper 14633, National Bureau of Economic Research.

Harttgen, K., S. Klasen, and M. Misselhorn. 2008. "Education for All? Measuring Pro-poor Educational Outcomes in Developing Countries." Background paper for EFA Global Monitoring Report 2009.

Hashim, I. 2005. "Exploring the Linkages between Children's Independent Migration and Education: Evidence from Ghana." Working Paper T-12, Sussex Centre for Migration Research, Brighton.

IMF. 2011. "Fifth Review Under the Three-Year Arrangement Under the Extended Credit Facility and Request for Modification of Performance Criteria (Ghana)." IMF Country Report No. 12/36, Washington, DC.

Innovations for Poverty Action. 2012. An Evaluation of the Teacher Community Assistant Initiative (TCAI) Pilot Programme in Ghana: Preliminary Impact Results.

JICA. 2008. "Final Report on Project to Support the Operationalization of the In-Service Training Policy." JICA, Accra, Republic of Ghana.

J-PAL and IPA. 2009. *An [Emergency] Primary School Quality Initiative*. Jameel Poverty Action Lab (JPAL) and Innovations for Poverty Action (IPA).

Joseph, George, and Quentin Wodon. 2012. "Test Scores in Ghana's Primary Schools: Measuring the Impact of School Inputs and Socio-Economic Factors." World Bank.

Kenny, Charles. 2011. "How 28 Poor Countries Escaped the Poverty Trap." *The Guardian*. Poverty Matters Blog. July 12, 2011.

King, Kenneth. 2011. "Eight Proposals for a Strengthened Focus on Technical and Vocational Education and Training (TVET) in the Education for All (EFA) Agenda." Background paper prepared for the EFA Global Monitoring report 2012, Paris, France.

Kingdon, Geeta, and Mans Soderbom. 2007. "Education, Skills, and Labor Market Outcomes: Evidence from Ghana." Centre for Study of African Economies, Department of Economics, University of Oxford, UK.

Klees, Steven. 2002. "World Bank Development Policy: A SAP in SWAPs Clothing." *Current Issues in Comparative Education* 3 (2): 110–21.

Klees, Steven, Joel Samoff, and Nelly Stromquist. 2012. *The World Bank and Education: Critiques and Alternatives*. Rotterdam/Boston/Taipei: Sense Publishers.

Lewin, Keith. 2007. "Improving Access, Equity and Transitions in Education: Creating a Research Agenda." CREATE Pathways to Access. Research Monograph No 1, University of Sussex, UK.

———. 2009. "Access to Education in Sub-Saharan Africa: Patterns, Problems and Possibilities." *Comparative Education* 45 (2): 151–74.

———. 2011. "Making Rights Realities. Research Insights into Educational Access, Transitions and Equity." Research Report of the Consortium for Research on Educational Access, Transitions and Equity, University of Sussex, Brighton.

Lewin, Keith, and Ricardo Sabates. 2011. Expanding Access: Who gets what? CREATE. CIES Conference. Montreal, 2011.

McKinsey and Company. 2010. "How the World's Most Improved School Systems Keep Getting Better." McKinsey.

Mereku, K., F. K. Amedahe, K. Etsey, J. Adu, E. Acquaye, W. Synder, A. Moore, and B. Long. 2005. "Opportunity to Learn: English and Mathematics in Ghanaian Primary Schools." USAID/BECAS, Washington, DC.

Mingat, Alain, Blandine Ledoux, and Ramahatra Rakotomalala. 2010. *Developing Post-Primary Education in Sub-Saharan Africa: Assessing the Financial Sustainability of Alternative Pathways*. Washington, DC: World Bank.

Ministry of Education. 2008. "Education Sector Performance Report." Ministry of Education, Accra, July.

———. 2009a. "Education Sector Performance Report." Ministry of Education, Accra.

———. 2009a. Complementary Basic Education Policy (draft).

———. 2010a. "Education Sector Performance Report." Ministry of Education, Accra.

———. 2010b. *Education Strategic Plan 2010–2020*. Accra: Ministry of Education.

———. 2010c. "Basic Education Comprehensive Assessment System: Report Summary 2009 National Education Assessment Primary 3 and Primary 6, English and Mathematics." Ministry of Education, Assessment Services Unit, Accra, June.

———. 2011. "Education Sector Performance Report." Ministry of Education, Accra.

———. 2012. "Education Sector Performance Report." Ministry of Education, Accra.

Ministry of Education, Youth and Sports. 2004. "White Paper on the Report of Education Reform Review Committee." Ministry of Education, Youth and Sports, Accra.

———. 2006. "Preliminary Education Sector Performance Report 2006." Ministry of Education, Youth and Sports, Accra.

Ministry of Education/Assessment Services Unit. 2005. "National Education Assessment 2005." Ministry of Education, Accra, Ghana.

———. 2007. "National Education Assessment 2007." Ministry of Education, Accra, Ghana.

———. 2009. "National Education Assessment 2009." Ministry of Education, Accra, Ghana.

———. 2011. "National Education Assessment 2011." Ministry of Education, Accra, Ghana.

Ministry of Education/Planning, Budgeting, Monitoring and Evaluation Unit. 2011. "Policy Evaluation Studies: Pro-Poor Interventions within the Education Sector." Ministry of Education, Accra.

Monk, David H. 1990. *Educational Finance: An Economic Approach*. New York: McGraw Hill, Chapter 2, Equity and the distribution of educational resources.

Moss, Todd, and Stephanie Majerowicz. 2012. "No Longer Poor: Ghana's New Income Status and Implications of Graduation from IDA." Working Paper 300 Center for Global Development, Washington, DC.

Motivans, Albert. 2010. "Education Investment and Commitment: Reassessing the International Benchmarks." UNESCO/UIS, Stockholm.

Mulkeen, Aidan. 2010. *Teachers in Anglophone Africa: Issues in Teacher Supply, Training and Management*. Washington, DC: World Bank.

Murphy, Patrick. 2009. *Teachers in Ghana; Summary and Observations*. Washington DC: World Bank, unpublished.

National Development Planning Commission. 2012. *Achieving the MDGS with Equity in Ghana: Unmasking the Issues Behind the Averages*. Accra: NDPC.

National Education Reform Implementation Committee. 2007. "Education Reform 2007 at a Glance." NERIC Secretariat, Accra, Ghana.

Nishimura, M., J. Ogawa, and J. Ampiah. 2009. "A Comparative Analysis of Universal Primary Education Policy in Ghana, Kenya, Malawi, and Uganda." *Journal of International Cooperation in Education* 12 (1): 143–58.

OECD. 2012. "Chapter V—Reducing Income Inequality while Boosting Economic Growth: Can It Be Done?" *Going for Growth: Economic Policy Reforms 2012*. OECD.

Oduro, A. D. 2000. *Basic Education in Ghana in the Post-Reform Period*. Accra: Centre for Policy Analysis.

Open Learning Exchange Ghana and Ghana Education Service, Teacher Education Division. 2011. "Study of the Multigrade Multilevel Situation in Ghana." OLE Ghana and GES Teacher Education Division.

Palma, José Gabriel. 2011. "Homogeneous Middles vs. Heterogeneous Tails, and the End of the 'Inverted-U': It's All About the Share of the Rich." *Development and Change* 42 (1): 87–153.

Participatory Development Associates. 2011. "Participatory Poverty and Vulnerability Assessment (PPVA)." UNICEF/World Bank/DFID.

Patrinos, Harry Anthony. 2007. *Demand-side Financing in Education*. Education Policy Series. Paris/Brussels: UNESCO/IIEP.

Perry, C. 2007. "MoESS/GES Staff Supply/Demand Forecasting Model, Final Report." Ministry of Education Science and Sports, Accra, Ghana.

Sen, Amartya. 2003. "Reflections on Literacy." In *Literacy as Freedom*. Paris: UNESCO.

Shimada, Kintaro. "Student Achievement and Social Stratification: A Case of Primary Education in Kenya." *Africa Educational Research Journal* (1): 92–109.

Snyder, C. W. 1999. "Strange Loops in Education: Problems for Planning and Progress." Development Discussion Paper no. 690. Harvard Institute for International Development, Harvard University,

Spaull, Nic. 2011. "A Preliminary Analysis of SACMEQ III South Africa." Stellenbosch Economic Working Papers: 11/11, University of Stellenbosch, South Africa.

Stapenhurst, Rick, and Mitchell O'Brien. 2007. "Accountability in Governance." World Bank Paper 4, World Bank, Washington, DC.

Steffensen, Jesper. 2006. "Study on Improving Basic Education through a more Transparent, Equitable and Better Financial and Performance Management: Review of the Funding Flows in Basic Education." Nordic Consulting Group, June.

Teacher Community Assistant Initiative. 2012. "Presentation at Evidence-Based Education: Policy-Making and Reform in Africa." Accra, Ghana.

Thompson, Nii Moi, and Leslie Casely-Hayford (RECOUP). 2008. "The Financing and Outcomes of Education in Ghana." RECOUP Working Paper Series, Cambridge, UK.

Transparency International. 2009a. *Corruption Perceptions Index 2009*. Berlin: Transparency International Press.

———. 2009b. *Africa Education Watch*. Berlin: Transparency International Press.

Tsang, Mun. 1995. "Public and Private Costs of Schooling in Developing Nations." In *International Encyclopedia of Economics of Education*, edited by M. Carnoy and H. Levin, 393-98. 2nd ed. Oxford, UK: Pergamon Press.

———. 1997. "Cost Analysis for Improved Educational Policymaking and Evaluation." *Educational Evaluation and Policy Analysis* 19 (4): 318–24.

———. 2002. "Economic Analysis of Educational Development in Developing Nations." In *Encyclopedia of Education*, edited by J. Guthrie. 2nd ed. New York: Macmillan.

UNDP. 2009. "Human Development Report (HDR) 2009." United Nations Development Program, New York.

UNESCO. 2007. "EFA Global Monitoring Report 2008: Education for All by 2015; Will We Make It?" UNESCO and Oxford publishers, Paris.

———. 2008. "EFA Global Monitoring Report 2009; Overcoming Inequality: Why Governance Matters." UNESCO, Paris.

———. 2010. "EFA Global Monitoring Report; Reaching the Marginalized." UNESCO, Paris; Oxford University Press, Oxford.

UNESCO/UIS. 2011. "Financing Education in Sub-Saharan Africa: Meeting the Challenges of Expansion, Equity and Quality." UIS.

UNICEF. 2007. *Achieving Universal Primary Education in Ghana by 2015: A Reality or a Dream?* UNICEF: New York.

———. 2010. "An Analysis of Out of School Children in Ghana: Ghana Demographic and Health Surveys (GDHS) 2003–2008." Accra, Ghana.

UNICEF Ghana. 2006. "Abolition of School fees," Issue Briefing Note 9.

———. 2011. "Bottleneck Analysis: Application to Education Sector—Ghana." Presented at MoE ESAR, June.

USAID. 2009. *Basic Education Quality in Ghana; Basic Education in Ghana: Progress and Problems*. Washington DC: USAID, June.

———. 2012. "Decentralized Education Framework for the Ghana Education Service Headquarters, the Regional Education Office and the Education Section of the Education, Youth and Sports Department of the District Assembly." Ghana Education Decentralization Project.

United Nations Department of Economic and Social Affairs (UNESA) Population Division. 2013. "Ghana Country Profile: Urban and Rural Populations." http://esa.un.org/unpd/wup/Country-Profiles/country-profiles_1.htm.

United Nations Educational, Scientific and Cultural Organization Institute for Statistics and United Nations Children's Fund. 2005. "Children Out of School: Measuring Exclusion from Primary Education." UIS Montreal.

United Nations Population Division. 2009. *World Population Prospects: The 2008 Revision.* Population Division of the Department of Economic and Social Affairs of the United Nations Secretariat, http://esa.un.org/unpp.

Weis, Lois. 1979. "Education and the Reproduction of Inequality: The Case of Ghana." *Comparative Education Review* 23 (1): 41–51.

Wodon, Quentin. 2009. *Improving the Targeting of Social Programs in Ghana.* Development Dialogue on Values and Ethics. Washington DC: World Bank.

Wodon, Quentin, and George Joseph. 2010. *School Level Analysis, School Lunch Analysis and NEA Analysis in Ghana.* Accra, Ghana: Commissioned by the World Bank for this Country Status Report, unpublished.

World Bank. 2004. *Books, Buildings and Learning Outcomes: An impact evaluation of World Bank support to basic education in Ghana.* Washington, DC: World Bank.

———. 2005. "World Development Report: Equity and Development." World Bank, Washington, DC.

———. 2009. "Review of the MTEF in Ghana: Making the Strategic Budgeting Process More Effective—External Review of Public Financial Management." World Bank, Washington, DC.

———. 2010. *Education in Ghana: Improving Equity, Efficiency and Accountability of Education Service Delivery.* Washington, DC: World Bank.

———. 2011a. *Republic of Ghana: Joint Review of Public Expenditure and Financial Management.* Washington, DC: World Bank.

———. 2011b. *Tackling Poverty in Northern Ghana.* Washington, DC: World Bank.

———. 2011c. "Aide Memoire: Identification mission for the Ghana Global Partnership for Education Fund Grant." December, 2011.

———. 2012. "Education Sector Project (Ghana): Implementation Completion and Results Report." World Bank, Washington, DC.

World Bank: Independent Evaluation Group. 2006. "From Schooling Access to Learning Outcomes: An Unfinished Agenda." An Evaluation of World Bank Support to Primary Education. World Bank, Washington, DC.

Yates, Chris. 2012. TED-UTDBE Support Services Consultancy Report No. 1. DfID-Ghana.

Environmental Benefits Statement

The World Bank is committed to reducing its environmental footprint. In support of this commitment, the Publishing and Knowledge Division leverages electronic publishing options and print-on-demand technology, which is located in regional hubs worldwide. Together, these initiatives enable print runs to be lowered and shipping distances decreased, resulting in reduced paper consumption, chemical use, greenhouse gas emissions, and waste.

The Publishing and Knowledge Division follows the recommended standards for paper use set by the Green Press Initiative. Whenever possible, books are printed on 50 percent to 100 percent postconsumer recycled paper, and at least 50 percent of the fiber in our book paper is either unbleached or bleached using Totally Chlorine Free (TCF), Processed Chlorine Free (PCF), or Enhanced Elemental Chlorine Free (EECF) processes.

More information about the Bank's environmental philosophy can be found at http://crinfo.worldbank.org/wbcrinfo/node/4.

www.ingramcontent.com/pod-product-compliance
Lightning Source LLC
Chambersburg PA
CBHW081939170426
43202CB00018B/2945